Greenhill Books

Special Men and Special Missions

Special Men and Special Missions

Inside American Special Operations Forces

1945 to the Present

Joel Nadel with J. R. Wright

Greenhill Books, London
Stackpole Books, Pennsylvania

In Memory of
Bruce W. Watson

Special Men and Special Missions
first published 1994 by Greenhill Books,
Lionel Leventhal Limited, Park House, 1 Russell Gardens,
London NW11 9NN
and
Stackpole Books, 5067 Ritter Road, Mechanicsburg, PA 17055, USA

British Library Cataloguing in Publication Data
Nadel, Joel
Special Men and Special Missions: Inside American Special Operations Forces,
1945 to the Present
I. Title   II. Wright, J.R.
356

ISBN 1–85367–159–2

Library of Congress Cataloging-in-Publication Data
Nadel, Joel.
Special men and special missions: inside Americal special operations forces,
1945 to the present/by Joel Nadel with J.R. Wright.
p.   cm.
ISBN 1–85367–159–2
1. Special forces (Military science)–United States–History–20th century.
2. United States–History, Military   I. Wright, J.R. (Jon R.)   II. Title.
U262.N34   1994
356'.167'0973–dc20   93-41727
                                               CIP

Typeset by DP Photosetting, Aylesbury, Bucks
Printed and bound in Great Britain by
Butler & Tanner, Caxton Road, Frome, Somerset

Contents

	Page
Preface	*11*
Chronology of Special Operations Covered in this Work	*15*

Part I. The Early Years: 1776–1959   **19**

1. From Seine to Saigon: Special Operations in the Cold War Transition 1776–1959   **21**
Special Operations in World War II, 1941–5
The Cold War Transition
Korean Interlude, 1950–3
Guerilla Warfare Plans in the European Theater, 1952–60
Southeast Asia, 1956–9

Part II. Forging the Capability: The Vietnam Years 1960–75   **37**

2. Phoenix from the Ashes: The Rebirth of Special Operations Forces 1960–75   **39**
Khrushchev's Challenge – 'Wars of Liberation,' 1961
President Kennedy's Initiative, 1961
The Vietnam Conflict, 1945–61
Low-Intensity-Conflict (LIC) Doctrine
Escalation and De-escalation, 1965–75
Military Assistance Command (Vietnam), Studies and Observation Group
Conclusions

3. America's Best: Army Special Operations in Vietnam 1959–75   **47**
Special Forces Accession and Training
Advisors: The Lone Wolves, 1957–75
Border Camps, 1964
The Greek Letter Projects: Special Reconnaissance, 1965–7
The Mike Forces, 1966
Rangers, 1968–9
Military Assistance Command (Vietnam), Studies and Observation Group
Strategic Direct Action: The Son Tay Raid, 1970
Conclusions

4. **Maritime Strike Force: The Advent of Naval Special Warfare 1943–75**   60
   UDT/Frogman Training, 1943–61
   Specialized SEAL Training, from 1961
   UDT/Frogman Operations, circa 1965
   Indigenous Special Warfare Organizations
   Unilateral SEAL Operations, 1966–71
   Riverine Interdiction
   POW Rescue Operation, 1972
   Conclusions

5. **Fire from the Sky: The Genesis of Air Force Special Operations 1961–75**   77
   Jungle Jim, 1961
   Fixed-Wing Gunships, 1961–75
   AC-47 'Spooky'
   Gunship Support to Special Forces Border Camps, 1965–6
   Air Force Support to MAC(V)SOG
   AC-130 Spectre
   AC-119G/K Shadow/Stinger
   Psychological Operations (Psyops)
   Special Operations Outside Vietnam, 1961–6
   Conclusions

Part III. Hardening the Steel: Transition and Evolution 1975–86   89

6. **Battles of Influence: American Special Operations in Transition 1975–86**   91
   Harbinger of the Future: Assault on the *Mayaguez*, 1975
   The Presidency of Jimmy Carter, 1977–81
   Iran, 1979–80
   Rebuilding Special Operations Forces, 1981–3
   Privately Funded Special Operations, 1984
   Lebanon, 1982–4
   Grenada, 1983
   A Unified Command for Special Operations, 1986

7. **Battles of Influence: Army Special Operations in Transition 1975–86**   114
   Hostage Rescue, 1975–9
   The Iran Hostage Rescue Mission, 1979–80
   Rebuilding the Capability, 1981–3
   Grenada, 1983
   Conclusions

Contents

8. Battles of Influence: Naval Special Warfare in Transition
   1975–86   128
   Coastal Piracy: The *Mayaguez* Operation, 1975
   The Transition of Naval Special Warfare, 1975–83
   Air Operations
   Combat Swimming
   Swimmer Delivery Vehicles
   Surface Operations
   Combatant Craft
   Grenada, 1983
   Lebanon, 1983–4
   Latin America, 1981–6
   Conclusions

9. Battles of Influence: Air Force Special Operations in
   Transition 1975–86   149
   Mayaguez, 1975
   Iran Hostage Rescue Mission, 1979–80
   Consolidation of Air Force Special Operations, 1983
   The Drug War, 1983–5
   Grenada, 1983
   Conclusions

Part IV. Honing the Edge 1987–92   163

10. The New Order: Special Operations in a Multi-Polar
    World 1986–92   165
    Panama, 1989–90
    Special Operations Forces Organization, 1987–93
    The Gulf War, 1990–1
    Kurdish Relief, 1991–3
    Conclusions

11. Swords to Plowshares: Army Special Operations in the
    New Order 1986–92   180
    Panama, 1989–90
    The Gulf War, 1990–1
    The Kurdish Uprising, 1991–3
    Conclusions

12. Naval Special Warfare in the New Order 1986–92   201
    Persian Gulf Operations, 1987–90
    Panama, 1989
    Philippine Insurrection, 1990
    The Gulf War, 1990–1
    Conclusions

13. Air Force Special Operations in the New Order 1986–92   **217**
   .   Panama, 1989
Air Force Special Operations Command, 1990
The Gulf War, 1990–1
Conclusions

Part V. Epilogue   **235**

14. Special Operations in the Next Century   **237**
Recent Special Operations
The Future of Special Operations

Glossary   *243*

Select Bibliography   *249*

Index   *251*

Illustrations

Pages 97–112

1. Major General Robert C. Kingston
2. General Carl Stiner
3. Navy SEAL patrol
4. SEAL patrol exercise
5. F470 Zodiac boat
6. Special Boat Unit craft
7. Special Boat Unit in Operation DESERT SHIELD
8. Seafox Special Warfare Craft, Light
9. Naval Special Warfare Mark III (Spectre Class) Patrol Boat
10. Scorpion and Fountain high-speed boats in Operation DESERT STORM
11. Special Forces soldiers on the Son Tay mission
12. Basic underwater demolition/SEAL training
13. BUD/S trainees on the 'Mud Flats'
14. DESERT STORM psychological operations leaflets
15. 5th Special Forces Group soldiers with Arab counterparts in Operation DESERT SHIELD/DESERT STORM
16. US Special Forces personnel delivering relief supplies to the Kurds
17. 5th Special Forces Group at Saudi frontier outposts
18. MH-53 Pave Low ready for a combat search and rescue mission into Iraq
19. AC-130 Spectre gunship firing its 20mm gatling gun
20. Helocasting: Navy SEAL team member entering the water
21. Special Forces Moblie Strike Force in Nha Trang
22. STABO rig extraction of soldiers from the jungle
23. Air Force SOWT member measuring wind velocity
24. MH-53 Pave Low winching in a Special Forces soldier
25. Air Force Special Operations Pave Hawk
26. MH-6 Little Bird Helicopters
27. AC-130H Spectre gunship in operation
28. US Army MH-47E Special Operations Chinook
29. MH-53 Pave Low moving in to refuel

Charts

		Page
1.	Naval Special Warfare Group Organization 1983	137
2.	USSOCOM Organization	172
3.	US Army Special Operations Command Organization	182
4.	Naval Special Warfare Command Organization	202
5.	US Air Force Special Operations Command Organization	223

Preface

We wrote this book as an objective insight into the world of American special operations, and we have made every effort to describe accurately the men, and recently the women, of special operations units, as well as their activities on a mission. Our intent has been to present the truly spectacular history of special operations through vivid action accounts from the special soldiers, sailors, airmen, and marines who have lived life 'on the edge.' The pages of this book tell a story of the unsung 'silent warriors' who go in harm's way to do America's bidding, risking all for their nation's defense. Many of the accounts come from those stalwart men who beat the odds, and pay tribute to those who did not. They depict a history and tradition of heroism and valor that have become the hallmark of America's special operators.

Since World War II, each of the military services of the United States has employed special operations forces (SOF) in a variety of situations. While many books have been written about single-service SOF, such as Army Special Forces or Navy SEALs, none has discussed how the US Army, Navy, and Air Force SOF have developed in relation to each other. With the recent establishment of the United States Special Operations Command to synchronize the joint service special operations, and recent spectacularly successful American special operations, a history of these organizations from the joint service perspective is essential to a complete understanding of the robustness and effectiveness of America's present special operations capabilities.

Beginning with a tradition of special operations that emerged in the American Revolution, the work goes on to cover three separate stages in the history of US special operations. In each stage, the roles of the Army, Navy and Air Force special operations components are discussed in detail in separate chapters. The first stage (see chapters 2–5) began with the advent of the American involvement in Vietnam in 1961 and ended with the American withdrawal in 1975. The second stage (see chapters 6–9) saw a drastic decline in American special operations capabilities, beginning with the *Mayaguez* incident in 1975, continuing with the aborted Iran hostage rescue mission (1980) and the Grenada military intervention (1983), concluding in 1986, when the US Congress mandated creation of a separate, joint-service headquarters for all American special operations forces. The most recent stage (see chapters 10–13) began with the establishment of the US Special Operations Command (USSOCOM) in 1987, has seen extensive special operations in the Panama intervention, the Gulf War, and in northern Iraq, and continues as of the publication of this book. The final chapter looks at potential special operations in support of evolving US policy into the twenty-first century. In this way, we have presented not only the individual service (ie army, navy or air force) perspectives of special operations in the great (and not so great) military campaigns over the past fifty years, but the overall strategic contribution of special operations to those campaigns.

There remain a great many secrets in the special operations community. Secrecy is essential to protect the lives of the men and women who are engaged in operations at great personal risk. While we wish to demonstrate to the reader the many outstanding attributes of America's special operators, we do not want to put them at risk by compromising their activities. Consequently, on-going special operations are not discussed, nor have we addressed organizations or capabilities that may be classified.

There are a great many people to whom we owe thanks for their assistance in this work and we will not be able to name them all. For that we are profoundly sorry, because without the help of everyone who contributed, this book would have been a significantly lesser work. At the United States Special Operations Command, we would like to express our thanks to General Carl Stiner and his staff, particularly Colonel Jake Dye and Mr George Grimes, for providing copious amounts of information on special operations forces, and for providing guidance on other potential sources of information. Our thanks to Mr Stephen Moore at US Army Special Operations Command and Ms Roxanne Merrit, at the Special Forces Museum and Mr Fred Fuller at the JFK Special Warfare Center Library, for photos and research assistance; to Dr Richard Stewart, at the office of the Command Historian, US Army Special Operations Command for his knowledge and the use of his extensive and well-catalogued archives; to Mr Clay McCutcheon at Air Force Special Operations Command; to Anita Parins, Carol Norton, Carol Wong, Deb Brannen, Russ McIntyre, Paul Vivian, Peter Tsouras, and Bill Baxter at the US Army Intelligence and Threat Analysis Center; to Major General (Retired) John Singlaub and Colonel (Retired) Fred Caristo for their kind indulgence; to Colonel David Grange Jr, for his inspiration; to Dr John Jandora for accommodations, research assistance, and good company; to Major (Retired) Clyde Sincere, Colonel (Retired) Charlie Norton, and John Haralson, of the Special Forces Association; to Lionel Leventhal for being patient; to Howard Nadel, for everything; to General (Retired) Bob Kingston, who served as an inspiration, a mentor, and a source of expert information on the history of Special Forces, much of which he made; and importantly, to those special operators who declined to be named, who provided so much insight into the inner workings of the special operations community.

We owe the men and women who have served in America's elite special operations forces, especially those who made the supreme sacrifice, for providing us the inspiration and motivation to undertake this project. Throughout our research and writing, we have been continually amazed and heartened by the imagination, resourcefulness, courage, and grim determination demonstrated time after time in their incredible exploits. We hope that this work does some justice to them and their contribution to our national defense.

Finally, and most importantly, we would like to thank our wives, Pat and Myong-Hi, and our children for putting up with our bad humor as we persevered to bring this work to fruition.

Joel Nadel
J.R. Wright

Chronology of Special Operations Covered in this Work

Date(s)	Theater	Action	Special Operators	Chapter
1776	American	Guerilla Warfare	The Swamp Fox Green Mountain Boys	1
1863–5	Virginia (USA) Tennessee Missouri/Kansas	Guerilla Warfare Raids Guerilla Warfare	Mosby's Partisans Forrest's Cavalry Quantrill's Raiders	1 1
1943	Southern Italy	Anzio Raids	1st Special Service Force (US/Canada)	1
June 1944	European	D-Day Assault on Pointe du Hoc	Darby's Rangers	1
1942–5	European	Agent Insertion Clandestine Resupply	Carpetbaggers (Army Air Force) Air Transport Command	1
1943–5	European China–Burma–India Philippines	Guerilla Warfare (CBI)	OSS Army	1 1
1943–4	CBI	Direct Action Raids	Merrill's Marauders	1
1943–4	CBI	Clandestine Infiltration/Resupply Precision Fire Support	Air Commandos	1
1951–3	Korea	Guerilla Warfare	8240th Army Unit	1
1952	Korea	Direct Action Sabotage	JACK	1
1951–3	Korea	Direct Action/Special Reconnaissance	Rangers	1
1959	Laos	Guerilla Warfare	Special Forces	1
Aug 1961	Mali	Mobile Training Team	Jungle Jim (USAF)	5
Aug 1962	Panama	Civic Action (Operation BOOKS)	Jungle Jim (USAF)	5
Nov 1962	Vietnam	Fire Support to Indigenous Force	Farmgate (USAF)	5
1964	Vietnam	ARVN Ranger Advisors	Special Forces	3
Dec 1964	Vietnam	Precision Fire Support	Farmgate	5
1964–9	Vietnam	Advisors to Indigenous Units	SEALs	4
1965–6	Vietnam	Special Reconnaissance	Special Forces (Project Delta)	3
1966	Vietnam	Riverine Operations	SEALs	4
Feb 1966	Vietnam	Clandestine Armed Recon	Air Commandos	5

Date(s)	*Theater*	*Action*	*Special Operators*	*Chapter*
Mar 1966	Vietnam	Battle for the A Shau Valley	Special Forces	3
			Air Commandos	5
1966	Laos/Thailand	Civic Action (Medical Relief)	Air Commandos	5
Mar 1967	Vietnam	Blackjack Operations	Special Forces	3
Dec 1968	Vietnam	Special Reconnaissance Tet Offensive	Long Range Patrollers	3
1969	Vietnam	Direct Action	SEALs	5
Nov 1970	Vietnam	Son Tay Raid	Special Forces	3
June 1972	Vietnam	POW Rescue	SEALs	5
May 1975	Cambodia (Mayaguez)	Recovery of Human Remains Special Reconnaissance	SEALs 1st Spec Ops Wing	8 9
Apr 1980	Iran	Hostage Rescue Mission	Special Forces Rangers 1st Spec Ops Wing	7 7 9
1981–4	Latin America	Mobile Training Teams	SEALs	8
Aug 1981	Honduras	Counter-insurgency	Special Forces	7
1983–4	Lebanon	Mobile Training Teams Direct Action	SEALs SEALs	8 8
1983–5	Caribbean	Narcotics Interdiction	1st Spec Ops Wing	9
Oct 1983	Grenada	Point Salines Airfield Seizure	Rangers 1st Spec Ops Wing	7 9
		Hostage Rescue/ Richmond Hill Prison	Special Forces Special Ops Aviation (Army)	7 7
		Special Reconnaissance	SEALs	8
		Hostage Rescue	SEALs	8
		Direct Action (Seizure of Radio Station)	SEALs	8
1985	El Salvador	Special Reconnaissance	SEALs	8
Sep 1987	Persian Gulf	Protection of Commercial Shipping	Special Boats	12
20 Dec 1989	Panama	Airfield Seizure/Hostage Rescue	Rangers	11
		Sniper Suppression Operations	Spec Ops Aviation	11
		Destruction of Noriega's Yacht	SEALs	12
		Blocking of Panama Canal	Special Boats	12
		Special Reconnaissance	Special Boats	12
		Direct Action – Pacora River Bridge	Special Forces	11
			16 Spec Ops Sqdn (USAF)	13
		Air Defense Suppression/Rio Hato	16 Spec Ops Sqdn (USAF)	13
		Attack on La Commandancia	16 Spec Ops Sqdn (USAF)	13
		Sabotage of Noriega's Jet/ Paitilla Airfield	SEALs	12
Dec 1989	Panama	Psychological Operations (Operation MA BELL)	Special Forces 16 Spec Ops Sqdn (USAF)	11 13
1989–90	Panama	Nation Building	Army Civil Affairs	11
1990	Philippines	Hostage Rescue Plan	Special Boats	12
Aug–Sep 1990	Gulf War	Mobile Training Teams	SEALs	12

Date(s)	Theater	Action	Special Operators	Chapter
Sep 1990– Mar 1991	Gulf War	Mobile Training Teams	Special Forces	11
		Advisors	Special Forces	11
		Advisors	SEALs	12
17 Jan 1991	Gulf War	Capture of Oil Platforms and		12
		Qaruh Island	SEALs	13
		Ambush of Air Defense	20th Spec Ops Sqdn (USAF)	
		Early Warning		
19 Jan 1991	Gulf War	Combat Search and Rescue Mission	21st Spec Ops Sqdn (USAF)	13
			20th Spec Ops Sqdn (USAF)	13
31 Jan 1991	Gulf War	Advisors/Khafji Battle	SEALs	12
		Precision Fire Support/Khafji	16th Spec Ops Sqdn (USAF)	13
Feb 1991	Gulf War	Precision Heavy Bombing (BLU 82s)	8th Spec Ops Sqdn (USAF)	13
23 Feb 1991	Gulf War	Special Reconnaissance Missions	Special Forces	11
27 Feb 1991	Gulf War	Direct Action – Scud Interdiction	Special Forces	11
29 Feb 1991	Gulf War	Psyops – Seizure of Tallil Air Base	Army Psyops	11
1991–2	Kuwait	Nation Building	Army Civil Affairs	11
1991–	Northern Iraq	Kurdish Relief	Special Forces	11
			Army Civil Affairs	11
			Army Psyops	11
			39th Spec Ops Wing/	
			352 Spec Ops Group	11
1991	Somalia	Embassy Evacuation	SEALs	14
1992	Former USSR	Humanitarian Aid	Special Forces	14
1992	Mongolia	Mobile Training Team	Army Spec Ops Command	14
Mar 1992	Cameroon	Humanitarian Aid (Medical)	Army Civil Affairs	14
1993	Somalia	Clandestine Beach Surveys	SEALs	14
Mar 1993	Former Yugoslavia	Humanitarian Aid Airdrops	435th Air Wing	14
June 1993	Somalia	Precision Fire Support	16th Spec Ops Sqdn (USAF)	14

PART I

The Early Years
1776–1959

CHAPTER 1

From the Seine to Saigon Special Operations in the Cold War Transition 1776–1959

Contingents of American Provincials fought under the British flag against France and Spain during the imperial wars from 1689 to 1762. These colonists learned the art of guerilla warfare from native Americans, whom they called 'Indians,' and so special operations entered the repertoire of American military art before the American revolution.[1] The most famous of these was Major Robert Rogers, who was commissioned in 1756 as a captain in command of a company of Rangers. Rogers' Rangers successfully fought both native Americans and French forces in the Great Lakes region of what is now the northern United States. The 75th Ranger Regiment of the present day is descended from this band of rugged frontiersmen and every graduate of the US Army Ranger School is well versed in the 'The Rules of Rogers' Rangers'.

During the American Revolution, the colonists capitalized on their 'Indian fighting' skills as their only means of prosecuting military action against the well established British Army, with its superior training, established leadership, and more robust resources. Thus, unconventional warfare was established as the 'underdog's' way of war some 150 years before Mao Tse-tung.

The American revolutionary war followed the classic pattern of insurrection. The first shots fired at Lexington and Concord were fired by partisans, 'skulking behind stone walls.'[2] As the colonists prosecuted the war to its conclusion, a combination of conventional operations conducted by mercenary armies (both American and French) and special operations conducted by American guerilla bands characterized the action. Major Francis Marion, the 'Swamp Fox', led partisans and guerillas in fierce combat against British forces in the southern colonies. British response to the American guerilla campaign included reprisals and increasingly repressive measures taken against the populace, serving only to fuel the revolutionary cause.

In the American Civil War, Union forces had the advantages of an established military system, natural resources, and the manufacturing capability to sustain protracted war. The secessionist southern states of the Confederacy had

21

a strong military tradition, but due to a lack of manufacturing capability and the unwillingness of European nations to provide economic assistance, they were poor in resources. Faced by several Union military expeditions onto their territory, the Confederacy engaged in both conventional and unconventional warfare to defend themselves and preserve their 'states' rights.' In Virginia, Colonel John Mosby, the Gray Ghost, raised a battalion of partisan fighters in 1863 and by the end of 1864 had killed, wounded or captured 1,200 Union soldiers and captured several hundred horses and cattle; all with a loss of only twenty men.[3]

As America grew economically she developed a conventional military capability equal to any in the world and, since 'Indian fighting' was the last resort of underdogs, America perceived no need to maintain its unconventional warfare capability. Special operations became more or less a thing of the past as America's military planners began to forget their roots.

The United States Army punitive expedition to Mexico in 1916 illustrated this fact perfectly. Since 1914, Pancho Villa, a bandit and political opponent of Mexican president Carranza, had been raiding American settlements in New Mexico to protest American recognition of the Mexican government. To put a stop to it, President Theodore Roosevelt ordered General John J. Pershing to lead his 8th Cavalry Brigade into Mexico to ferret out Villa and his men and put a stop to his banditry. Pershing never found Villa, but he did succeed in angering the Mexican government with his flagrant violation of Mexico's sovereignty.

Not until World War II was the United States to see a need to rebuild her special operations capability. Because of the strong strategic positions of Japan and Germany, America and her allies found themselves the underdogs in Asia and Europe and were forced to turn to special operations to resist Axis expansion. After 125 years, the United States had no unconventional warfare experience or doctrine. But, paradoxically, the British had learned well the lessons of special warfare not only from the American colonials, but from the other colonial wars they had fought. Since 1940, the British had been engaged in special operations in France, collecting intelligence, organizing resistance groups, and conducting sabotage operations, under the supervision of their Special Operations Executive.

Beginning with the declaration of war against Japan in 1941, the United States began providing men and material to Britain's special operations campaigns both in Europe and the Far East.

Special Operations in World War II, 1941–5

EUROPEAN THEATER

Special operations in World War II fell into two basic types: direct action and unconventional warfare. Special operations units engaged in direct action missions, such as raids and reconnaissance, in support of divisions and Corps. Those units engaged in unconventional warfare were part of the Office of Strategic Services (OSS), the forerunner of the Central Intelligence Agency (CIA), under Major General William Donovan. Although these units supported theater campaign plans, Donovan worked directly for President Franklin D. Roosevelt, supervising operations in North Africa, India, Burma, and China.

One of the more colorful direct-action commando outfits was the 1st Special Service Force, also known as the Devil's Brigade; a joint Canadian–American venture that began 9 July 1942 at Fort William Henry Harrison, in Montana. Trained in airborne operations and particularly skilled in close combat, the Devil's Brigade saw combat primarily in Italy, and later in France.[4] Bill Mauldin, the famous cartoonist for the newspaper *Stars and Stripes*, encountered the Devil's Brigade at the Anzio beachhead, in Italy. Formally designated the 1st Special Force, the Devil's Brigade was composed of volunteers from US and Canadian paratrooper and ranger units. With special training in para-ski operations, explosives, and sabotage they were supposed to be dropped into Norway on essentially a suicide mission: to destroy hydroelectric plants and harass the Germans.

When the Norway operation was cancelled, the unit was deployed to Anzio because of their reputation as tough seasoned fighters. They were an unusual outfit: they called their officers by their first names, designed their own uniforms, and chose their own weaponry. Many were known violent criminals.

They occupied the extreme southern flank at Anzio, which was the only quiet sector on the beach. Essentially, they kept the Germans terrorized at night by forming up huge patrols of some three hundred men. These nocturnal expeditions would venture forth toward the German positions and wreak utter havoc with Tommy guns (.45 caliber Thompson sub-machineguns), knives, grenades and sniper rifles.

The activities of the Devil's Brigade forced a salient in the German position that was as much as five miles deep while other sectors resembled the trench warfare that characterized World War I. The 1st Special Service Force used this to advantage, and lived comparatively well. Men sunbathed next to their foxholes, fished with hand-grenades, and searched for buried wine casks with metal detectors.[5]

As the second front in France opened up, the brigade left Italy and continued to distinguish itself in close quarter combat until it was inactivated in 1944.

The 1st Ranger Battalion, commanded by Major William O. Darby and hence known as Darby's Rangers, was activated in Carrickfergus, Ireland on 19 June 1942. These Rangers were trained as elite infantry and fought in North Africa, Sicily and throughout western Europe. Their most noteworthy achievement was their assault against the cliffs of Pointe du Hoc during the D-Day invasion at Normandy, France.

On the unconventional warfare side, the OSS set up intelligence nets and resistance movements throughout Europe, but nowhere was it more active than in German-occupied France. The Jedburgh mission consisted of dropping three-man teams into France, Belgium and Holland, where they trained partisans to conduct guerilla operations against the Germans in preparation for D-Day.

The OSS also deployed units, called operational groups or OGs, into Europe to conduct bi-lateral and unilateral intelligence and sabotage missions against high priority targets. Although these units occasionally relied on local resistance movements for logistical support, they were operationally independent of the resistance for security reasons.

Initially to support the Polish underground, the Eighth Air Force organized the 801st Bomb Group, and later the 492d Bomb Group, which would get OSS agents into and out of occupied Europe and provide logistical support to both the OSS and friendly resistance movements. The forerunners of today's 1st Special Operations Wing infiltrated OSS agents into and out of occupied Europe and provided these agents and their resistance units with all manner of supplies during their missions.

The United States Air Transport Command (ATC) flew clandestine infiltration missions to resupply resistance forces fighting throughout Europe. One such operation was staged out of Leuchars Airfield, near Edinburgh, Scotland, where unarmed B-24 Liberator and B-26 Martin-Marauder Long-Range Bombers would drop supplies to the Norwegian underground, conduct photoreconnaissance, and drop agents into German-occupied territory. Upon completion of their missions over hostile territory, the aircraft would refuel in neutral Sweden, at two airfields near Stockholm that were used by both allied and German air crews. Because of Swedish neutrality, the antagonist air crews were prohibited from engaging in combat with one another while they were on or over Swedish territory, but both sides were constantly trying to use this unusual arrangement to their advantage.

THE ASIAN THEATER

On the other side of the globe, in the China–Burma–India Theater or CBI, the men of the 5307th Composite Unit waged a fierce war against the Japanese forces occupying Burma. Known as Merrill's Marauders, in honor of their commander, Colonel Frank D. Merrill, the 5307th fought and won five major battles and seventeen minor engagements against the Japanese.

Formed as the Galahad Force in September 1943, the Marauders were composed of three battalions of volunteers who were primarily veterans of the Solomon–New Guinea campaigns. After training under the supervision of British Brigadier Orde C. Wingate and his Chindits, Merrill's Marauders entered combat on 9 February 1944. Their mission: in support of a general offensive by two divisions of Chinese troops, to infiltrate from India through Japanese lines deep into mountainous north Burma and seize Myitkina (pronounced *Mi' chin ahr*) Airfield on the Irrawaddy River. The mission was essential to support construction of the Ledo road, which would reconnect Chinese forces with allied logistics bases in India.[6]

Beginning their campaign, the Marauders infiltrated Japanese defensive positions in the Hukawng Valley and established blocking positions to the Japanese rear. The Japanese fought fiercely to dislodge the Marauders but were unsuccessful, breaking contact on 6 March and withdrawing. The Marauders pressed their attack against the Japanese 18th Division through heavy jungle and steep, narrow ravines until the end of March, when losses to enemy and disease caused the advance to bog down. Then, on 31 March, the 2d Battalion found themselves surrounded after fending off several Japanese attacks. Simultaneously, the 3d Battalion began a series of assaults against the Japanese to relieve its sister unit, and on 9 April were able to break through to the 2d Battalion as the Japanese withdrew.

After being reinforced by 300 Kachin tribesmen (provided courtesy of OSS Detachment 101) and two Chinese Regiments, the Marauders continued the mission to Myitkina on 27 April. Through the summer of 1944, the Marauders scaled the Kumon Mountain range and slogged through triple canopy jungle, arriving at Myitkina on 17 May, completely exhausted. Myitkina was not actually secured until 3 August, after the Marauders received Chinese reinforcements.

This campaign was costly; the Marauders suffered 424 battle casualties and 1,970 casualties from dysentery, typhus, malaria, psychoneurosis and other diseases. But they established a reputation and tradition for tough, determined fighting that served to inspire the Ranger units that were their legacy in Korea, Vietnam, Grenada, and Panama.

As mentioned earlier, OSS Detachment 101 executed highly successful unconventional warfare operations complementing the Chindit/Marauder campaign in Burma. At the height of their activity, Detachment 101 had trained and armed a force of 11,000 Kachin tribesmen who waged a fierce and ruthless battle against the Japanese. The victims of vicious Japanese atrocities, the Kachin people were only too glad to throw in their lot with the allies in their battle for Burma. With US training, arms and supplies, the Kachins killed over 10,000 Japanese while their own losses amounted to only 206.[7]

The 1st Air Commando Group provided air support to the allied forces engaged in the Burma campaign. This outfit was the genesis of a concept developed in August 1943 by two legendary figures: Army Air Corps General Henry H. 'Hap' Arnold and British Admiral Lord Louis Mountbatten, the Supreme Allied Commander, Southeast Asian Command. Under co-command of Colonels Philip G. Cochran and John R. Alison, some 500 Air Commandos provided special operations aviation support to General Wingate, his Chindits, and Merrill's Marauders in their campaign to re-take Burma. These airmen and their equipment embodied the spirit and capabilities later found in the United States Air Force's 1st Air Commando Wing, established in 1963, and its successor, the 1st Special Operations Wing.

A fighter squadron of P-51 Mustangs provided the 'airborne artillery' support the Chindits needed as they operated out of range of their own tube artillery. Squadrons of C-47 Dakota 'Gooney Birds,' CG-4A Gliders, and a variety of light planes provided transportation and logistical support. Light planes and the newly developed helicopter delivered light cargo and pioneered air medical evacuation operations. The Dakotas were used both as troop transports and glider 'tugs.' Gliders hauled artillery, troops, and pack-mules. This latter requirement caused some concern among Colonel Cochran's men and so the concept was tested:

> ... it was finally decided on the night of 10 January 1944 to see if the animals could be transported without them kicking holes in the side of gliders. For this test ... the glider floors were reinforced, the mules' legs were hobbled, their heads were tied down to keep the ears out of the control cables, and they were restricted in a sling-like contraption ... Last minute instructions were given muleteers to shoot the animals if they became unmanageable. The worries were all in vain; the mules performed well, reportedly even banking during turns![8]

On the evening of 5 March 1944, the Air Commandos executed the very first airmobile insertion when they penetrated Japanese airspace over Burma, descended on a remote jungle clearing code named 'Broadway,' and carved an airfield out of the jungle. Air Commando engineers prepared the landing strip as Colonel Alison became the first air force combat controller, directing the landing of some forty gliders in the clearing. Although glider losses were heavy, personnel losses were relatively light (twenty-four killed out of 539 deployed); by the following night, C-47 Dakotas were landing the first of some five brigades of Chindits, who would melt into the jungle and raid Japanese lines of communication and supply bases.

Meanwhile, the Air Commando assault groups roamed the skies over Burma, attacking Japanese airfields, fighter patrols, and bombers, thus crippling the enemy capability to react to this tour-de-force. During this one day, the assault force destroyed forty-eight aircraft: forty percent of all the aircraft destroyed by the allies in the month of March.[9]

THE PHILIPPINES

By the spring of 1942, Japanese armies had occupied all of Southeast Asia, incorporating the Philippines and Dutch East Indies into their 'co-prosperity sphere.' However, not all of the American–Filipino garrisons surrendered after the fall of Corregidor and some fifty guerilla groups formed in the islands before the Japanese could consolidate their gains. Guerilla groups began harassing the Japanese on all the major islands: Luzon, Leyte, Samar, and Mindanao.

MacArthur recognized Lieutenant Colonel Kangleon, a Filipino, as the guerilla commander on Leyte when he dispatched Navy Commander Charles Parsons and his team of officers to Leyte in the spring of 1943. Parsons and his men brought communications gear and other military supplies and provided Kangleon with logistics and training support. These guerillas eventually forced the Japanese out of the countryside and into the coastal villages. The Japanese were so intimidated that they would not even send patrols into the rural countryside.[10]

In Luzon, US Army Lieutenant Colonel Russell Volckmann equipped, trained and commanded five Filipino regiments that successfully engaged the Japanese in combat. On Mindanao, Lieutenant Colonel Wendell Fertig eventually recruited some 37,000 guerilla troops and occupied ninety percent of that island until the end of the war. Both Fertig and Volckmann were instrumental in the formation of Army Special Forces in the early 1950s.[11]

NAVAL CAMPAIGNS

Seventy percent of the surface of the planet Earth is covered with water. This fact has been evident to military leaders and planners throughout recorded history. But it was not until World War II that the most capable military forces in the world began to appreciate truly the need for military units that were *dedicated* to operating in maritime and riverine environments at the individual or small unit level. For a country's armed forces to control effectively the sea lines of communication, take advantage of amphibious approaches to military objectives and operate effectively in coastal and inland waterways, it became evident that conventional naval and marine forces needed an added capability. Soon after World War II began, the United Kingdom found that small, non-traditional units engaging in special operations could significantly enhance the success of amphibious operations.

The United States Navy began in 1943 to see the value of special operations in support of US Marine and Army amphibious operations. Britain and several of her allies had pioneered the use of special operations units in support of amphibious operations. Hundreds of training landings were played out on the beaches of Florida (Ft Pearce), Virginia (Little Creek) and California (Coronado) as well as along the coastlines of San Clemente Island, off the west coast of California, and Vieques Island, east of Puerto Rico. These and hundreds of other realistic, but simulated, combat scenarios were part of the basic training that prospective UDT (Underwater Demolition Team) and, in later years, SEAL (Sea, Air, Land) Team combat swimmers had to experience before being considered basically proficient enough to matriculate to the operational units of naval special warfare, often referred to simply as the 'Teams.'

Although formally recognized by the US Navy as a military necessity earlier in the year, events that began on the morning of 20 November 1943 on a semi-circular collection of coral specks in the Gilbert Islands, in the western Pacific Ocean, were to prove sufficient to justify the need for units such as the underwater demolition teams. On this date elements of the 2nd Marine Division, 5th Amphibious Corps, US Navy 5th Fleet assaulted Tarawa Atoll as part of Operation GALVANIC. The assault force, especially those elements assigned to capture Betio island, suffered over 1,000 dead and 2,000 wounded over a three-day campaign. A majority of the losses were attributed to the assault force's need to cross over 700 yards of shallows leading to assigned beachheads (which could not be negotiated by all available landing craft) under continual machinegun and artillery fire from the determined and well dug-in adversaries of Japan's Special Naval Landing Force. Had a clandestine, night-time, pre-assault reconnaissance been done by a small group of combat swimmers, more acceptable routes to the beaches may have been found that could have helped reduce Marine casualties.

Thus, the concept of naval special warfare was born, but it would not be until America entered the Vietnam conflict that a true naval special warfare capability would develop from this seed.

The Cold War Transition

As the blinding flash and roar of the atomic bomb brought World War II to a close, it looked as if special operations forces would fade into history. The apocalyptic destructive power of the bomb now called into question the wisdom of any future combat, at least involving the United States.

But the Soviet Union maintained a high state of readiness in its conventional forces occupying eastern Europe, Korea and Manchuria as it raced to produce its own atomic device. Finally, in August 1949, the first Soviet atomic device shattered the equilibrium created by sole American possession of 'the bomb.' By the 1960s the proliferation of Soviet nuclear weapons led to the concept of MAD – mutually assured destruction – and reestablished the need to maintain a strong conventional deterrent against Soviet aggression in Europe.

The Soviets had already amassed large armored formations in eastern Europe, at a high state of readiness. The United States and the newly formed North Atlantic Treaty Organization, formed four months before the Soviets exploded their first atomic bomb, had maintained only a token presence; the Americans again found themselves in the position of underdog, and they began a return to their military roots.

But Korea intervened.

KOREAN INTERLUDE, 1950–3

At approximately 0400 hours on 25 June 1950, the roar of artillery shattered the dawn as the North Korean Army opened fire on South Korean units standing watch south of the 38th parallel in Korea. Within thirty minutes the first of four North Korean Field Armies composed of some 80,000 troops crossed the border. Proceeding unilaterally on 30 June, US President Harry Truman directed General of the Army Douglas MacArthur, the American commander in East Asia, to commit his ground, air, and naval forces against the North Koreans. This led to a full US military effort to restore the South Korean state; an objective that was achieved, in spite of Communist Chinese intervention and phenomenal suffering and bloodshed on all sides, on 27 July 1953 when China, the US, and North Korea signed an armistice.

8240TH ARMY UNIT

In early 1951, Eighth United States Army took control of partisan operations with the objective of establishing a resistance net in North Korea. Some 6,000 to 10,000 Koreans had fled the Chinese onslaught and had declared their willingness to continue the fight against the Communists.[12] To coordinate their efforts, Eighth Army created the Combined Command for Reconnaissance Activities in Korea (CCRAK). Using OSS and Ranger veterans of World War II, CCRAK established the 8240th Army Unit, under the command of Lieutenant Colonel Jay D. Vanderpool, to train, equip, and in many cases lead, these partisans.

Lieutenant Colonel Vanderpool's objective was to degrade North Korean logistics capabilities, undermine their government, and collect critical intelligence. As the 8240th provided training, air support and supplies, the partisans were expected to steal supplies from North Korean coastal shipping, recruit Chinese partisans, rob banks for North Korean currency, steal enemy radar equipment and aircraft, interdict supply lines, and assassinate Korean Communist leaders.[13] Although this program had only minor impact on enemy combat readiness, it provided valuable lessons that would be implemented over a decade later in Vietnam. One excerpt from Lieutenant Colonel Vanderpool's 1952 Guerilla Operations Outline may have provided the seed of inspiration for the American Phoenix program in Vietnam:

Assassinations. Primary assassination targets are Korean Communist leaders. Communist or North Korea Labor Party leaders who will not render partisan assistance to our forces will be assassinated. If succeeding Communist leaders are assassinated, the ambitions of minor leaders will be dampened. This has already been demonstrated by our efforts in some sectors. Terrorist tactics of focussing attention on the high mortality rate of enemy leaders are to be encouraged. Only selected Soviets should be assassinated. They should be of sufficient rank or possess sufficient technical knowledge that the gain will compensate for the resultant counter-measures that will be taken by the enemy. Soviets should be assassinated in areas that abound with pro-Communist. This creates suspicion and doubt between the Soviets and their satellite Korean followers. Korean Communists leaders should be assassinated wherever found.[14]

The 8240th normally provided only logistics support for partisan operations but occasionally it provided advisors to coordinate resupply, air, artillery, or naval gunfire support on an exceptional basis. This procedure was highly risky since Caucasian males could easily compromise a group of Korean partisans operating in enemy territory.

An example of one of these operations took place on the west coast of North Korea in October 1952. To coordinate naval gunfire support from British and New Zealand cruisers as well as air strikes from Navy aircraft, American advisors accompanied the partisans on a raid. The operation was supposed to be a two-pronged raid against an enemy troop concentration.

The partisans commenced their operation at 0200 hours as they left their island base and approached the enemy shore in an unlikely armada of motorized junks, sail boats and 'wiggle-boats' (a form of Korean sampan that is propelled by a long oar extending off the stern that is 'wiggled' back and forth). An hour from shore the junks cut their motors to begin their final approach. The element in the supporting attack hit the beach at 0400 followed by the main attack at 0500 hours.

As the sun rose, it became apparent that operational security had been breached as both groups were ambushed en route to their objectives and came under intense fire. The partisans and their advisors were caught in a deadly cross-fire of mortars and small arms. Most of the partisans fled into the countryside with only a few staying with the advisors to make their way back to the beach. In a panic, the remaining partisans bolted for the beach, bypassing several pre-designated emergency assembly points (called rally-points) only to find that their boats were not scheduled to meet them for several hours.

Badly outnumbered, one of the American advisors called in some pre-planned air strikes as the boats were called forward for an early extraction of the raiding force. With the enemy in hot pursuit the raiding party took to the water, under fire from the enemy force, and swam out to meet their transportation. The New Zealand cruiser had monitored the call for air strikes and began shelling the beach, effectively suppressing the enemy fire so that the junks could pick up the survivors.

Ten partisans had been killed and seventeen wounded. The survivors were fished out of the water by the British cruiser, whose personnel provided medical support for the wounded and excellent hospitality for the advisors.

Unfortunately, the American inexperience in unconventional warfare on the

Asian land mass contributed to the overall lackluster performance of the Korean partisans. As the Korean war progressed, these partisan activities served as a sort of trial-and-error proving ground for the development of unconventional warfare doctrine. The Americans documented the mistakes made while training, leading and resourcing the Korean partisans and corrected their doctrine accordingly. As a result, the harrowing experiences of Korea led to much improved unconventional warfare policies and operations undertaken six years later as American Special Forces deployed to Laos, in Southeast Asia, to raise an indigenous guerilla army to fight the Communist Pathet Lao.

JACK

In an inexplicable paradox, the CIA, as the successor to the OSS, did not engage in extensive partisan operations; that was left to CCRAK. Joint Advisory Commission Korea, the cover name for CIA activities in Korea,[15] planned and executed direct action and intelligence collection operations throughout North Korea.

JACK maintained a network of covert bases on islands off the west coast of North Korea and one base off the east coast on Yodo Island, in Wonsan harbor, from which they recruited and dispatched young Korean agents into North Korea by either boat or parachute. These agents performed a variety of missions, such as observing troop movements and ambushing trucks and trains. Although JACK attempted to set up a resistance movement similar to the one established in France in World War II, they were unsuccessful principally because relatively few anti-Communists chose to remain in the north after the United States extended an open invitation to them to come south. Retired Major General John Singlaub tells of one particularly successful JACK operation he directed:

> One of my most successful ... operations in Korea involved a tough Air Force Master Sergeant who ran a converted wooden junk out of our bases on the west coast islands. He lived with his crew, had a Korean 'wife,' and was bound and determined to raise hell with the enemy. The sergeant had learned from Korean seamen that there was a marine telephone-telegraph cable connecting the Shantung peninsula in mainland China with Dairen in Manchuria. He realized this had to be one of the main telecomm links between CCF (Chinese Communist Forces) in Korea and Peking. The Yellow Sea is generally shallow; the sergeant was enterprising. Early one May morning, his trailing grapples fetched up the thick, weedy cable ... the sergeant wielded a fire ax, whacking out a three foot length of cable. He then ran to the wheelhouse, called for maximum speed, and hightailed it back across the Yellow Sea.[16]

The upshot of this operation was that the Chinese had to resort to radioteletype to communicate with Peking, thus providing a gold mine of new information derived from signal intercepts.

JACK procured two B-26 Martin Marauders which they modified to support agent operations in North Korea. Thus, under the direction of (then) Major Singlaub, JACK had acquired its own Air Force. Singlaub put his experience with JACK to use fifteen years later when he became commander of Military Assistance Command (Vietnam), Studies and Observation Group (MAC(V)SOG), the cover name for the special operations command whose mission it was to interdict the Ho Chi Minh trail, North Vietnam's principal line of communication into South Vietnam. There too, Singlaub had not only his own army, but also his own air force and navy.

RANGERS

The Rangers of the Korean War commenced service as *ad hoc* or field-expedient organizations. The Eighth US Army's Ranger company was called the 8213th Army Unit; it activated on 25 August 1950 in Japan and, after completing intensive training, entered the war in November of that year. Initially, the Rangers conducted anti-guerilla operations inside the Pusan perimeter.

Later, they supported one of the thrusts to the Yalu River when they got caught up in the Chinese intervention. The company was almost completely wiped out as it defended a hill at Ipsak against almost overwhelming odds. The commander was critically wounded and the unit was withdrawn to Kanghwa-do island off Korea's east coast where it provided support to the Turkish Brigade until its discontinuance in March 1951.

X Corps, under Major General Edward M. Almond, raised a provisional raider company designated the 8245th Army Unit. In preparation for the 1st Marine Division landings at Inchon, the raiders conducted a raid at Kunsan to deceive the enemy as to the actual landing sites. When X Corps landed in Northeast Korea in November, the company began conducting screening and reconnaissance operations north of the eastern port city of Hamhung. They were later formed into a special attack battalion and conducted mountain warfare in support of Eighth Army in December.

From October 1950, Divisional Ranger companies were activated at Fort Benning, Georgia, and then attached to combat divisions. Their mission was to infiltrate enemy lines and attack command posts, artillery positions, vehicle parks, key communications centers and other facilities. These were essentially the same tasks the Rangers would be assigned in Vietnam.[17]

AIR FORCE SPECIAL OPERATIONS

The Air Force supported JACK and CCRAK with C-47 'Gooney Birds,' C-119 'Flying Boxcars,' and A-26 Marauders. In response to the highly specialized requirements of unconventional warfare, the Air Force activated, trained, and equipped three special operations wings called the 580th, 581st, and 582d Air Resupply and Communications Wings, although only one wing saw service in Korea. Immediately following the conflict, all three wings were deactivated and the Air Force special operations capability would lie dormant until revitalized in response to President Kennedy's low-intensity-conflict initiatives in 1961.

Guerilla Warfare Plans in the European Theater, 1952–60

10TH SPECIAL FORCES GROUP

Colonel Aaron Bank, a Jedburgh veteran of World War II, is considered the father of modern Special Forces. In April 1952, Bank was reassigned from the Pentagon to the Psychological Warfare Center at Fort Bragg, North Carolina. On 20 June, he established the 10th Special Forces Group with a strength of ten men.[18] Two of those men, Clyde Sincere and Charlie Norton, would figure prominently in Special Forces in Vietnam and on into the 1970s; Norton would ultimately command the 7th Special Forces Group in 1977.

The workers' revolt in East Berlin in June 1953 (which was brutally suppressed) pointed out to the Joint Chiefs of Staff the potential for revolution simmering behind the Iron Curtain. The new Special Forces were being formed to provide the resources, training and leadership to help oppressed populations, such as the East German workers, to throw off the shackles of tyranny. At Fort Bragg, the 10th Group was in no position to exploit any future turmoil so the Group sailed for Germany in November 1953 where they occupied an old German Army garrison at Bad Tolz, in the Bavarian Alps.

Destined never to perform its wartime mission, the 10th Special Forces Group was expected to exploit the resistance potential in eastern Europe if the Soviets attacked the west. The Special Forces teams would infiltrate target countries, make contact with agents recruited by the CIA,[19] who would assist them in establishing a resistance movement. A Special Forces FA Team (later called simply A Teams) was composed of ten men and designed to raise and support a guerilla regiment of up to 1500 indigenous personnel.[20]

The 10th also trained in direct action missions, whereby they would infiltrate a target country by air and destroy key facilities and interdict rail and road networks. Blowing up bridges and destroying railway tunnels required tremendous amounts of conventional explosive, requiring each man in the Special Forces team to carry a staggering load. To alleviate this problem, atomic demolition charges weighing about sixty pounds and capable of destroying the most massive highway bridges, were developed for the 10th Group.[21]

Realizing his embryonic Special Forces Group lacked experience in special operations, Colonel Bank trained his group with a variety of special operations forces from the United Kingdom, France, Norway, Germany, Greece, Spain, Italy, Turkey, Pakistan, Iran, Jordan, and Saudi Arabia. Each of these nations had highly developed and specialized forces that exposed the Americans to a wide variety of techniques and tradecraft that would eventually be incorporated into American doctrine. The Greeks' experience in waging guerilla warfare against the Germans and in counter-insurgency operations against the Communist guerilla movement proved invaluable in operations later undertaken in Southeast Asia. The British Special Air Service (SAS) taught the Americans the art of stealth and completely clandestine warfare necessary for direct action in denied areas. The Norwegians demonstrated how to set up an almost foolproof rear area protection system by co-opting a friendly populace. All these techniques remain a part of American Special Forces doctrine to this day.[22]

Southeast Asia, 1956–9

In 1956, Special Forces began training and operations in Asia, a sixteen man detachment was deployed to Hawaii and a twenty-two man detachment deployed to Camp Drake, Japan. These units consolidated into the 1st Special Forces Group in Okinawa. Their mission, like that of the 10th, was to prepare to conduct guerilla operations and so they trained with Taiwanese, Korean, Malaysian, and Filipino troops.[23] In addition to conducting joint exercises, the men of the 1st Group deployed in Mobile Training Teams throughout Asia to South Vietnam, Thailand and Indonesia.

As the men of the 1st Special Forces Group prepared for a future conflict in Southeast Asia, the legendary Lieutenant Colonel Arthur 'Bull' Simons and 120 Special Forces troops deployed from Fort Bragg to Laos in the summer of 1959 in an operation code named WHITE STAR. Infiltrating in civilian clothing, with civilian identification, and carrying hunting rifles, the men infiltrated Laos with a variety of cover stories.[24] Their mission was to link up with Laotian hill tribes the CIA had identified and, if they proved willing, train and arm them to fight the Communist Pathet Lao guerillas in the north.

Thus began the American military involvement in Southeast Asia.

NOTES

1. Shelby Stanton, *Rangers at War; Combat Recon in Vietnam* (New York, Orion, 1992), p. 1.
2. Barbara W. Tuchman, *The First Salute* (London, Sphere, 1990), p. 254.
3. James J. Worsham and Major R.B. Anderson, 'Mosby: The Model Partisan,' *Special Warfare Magazine* (Winter 1989), pp. 36–7.
4. Author unknown, *To Free the Oppressed; a Pocket History of the U.S. Special Forces* (The John F. Kennedy Special Warfare Center and School Public Affairs Office, October 1990).
5. Bill Mauldin, *The Brass Ring* (New York, W.W. Norton & Company, 1971), pp. 218–9.
6. Stanton, *Rangers at War*, pp. 2–6.
7. *To Free the Oppressed*, p. 7.
8. R.D. VanWagner, *1st Air Commando Group; Any Place, Any Time, Any Where, Military History Series 86–1* (Maxwell Air Force Base, USAF Command and Staff College, 1986), p. 51.
9. Ibid, p. 76.

10. General Robert C. Kingston, Notes from the Introduction to Special Operations Course, 1992, taught at the US Air Force Special Operations School, Hurlburt Field, Florida.
11. Alfred H. Paddock, Jr., *US Army Special Warfare; Its Origins* (Washington, DC, National Defense University Press, 1982), p. 30.
12. Frederick W. Cleaver, et. al., *U.N. Partisan Warfare in Korea, 1951–1954* (Chevy Chase, Maryland, The Johns Hopkins Research Office, June 1956), p. 1.
13. Memorandum, Subject: Guerilla Operations Outline, 1952, Headquarters, Far East Command Liaison Detachment (Korea), Guerilla Section, 11 April 1952.
14. Ibid.
15. Major General John K. Singlaub, US Army (Retired) with Malcolm McConnell, *Hazardous Duty; an American Soldier in the Twentieth Century* (New York, Summit, 1991), p. 181.
16. Ibid, p. 183.
17. Stanton, *Rangers at War*, pp. 7–11.
18. Charles M. Simpson III, *Inside the Green Berets; the First Thirty Years* (Novato, California, Presidio, 1983), p. 20.
19. Interview with Colonel Charles Norton, US Army (Retired), 22 September 1992.
20. Simpson, p. 36.
21. Ibid.
22. Ibid, p. 47.
23. Ibid, p. 50.
24. Cadet Kristen Morton, Monograph: *CIDG; Civilian Irregular Defense Group, Vietnam* (Colorado Springs, United States Air Force Academy, 1984).

PART II

Forging the Capability
The Vietnam Years
1960–1975

CHAPTER 2

Phoenix from the Ashes
The Rebirth of Special
Operations Forces 1960–75

The intensification of the Cold War sparked President John F. Kennedy's decision to reinvigorate the unconventional warfare and special operations capabilities of the United States. Vietnam, a small nation in southeast Asia in the throes of a hot civil war, became America's chosen battleground to prosecute surrogate warfare, a new type of conflict with international Communism. The history of the Vietnam conflict serves as backdrop for the development of America's special operations capability. Special operations forces (SOF) were involved elsewhere in the world during the period of American involvement in Vietnam, but it was in the crucible of Vietnam that their doctrine and techniques were developed and refined.

Khrushchev's Challenge – 'Wars of Liberation,' 1961

Nikita Khrushchev threw down the gauntlet on 6 January 1961, two weeks before President Kennedy took office, when he openly announced that while the Soviet Union and its satellites opposed world wars and local wars, they would support 'just wars of liberation and popular uprisings.' Using a technique that would become all too familiar over the Cold War years, Khrushchev's bluster inadvertently belied his frustration at being unable politically or militarily to gain the upper hand against NATO and the US. Stalin's ruthless suppression of the East Berlin workers' revolt in 1951 and Khrushchev's own cold-blooded suppression of the Hungarian revolution in 1956 prompted the NATO nations to accelerate rearmament to mitigate the overwhelming numbers of troops Moscow had left deployed throughout eastern Europe following the conclusion of World War II.

Systematically, the West maintained parity or superiority over Soviet conventional and strategic nuclear capabilities. Consequently, Khrushchev began to seek ways to break the deadlock and came up with a military doctrine that emphasized maintaining the status quo in Europe, expanding Soviet influence in the third world through the arming of surrogates, and striving initially for parity and eventually for superiority in the nuclear arms arena.

President Kennedy's Initiative, 1961

At the age of forty-three, John Fitzgerald Kennedy became the thirty-fifth president of the US and the youngest man ever elected to the presidency. Although a relatively lackluster senator, Kennedy proved to be an innovative and particularly dauntless leader and statesman. A bona fide naval hero of World War II, Kennedy would pursue an active foreign policy.

Picking up the gauntlet thrown by Khrushchev, Kennedy immediately struck at one of Khrushchev's most important satellites, Cuba, in April 1961. First authorized under the Eisenhower administration, Kennedy continued an operation in which the Central Intelligence Agency (CIA) armed and trained a brigade of Cuban exiles to invade Cuba and oust the Cuban dictator Fidel Castro. Unfortunately, due to poor security, Castro's forces learned of the invasion and proceeded to cut the brigade to ribbons as they assaulted the beach at the Bay of Pigs. Kennedy sealed the fate of these hapless irregulars when he withdrew US air support from them at the last minute after being convinced that the entire endeavor was a mistake.

Chastened and learning from his experience, Kennedy and his advisors turned to the problem of spreading communism in Southeast Asia. Maoist Communist movements were springing up throughout Asia and in the 1950s, two had been successfully suppressed; the Malayan insurgency by the British, and the Huk insurgency in the Philippines by the US. Retired Air Force General Edward Lansdale was the chief American military advisor to the Philippine government and instrumental in the successful suppression of the Communist Huk movement. Impressed with Lansdale's combination of experience and success, Kennedy sent him to South Vietnam as an advisor to the Saigon government.

Under Kennedy's leadership, the Departments of State and Defense formulated a comprehensive strategy for Vietnam in which the military action should have almost perfectly complemented the political initiatives. The strategy had but one serious flaw, which proved fatal: it assumed that through the correct application of political, economic, and military power, North and South Vietnam could peacefully coexist. Although peaceful coexistence was amenable to many South Vietnamese, it was absolutely unacceptable from the North Vietnamese perspective. Adhering to the most stringent interpretations of Maoist–Leninist doctrine, the North Vietnamese could not tolerate political dissent within the framework of their political system. They believed that as long as a free south existed, it would be a subversive influence; its existence was intolerable. Many South Vietnamese believed the same regarding the north, but the Kennedy administration believed in peaceful co-existence, and they were 'calling the shots.'

The Vietnam Conflict, 1945–61

When World War II ended, the allies were in disagreement over the administration of former Japanese holdings throughout Asia. In Vietnam, Ho Chi Minh, a dedicated Communist guerilla leader in Vietnam, had gained considerable popular support. The former colonial power in Vietnam, the French, formed a government led by the Emperor Bao Dai. Bent on establishing his own Communist regime, Ho Chi Minh took to the jungle again in 1947 with his band of Viet Minh supporters and conducted a guerilla war to oust both the French and Bao Dai.

By 1953, with eighty percent of the war effort in Vietnam subsidized by the Americans, the French appeared to be gaining the upper hand. However in 1954 this proved wrong when the French lured the Viet Minh into what they thought would be a conventional, set-piece battle at Dien Bien Phu, only to find themselves besieged and forced to surrender by the wily Communist general Vo Nguyen Giap, and his guerillas. This major defeat caused France to re-evaluate her objectives in Indochina, withdraw her forces and disengage completely.

The terms of the Geneva conference of 1954 were a mixed victory for the Viet Minh since Ho Chi Minh's Chinese and Soviet allies forced him to concede significant amounts of the territory his forces had captured in order to establish a temporary partition of Vietnam along the 17th longitudinal parallel. On the plus side, Laos, Cambodia, and Vietnam were granted independence, and no foreign troops were to be stationed there. Neither the South Vietnamese government in Saigon under Ngo Dinh Diem nor his new backers, the Americans, signed the accords.

With American CIA support, Diem began a systematic 'pacification' campaign to destroy the remaining Communist infrastructure and its political base, which opposed the stability of his government. To replace the vacuum left by the withdrawal of the French, American President Dwight D. Eisenhower's administration deployed some 700 regular and Special Forces soldiers to advise and train Diem's Army of the Republic of Vietnam (ARVN). This would remain the extent of America's involvement in Vietnam until 1961, when a new American President would take office.

In these early days of American involvement, American idealism stood out in stark contrast to a Vietnamese cynicism and pragmatism that would never be clearly understood by America's senior political and military leadership. The Vietnamese adopted US Army force structure, doctrine, and equipment designed for battle on the north German plains, but selected their leadership on the basis of political connections and loyalty to the current regime.

Low-intensity-conflict (LIC) Doctrine

In 1961, Kennedy's plan was to provide increased military aid to the regime of President Diem in its fight against the Communist insurgency, but to avoid direct US military involvement. But as a demonstration of American commitment to the region, Kennedy ordered a brigade of US Marines to Thailand to deter North Vietnam from expanding its operations against the south. This deployment also threatened the Ho Chi Minh trail, North Vietnam's major supply line to its forces fighting in South Vietnam, which crossed Laos and Cambodia.

Taking advantage of rural dissatisfaction with Diem's land reform policies, the old soldiers of the Viet Minh renamed themselves the Viet Cong (Vietnamese Communists in the Vietnamese language) and organized armed resistance to Diem. Communist-led and directed by Hanoi, the Viet Cong (called VC in the vernacular of the American GI) included all groups opposed to the Diem regime and its US ally. Later, in 1969, the VC reorganized into the National Liberation Front (NLF) in an effort to appear as a legitimate political opposition movement.

The VC adopted the 'people's war' strategy favored by Chinese Communist leader Mao Tse-tung: guerillas used the civilian population as cover to engage in protracted warfare, avoiding direct combat with conventional forces except in advantageous circumstances. As mentioned earlier, the North Vietnamese government provided resources for the VC effort by infiltrating men and supplies through Laos and Cambodia along the network of trails that comprised the Ho Chi Minh trail. The fact that this network crossed the sovereign nations of Laos and Cambodia would later present a significant dilemma to American military planners who were under direction not to the 'widen the war.'[1]

The VC used any means they deemed necessary to expand control in government villages: assassinations, atrocities and other terrorist activity were common methods of dissuading villagers from supporting the South Vietnamese government. Using a technique pioneered by the British in Malaya in the 1950s, Diem moved peasants into 'strategic hamlets' to separate and protect them from the guerillas. The peasants had mixed feelings about this policy: on the one hand they were relatively safe from VC atrocities, but on the other they were unhappy with the replacement of elected village officials with Diem appointees.

Responding to Diem's requests for additional help, President Kennedy gradually increased the number of US advisors in Vietnam to over 16,000 as the VC continued to expand their recruitment and the North Vietnamese provided ever more extensive aid. Introduction of helicopters and more advisors briefly boosted morale in Saigon, but the ARVN continued to lose battles in 1963 in spite of the American advice and superior technology.

By the summer of 1963, the political situation in South Vietnam became critical. Buddhist monks immolated themselves in the streets to protest Diem's religious persecution, drawing extensive world media attention. Diem refused any accommodation with the Buddhists, who numbered some ninety-five percent of his population. Frustrated by Diem's intransigence and the political damage it was doing, the US threw their support behind a successful coup launched by General Duong Van 'Big' Minh, who was overthrown by another group of officers in January 1964. A period of intense political turbulence followed, in which South Vietnam had seven different governments in sixteen months. Finally, in June 1964, Army General Nguyen Van Thieu and Air Force General Nguyen Cao Key seized power as chief of state and premier, respectively.

Ironically, the pacification program (that would later evolve into the controversial Phoenix program) enacted by Diem with CIA help was beginning adversely to affect VC recruiting. In spite of a series of coups over the next two years, the pacification and strategic hamlet programs began to improve government control in the rural areas. With their guerilla campaign becoming bogged down, Hanoi decided to raise the stakes and deploy some thirty-five to forty People's Liberation Armed Forces (PLAF, but more commonly referred to as the North Vietnamese Army or NVA) main force battalions, 35,000 guerillas and 80,000 irregulars down the Ho Chi Minh Trail into central South Vietnam. In December 1963, shortly after the death of President Kennedy, the first North Vietnamese main force (conventional) unit arrived in South Vietnam.

Throughout the 1960s, the US military leadership considered the Vietnam involvement a distraction from the principal threat: the massive Soviet formations remaining in Eastern Europe. The US military strategy was initially to prop up the South Vietnamese Army by assisting them in building a strong conventional deterrent along the lines of the US European combat divisions. Ironically, the ineffectiveness of this approach resulted in later deployment of US combat divisions – also tailored for European combat.

Consequently, the majority of Americans and South Vietnamese sent to fight the NVA were organized, trained and equipped for a European war. The business of fighting the unconventional, guerilla, and psychological operations (known as the Low-Intensity Conflict, or LIC threat) was detailed to a small core of army, navy and air force special operations units. As such, the majority of US and South Vietnamese combat power was focused against what was arguably the wrong threat.

But the specialized forces necessary to deal with a LIC threat were not lost on the Kennedy administration, which directed a revitalization of SOF. Unfortunately, Defense Department planners saw this, too, as a distraction from the European focus and failed to provide adequate resources for revitalization. Thus, the American SOF and ARVN Rangers were vastly under-resourced, but bore the brunt of the action in this jungle war. As a consequence, they were frequently committed against superior numbers of well-trained enemy jungle fighters. While there is no question that these units fought valiantly, they suffered high losses of very fine, courageous and well-trained personnel.

Escalation and De-escalation, 1965–75

In Washington, Kennedy's successor, Lyndon Johnson, moved rapidly to neutralize the insurgent movement. CIA operatives and SOF conducted covert diversionary raids on the northern coast, while the navy conducted electronic intelligence missions in North Vietnam's Gulf of Tonkin. Johnson appointed General William Westmoreland (to this day known affectionately as 'Westy' to the thousands who served under him) to command Military Assistance Command, Vietnam (MACV), increased the number of advisors to 23,000, and expanded economic assistance. Simultaneously, Johnson warned Hanoi that continued adventurism in South Vietnam and revolutionary support would elicit a strong US response. Thus, the Pentagon began planning bombing raids on the North.

Johnson justified escalating US involvement in Vietnam because of an incident in the Gulf of Tonkin. On 2 August 1964, North Vietnamese torpedo boats attacked a US destroyer conducting intelligence collection in international waters in the Gulf of Tonkin. A second destroyer rushed at flank speed to its aid and was reportedly attacked; however, this report later proved erroneous. Nevertheless, Johnson ordered retaliatory air strikes and urged congressional support for the Tonkin Gulf Resolution, authorizing him to conduct extensive retaliatory military operations.

Tactical and strategic bombings became an integral part of US policy to demoralize the North Vietnamese. Forgetting the lessons of World War II, the bombing campaign was predictably counter-productive and served only to strengthen enemy resolve.

In spite of American bombing and deployments, by the summer of 1965 an entire main force North Vietnamese division was operating in South Vietnam with two more working their way through Cambodia and Laos along the Ho Chi Minh trail. With Westmoreland desperately requesting more troops, Secretary of Defense Robert McNamara convinced Johnson that an additional 70,000 troops should be deployed to South Vietnam and that their mission should be expanded from air base defense to 'search and destroy.'[2]

With this, the nature of the US military involvement fundamentally changed from air base defense to the offense – search-and-destroy, but it was done secretly, without congressional debate. The results of this strategically naive and clandestine attempt at an 'economic' escalation was an extremely costly loss of lives, and the near destruction of the American military institution.

Military Assistance Command (Vietnam), Studies and Observation Group

One of the results of the policy to prosecute the war within the confines of Vietnam was a major clandestine campaign to abate the flow of troops and supplies coming through Cambodia and Laos by interdicting the Ho Chi Minh trail. This campaign was carried out by the MAC(V) Studies and Observation Group, or MAC(V)SOG; the cover name for the first truly joint US Special Operations Command, whose exploits are discussed in subsequent chapters. In this unified command, army, navy and air force special operations units conducted a secret war in Cambodia and Laos to interdict activity along the trail.

Simultaneously, special operations units of all three services took the war deep into North Vietnam to attack the enemy in his staging areas and along his lines of communications. SOF penetrated deep into North Vietnam to raid staging and supply bases, collect intelligence, snatch key enemy personnel and rescue allied prisoners-of-war.

The Operations Staff Directorate of MAC(V)SOG was composed of five divisions called Op-31 through 35. Op-31 was the naval component, conducting maritime special operations out of Danang. Op-32 was the secret air force, providing a clandestine resupply and infiltration capability. Op-33 conducted psychological operations (Psyops). Op-34, out of Long Thanh, attempted to organize resistance groups and collect intelligence in the North. Op-35 was responsible for cross-border operations into Cambodia and Laos.

Although at the tactical level, MAC(V)SOG activities proved quite successful, the overall US strategy was foundering.

Conclusions

The fumbling withdrawal from Vietnam left particularly deep marks on the special operations community. It was the men who had worked closely with and befriended the dedicated, idealistic South Vietnamese, who had a dream of a better Vietnam. These men lost many American and Vietnamese friends in a cause that their country cynically abandoned.

The impact of the American experience in Vietnam proved disastrous for American SOF for several reasons. First, the image of SOF had been tarnished as a consequence of adverse media coverage as had that of the overall military as an institution. As a result of this adverse impression, the Congress and incoming administration were unwilling to devote funding to the special operations capability, seeing this as throwing good money after bad. Most tragically, a great many fine special operators had been either killed or disillusioned by their Vietnam experience; the latter opting out of the service. The result was that the capability eroded and ultimately was not there when needed.

Fortunately, not all was lost: the lessons of Vietnam were well-documented in Defense Department historical records enabling the American political leadership to reinvigorate special operations in the mid-1980s.

NOTES

1. Major General John K. Singlaub with Malcolm McConnell, *Hazardous Duty; an American Soldier in the 20th Century* (New York, Summit, 1991), p. 271.
2. Ibid, pp. 273–4.

CHAPTER 3

America's Best
Army Special Operations in
Vietnam 1959–75

Army special operations forces (SOF) waged a fierce and unrelenting war focused against the Viet Cong (VC) and strategic rear areas of the North Vietnamese Army (NVA). In operations characterized by innovation, courage, and tenacity, army SOF consistently seized the initiative from the VC, usually annihilating them in the process. As the war progressed into the late 1960s and early 1970s, the conventional leadership in Vietnam took note of these successes and increasingly committed these men against more conventional forces, believing that SOF could achieve similar successes against regular units.

But the soldiers of SOF were not 'Supermen' and were ill-equipped to deal with large, conventional forces in set-piece battles; consequently, many were killed simply because they were hopelessly outnumbered.

The initial strategy of the American leadership in Vietnam was to fight NVA main force units with South Vietnamese and American conventional units, while SOF undermined the Communist infrastructure. Within this strategy, SOF were expected to mobilize indigenous resistance to the Communists, which they did effectively. Their success prompted the Communists increasingly to engage in terrorism, for which the Americans initially were ill-prepared. But the men of SOF learned quickly, and began neutralizing the instruments of terror via programs such as Phoenix.

Special Forces Accession and Training

Special Forces were the spearpoint of army special operations in Vietnam. Since the early 1950s, these men had prepared to recruit, train and equip bands of indigenous guerilla fighters and lead them in combat in enemy rear areas. This type of mission required rugged individuals who could master tactical skills not only for their own use, but also to such a degree that they could use them to transform foreign civilians into effective partisans and guerillas. Special Forces soldiers had to be tough, smart, innovative, diplomatic, and able to survive under the harshest of conditions in hostile territory with little or no outside support.

The Special Forces volunteer, after meeting rigorous accession standards, underwent rigorous physical conditioning and testing to assess his physical and mental strengths and weaknesses. After paratrooper training, the Special Forces recruit went on to comprehensive instruction in one of five specialties: intelligence, weapons, demolitions, medicine or communications. Weapons and demolitions training would take four weeks with specialists training on both US and foreign weapons and explosives. Medical specialists would train for almost forty weeks. Team and intelligence sergeants were already senior non-commissioned officers before they received formal training in those specialties.[1] Soldiers who did not already speak a second language would be sent for additional foreign language training. Some soldiers underwent SCUBA, High-Altitude Low-Opening (HALO) parachute and hand-to-hand combat training. After completing seven more weeks of Special Forces branch training, they were assigned to an A Detachment, also known as an A Team.

The A Detachments maintained a high training tempo. Here the soldiers underwent specialized team training in such areas as arctic, mountain, or jungle operations. To keep their language and instruction skills honed, they trained extensively with indigenous forces in Europe and Asia.[2] Most of the Special Forces soldiers who deployed to Vietnam already had extensive experience training in other Asian countries, such as Taiwan and Laos.

Advisors: The Lone Wolves, 1957–75

The first Special Forces personnel arriving in Vietnam in 1961 were the advisors. These men (who were usually quite young and learned the art of oriental jungle warfare through on-the-job training) were assigned to Vietnamese units to provide advice and assistance in leadership techniques, fieldcraft, and operational planning as well as communications with US Army and Air Force fire support. As early as 1957, Special Forces advisors helped form the Vietnamese 1st Observation Group, a politicized 'special intelligence' unit directly subordinate to President Diem. In 1960, the US established three Vietnamese Ranger training centers, staffed by Special Forces advisors, to raise sixty indigenous Ranger companies.[3]

One of many such advisors was First Lieutenant Fred Caristo, who advised the 37th Ranger Battalion (ARVN) in 1964 and 1965 (which secured the beach for the first US Marines when they landed at Danang). The Vietnamese Rangers were used to fight the budding VC movement in South Vietnam and essentially were called in when regular units found themselves being overpowered. Although these Rangers were very tough, tenacious fighters, this employment practice led to crippling personnel losses. When Caristo was reassigned to MAC(V)SOG in 1965, fierce combat had reduced his battalion to less than forty percent of its original strength.

Caristo, who went on to perform a number of remarkable feats of heroism, developed a strong bond with his indigenous comrades in arms, and went on to spend a total of eight years in Vietnam, more continuous combat time than any American soldier in history. He is also the recipient of America's second highest award for gallantry, the Distinguished Service Cross.

Border Camps, 1964

Ho Chi Minh and his government began steadily to escalate their campaign to undermine the newly formed South Vietnamese government of President Thieu and Vice President Key in 1964. Increasing amounts of troops and military supplies began flowing down the Ho Chi Minh trail in Cambodia and Laos in an effort to reinvigorate the Viet Cong movement. To counter this initiative, US Army Special Forces began establishing border camps near the South Vietnamese border along the main Communist infiltration routes.

These camps were administered by Special Forces A Detachments who supervised, trained and equipped indigenous South Vietnamese Montagnard Civilian Irregular Defense Group (CIDG) units, Nung tribesmen, and Airborne Special Forces (abbreviated LLDB after the Vietnamese translation). These Special Forces detachments were composed of ten to twelve highly trained non-commissioned officers and officers who provided expertise in tactics, medical aid, demolition, communications, fieldcraft (the art of survival), and military endeavor at the small unit level.

The Montagnards (mountain people) of the western highlands were a primitive tribe of people who harbored an intense dislike for both the North and South Vietnamese. Seeing the combat potential of these people, the Special Forces sought them out, learned their customs and recruited them to fight against the NVA and VC. Once recruited, the Americans trained them, formed them into units and led them.

The Nung were mercenaries of Chinese extraction that were used to guard the camps and the Detachment Commanders. Both Nungs and Montagnards were intensely loyal to their Special Forces benefactors.

The Nam Dong CIDG camp in Thua Thien Province was typical of the early border camps. Commanded by Captain Roger H.C. Donlon, the camp was located at the junction of two mountain valleys that served as VC infiltration routes and protected some 5,000 Montagnard villagers who lived in the valleys. The camp was garrisoned by Captain Donlon and his team, 381 CIDG troops, fifty Nungs, an Australian advisor and a pathologist.[4] Because it had become a prime VC target and its location was so vulnerable, by July 1964 the Special Forces had decided to close the camp, and were preparing to do so.

Then, on 6 July 1964, at 0230 hours, the camp was attacked by a battalion of Viet Cong. Achieving complete surprise, the attack began with a devastating mortar barrage followed by a human wave of screaming Viet Cong. VC loudspeakers harangued the defenders in English and Vietnamese to surrender.

Because Nam Dong was initially established as a small French outpost and had subsequently expanded, it had an outer and an inner perimeter. The VC overwhelmed the outer perimeter but were raked with exploding grenades and machinegun fire before they achieved the inner perimeter. The Nungs and Montagnards fought viciously.

As a VC demolition team tried to force the main gate, Captain Donlon charged through intense rifle fire and grenade detonations and single-handedly killed them all. Wounded in the stomach, he covered the withdrawal of other wounded Special Forces soldiers from one of his own mortar positions. Carrying out his team sergeant, he was wounded again. He recovered the mortar, administered first aid to his wounded and continued to direct the defense of the outpost. He was wounded four times during the course of the battle, and was largely responsible for the successful defense of the camp.[5]

Captain Donlon received the first Medal of Honor, America's highest award, of the Vietnam conflict. The construction of Nam Dong, with inner and outer perimeters, became the standard for border camps. Camp Nam Dong was eventually closed by another A Detachment on 4 September 1964.[6]

The Greek Letter Projects: Special Reconnaissance, 1965–7

As Phoenix and the US-backed South Vietnamese civic action programs applied a brake to the expansion of the Communist power base in Vietnam, the North Vietnamese leadership began sending ever increasing numbers of troops and equipment down the Ho Chi Minh Trail into South Vietnam's 'soft underbelly.'

American and Vietnamese special forces teams were the first units to encounter the main force NVA battalions and regiments that infiltrated South Vietnam. Project Delta, or Detachment B-52, 5th Special Forces, commanded by Major Charlie Beckwith among others, was the first unit to find and engage a NVA unit on the territory of South Vietnam.[7] Beckwith's unit was composed of six reconnaissance/hunter-killer teams; each consisting of eight South Vietnamese Airborne Special Forces soldiers and two Americans. A Strike/Recondo platoon had sixteen teams which infiltrated into enemy held areas to gather intelligence, target artillery, and 'snatch' the odd prisoner. A Roadrunner platoon travelled the roads in enemy garb, with cover stories, to collect intelligence and monitor enemy activities.[8]

It was in October 1965 that Project Delta found its first NVA main force unit in South Vietnam.[9] Colonel Bill McKean, Commander of the 5th Special Forces, directed Major Beckwith to conduct a reconnaissance of the northern II Corps area near the village of Plei Me. The mission was to determine the size, composition and disposition of enemy units already reported to be operating in the area.

The Special Forces camp at Plei Me was defended by some 400 Montagnard tribesmen and their families, supported by a twelve-man Special Forces A Detachment and an equal number of Vietnamese Special Forces. On the evening of 19 October, while Beckwith was planning the reconnaissance mission, Plei Me was attacked by a force of indeterminate size. Project Delta was ordered to accelerate its timetable and get to the area immediately.

On 20 October Beckwith assembled four recon teams and two companies of Vietnamese Rangers and staged them at Pleiku, ready for action. He then conducted an aerial recon of Plei Me, to assess the situation and find a suitable landing zone. At first light the next day, Project Delta and the Rangers boarded helicopters and flew to a landing zone near Plei Me. They began the hot, arduous trek toward the embattled camp.

At about noon, the force entered a deserted hamlet. With cooking fires still smoldering, it was apparent that some unit had entered the hamlet eight to ten hours earlier and taken the inhabitants along with them.

Continuing through the jungle, in single file, two shots rang out from the vicinity of the point man (lead man in the file). One of the Delta troops had killed a soldier in a khaki uniform and pith helmet, the uniform of a North Vietnamese Army regular. Up until this point, there had been unconfirmed reports of NVA presence in the south, but this was the first face-to-face encounter with them. The Vietnamese Rangers began to get nervous and refused to proceed. Delta went on without them.

By 2000 hours that night, the Americans were close enough to hear gunfire coming from Plei Me. Rather than enter the camp at night and risk being shot on the basis of mistaken identity, Beckwith bedded his people down, with fifty percent of the unit on watch while the remainder slept, conducted a reconnaissance of the area, and planned how he would enter Plei Me the next morning. That evening, the Vietnamese Rangers caught up with Delta; their commander had decided he did not want to lose face by fleeing in the face of the enemy.

The plan was to infiltrate the unit undetected through the jungle to the dirt road leading into the camp, then dash down the road, through the gate, and into the camp. Catching the NVA off guard, within thirty minutes Delta and the Rangers were inside the compound. Casualties included a Vietnamese lieutenant and a newspaper reporter who had stowed away aboard one of the helicopters at Pleiku.

The combined might of the defenders was then able to break the siege.

The successes of Project Delta as a country-wide strategic reconnaissance unit led to the formation of Projects Omega and Sigma, which provided long-range reconnaissance support to I and II Field Forces in the more southerly regions of South Vietnam. Each of these special reconnaissance units was 'tailored,' or specially configured and organized, for the missions they conducted.

The Blackjack operations conducted in the spring of 1967 also proceeded from the successes of the strategic reconnaissance units. These operations were conducted by Mobile Guerilla Force companies (composed of Nung or Montagnard tribesmen) under the command of an American Special Forces officer in support of the American 1st Cavalry Division (Airmobile).

Blackjack 23, led by Captain Clyde J. Sincere Jr., was essentially a deep reconnaissance operation to find enemy main force units so that the 1st Cavalry Division could effectively attack them. Deploying on 5 March 1967, Mobile Guerilla Force 876 endured enemy hit and run attacks and one attack by US aircraft before it hit pay dirt almost a week later, on 11 March. It was that day that Captain Sincere climbed Hill 709 to get a view of the surrounding terrain.

> Hill 709 was the highest terrain in the area. Observation of the river junction was excellent, but long range. Using binoculars, it was easy to observe platoon size forces bathing at different intervals at the base of Hill 242. Barges, approximately eight by eight feet with outboard motors were seen moving in the area loaded with equipment. Generator engines were heard starting at 1700 hours and continued throughout the night from the direction of Hill 242 ... Mobile guerilla force radios were jammed ... Large searchlights were observed during the night. Apparently the NVA/VC made no attempt to hide their location ... It was apparent that 13 March would prove to be interesting as the Mobile Guerilla Force moved toward Hill 242.[10]

The enemy spotted by the Mobile Guerilla Force was successfully attacked by air strike, but the Blackjack force never got near Hill 242. In the subsequent two days, Hill 709 was attacked by successively larger enemy formations forcing Captain Sincere to break off the operation and call for extraction.

The Mike Forces, 1966

To provide emergency reinforcement of the border camps if they came under concerted attack, the 5th Group established the Mike Force (short for Mobile Strike Force) at Nha Trang. Mike Force was ready to go at a moment's notice to reinforce a border camp in peril.

In March 1966, a reinforced NVA regiment moved up the A Shau valley, two miles from the Laotian border in South Vietnam, to attack a border camp named for the valley in which it lay. The camp was garrisoned by a rather motley South Vietnamese Civilian Irregular Defense Group (CIDG) company of two hundred soldiers and a group of South Vietnamese Special Forces soldiers. Supervising the activities of this group, and providing much needed leadership, was Detachment A-102 of the 5th Special Forces Group, commanded by Captain John D. 'Dave' Blair. This small group of Americans and South Vietnamese had been regularly disrupting the flow of men and supplies coming down the Trail, and the NVA had come to put a stop to it, permanently.

By 7 March, Blair had received enough intelligence on the NVA buildup to have the Nha Trang Mike Force dispatched to Camp A Shau. The force that arrived by helicopter was composed of 143 indigenous Nung tribesmen led by a team of Special Forces NCOs under the command of Captain Tennis 'Sam' Carter. The Nung were a Vietnamese hill tribe of Chinese ancestry known for their fighting prowess and intensely loyal to their Special Forces advisors. The Mike Force pitched in and helped Camp A Shau prepare for the onslaught.

The thunder of recoilless rifles and the 'crump' of mortars heralded the beginning of the assault at 0400 hours on the morning of 9 March. Forty minutes later, under cover of the heavy weapons, two NVA companies assaulted the south wall of the camp, only to be thrown back by the tenacious resistance they encountered.

The barrage continued for two and a half hours, killing one Special Forces soldier and blowing off the legs of Staff Sergeant Billie Hall, the senior Mike Force medic. Demonstrating the courage, tenacity, and selflessness that became commonplace among Special Forces medics, Hall applied tourniquets to the stumps of both his legs and continued to administer aid to the wounded until he passed out and died.

Cloud cover severely hampered air support to the Special Forces. Although two light observation helicopters were able to take out two of the wounded, a Marine CH-34 crashed while attempting to land and a second CH-34 retrieved the crew of the first and disappeared into the clouds. An AC-47 'Spooky' (modified Douglas DC-3) gunship trying to provide fire support was destroyed by anti-aircraft fire. Supply drops landed outside the camp and were lost to the enemy. Finally, at dark, an HH-3 Jolly Green Giant helicopter was able to land and evacuate twenty-six of the wounded.

At 0400 hours the next morning, after regrouping under the light of American parachute flares, the NVA began another of their devastating barrages. This time the NVA simultaneously assaulted across the airstrip against the east wall and against the south wall of the camp.

As the NVA were about the breach the wall, the CIDG company turned its weapons on the Americans and the Mike Force. For three hours, Nung and American fought the NVA and their traitorous allies in a fierce battle. As the fighting became hand-to-hand, the Americans and their remaining Nung and CIDG allies withdrew to the camp communications bunker in order to withstand a fresh enemy assault that began at 0830.

Simultaneously, Blair and his men were able to call in an air strike by B-57 Canberra bombers against an NVA battalion that was massing on the airstrip. The Canberras dropped cluster munitions that inflicted severe casualties on the battalion and shattered their attack.

Captain Carter and his NCOs now tried to mount a counter-attack to regain some ground, but the situation was desperate. Blair called in another air strike, this time against the south and east walls of the Camp itself.

Four old A1E Skyraiders, single-engine, propeller-driven aircraft with twenty-millimeter cannons, came in low, raking NVA attackers with cannon fire. As the aircraft made their run, one was hit by anti-aircraft fire and forced to return to base. A second was hit and caught fire, forcing the pilot to crash land on the air strip. As they were joined by two more Skyraiders, Major Bernard Fisher called for a rescue helicopter to assist the downed aircraft. Learning that the helicopter was at least twenty minutes away, Fisher landed on the airstrip amid a hail of bullets, retrieved his colleague, and took off with nineteen bullet holes to show for it. Fisher was later awarded the Medal of Honor, America's highest military decoration, for his heroism.

Although the air strikes kept them pinned down, the enemy continued to press their attack by fire. Out of food and water, short of ammunition and sleep (the battle was half-way through its second day) Captain Blair decided to abandon the outpost.

As the Marine helicopters arrived, amid heavy ground fire, to evacuate the post, they were mobbed by the remaining CIDG and Vietnamese Special Forces troops while the Mike Force laid suppressive fire on the NVA. The Marines had to shoot into the mob to get them under control. Only sixty personnel were evacuated; among them were one wounded American and seven crew from two of the helicopters that had been shot down. One chopper carrying wounded was shot down in flames, with no survivors.

After this evacuation, a Huey helicopter gunship spotted fourteen of the survivors, jettisoned its rocket pods, and rescued them. That night, the remaining survivors escaped through the jungle, but some were not seen again.

The battle was costly: five Americans and seventy-five of the Nung were killed. Thirty-three Nung were wounded and another fifteen were missing – an eighty-six percent casualty rate for the Mike Force. The NVA suffered 800 killed and scores of others wounded, out of a regiment of 2000.[11]

Rangers, 1968–9

Recognizing the need for a long-range patrol capability in his conventional units similar to that possessed by the Special Forces, General Westmoreland ordered the formation of long-range patrol detachments in each division. In most cases, this simply codified a requirement the divisions had already identified and supplied on their own in various ways. During the course of the war, the Long-Range Reconnaissance Patrol (LRRP) detachments evolved into the ranger companies that would one day be consolidated into the battalions of the 75th Ranger Regiment.

One of the more successful examples of a Ranger operation was conducted by Company F (Long Range Patrol), 52d Infantry Regiment, of the 1st Infantry Division just before the NVA Lunar New Year or Tet offensive of 1968.[12]

Nicknamed the 'Danger Forward Patrollers' because of their radio call sign, Company F successfully foiled the main NVA assault against their division.

In response to division intelligence assessments in January 1968, Company F withdrew from its routine patrol assignments and established a security screen around several critical 1st Division installations. On 31 January 1968, one of the patrols established an observation post outside the division aviation base at Phu Loi. At 2005 hours the patrol leader, Sergeant Ronny O. Luse, observed some twelve VC approaching his position. As the patrol prepared an ambush, the VC moved off into the forest before they came in range. Rather than pursue, the patrol waited to see what else might come along.

They did not have to wait long.

A full battalion of VC emerged from the jungle about an hour later, much to the astonishment of the patrol, and began to work their way across the rice paddies. Luse reported the activity to the division tactical operations center, who in turn ordered the Rangers to break contact and withdraw inside the friendly security perimeter. Simultaneously, a helicopter equipped with a search light was dispatched to the area to direct an artillery strike which scattered the VC formation into the village of An My.

As the artillery pounded the VC positions, the division assaulted the outskirts of Phu Loi and the village of An My, concluding the battle on 3 February. Three VC battalions were thwarted from their Tet objective because of the efforts of one patrol.

Special Forces and Ranger reconnaissance performed valiantly in finding the enemy so that conventional forces could more effectively deal with them. Unfortunately, the fruits of this reconnaissance were seldom reaped as the supported conventional forces were rarely able to deploy maneuver units against the enemy before he could escape into the jungle. Consequently, as air and artillery strikes were directed against the enemy formations detected by special and long-range reconnaissance units, the enemy formations would flee into the relative security of the jungle to regroup. Upon regrouping, these formations would frequently continue their operations while searching with a vengeance for the reconnaissance units that targeted them.

The American response to this was to put more firepower with the Rangers, eventually forming Ranger Companies in 1969. This only served to reduce the effectiveness of Ranger Recon since the larger units were more easily detected and more prone to become decisively engaged.

Military Assistance Command (Vietnam)(MACV), Studies and Observation Group (SOG)

They effectively attacked and captured our soldiers and disrupted our supply lines. This weakened our forces and hurt our morale because we could not stop these attacks. We understood that these American soldiers were very skillful and very brave in their tactics to disrupt infiltration from the north.[13]

Nguyen Tuong Lai
Former NVA Officer

Three of the functional directorates of SOG were composed primarily of army special operations personnel and units: Op-33, Op-34, and Op-35. Op-34, as mentioned in the previous chapter, attempted to organize resistance to the Communist government within North Vietnam. Unfortunately, as with JACK operations in North Korea, this proved virtually impossible due to the extremely tight security maintained by the Ho Chi Minh regime. Undaunted by this lack of success, Op-33, the Psyops directorate, launched a deception operation in which they fabricated a resistance movement, called the 'Sacred Sword of the Patriot,' complete with a clandestine radio station. Using a careful mix of intelligence gained from linecrossers and agents combined with artful fabrication, the radio station broadcast factual North Vietnamese casualty figures and both factual and fictitious reports of corruption within the Communist leadership. The 'Patriot' station also exposed immoral cadre who not only embezzled public funds but cavorted with the young wives of soldiers fighting in the south. According to reliable agent reports, those personnel actually engaged in corruption reported by the station, as well as those slandered by the station but innocent of any corruption, were removed from their positions.

As the 5th Special Forces Group attempted to interdict the Ho Chi Minh trail in South Vietnam, Op-35, led by Colonel Arthur D. 'Bull' Simons (who had been working the area since the 1950s with the WHITE STAR Special Forces deployment in Laos), interdicted the trail in Laos and later, in Cambodia. As these nations were politically neutral, Op-35's operations had to be conducted discreetly.

Operation SHINING BRASS (later called PRAIRIE FIRE) was the code name for the Trail interdiction campaign. Op-35 interdicted the Trail by inserting reconnaissance teams (which were called 'Spike' teams) by Vietnamese Air Force helicopter into critical road junctions and bottlenecks on the trail. Usually inserted at dusk, the teams would disembark their helicopters rapidly and immediately set up ambushes in case any NVA security troops heard the insertion. After spending the night near their landing zone, they would begin their patrolling operations which could last anywhere from one or two days to several weeks. Extraction would be accomplished by a 'Maguire rig,'(named after a Special Forces NCO) which was a long sling dangled through the jungle canopy by a helicopter.

Op-35 recon teams conducted not only reconnaissance, but prisoner 'snatches.' Master Sergeant Dick Meadows (who would later plan the Son Tay Raid and be the first Special Forces operative on the ground in Tehran for the aborted 1980 hostage rescue mission) and his team held the record of thirteen 'snatches.' 'Snatched' prisoners were rapidly moved from the scene of their capture, trussed up into a 'Maguire' or the follow-on STABO (initials of the developers) rig and extracted. After the experience of being literally 'snatched' away from their units and out of the jungle, the prisoners were usually quite cooperative and provided valuable intelligence.

Op-35 also dispatched 'Hatchet' teams, composed of Nung or Montagnard mercenary tribesmen led by an American Special Forces NCO. These teams were dispatched into Laos and Cambodia to attack NVA units moving along the Trail. The operation was designed to deprive the NVA of their sense of sanctuary in these neutral countries. These teams conducted 'hit and run' raids against NVA main force units and occasionally got into protracted battles.

SOG operations were highly effective against the NVA and VC, but SOG itself was too poorly resourced to make a real impact on the outcome of the war. Unfortunately, the European war mindset of the Pentagon planners ensured that the conventional divisions were the priority for resources in spite of their relatively poor performance in comparison to SOG and the Special Forces. Consequently, the priority for resources was with the units that were the least effective.

Strategic Direct Action: The Son Tay Raid 1970

By May of 1970, American intelligence had identified Son Tay Prison, twenty-three miles west of Hanoi, North Vietnam, as a prisoner-of-war detention camp. As a result of that intelligence, Brigadier General Donald D. Blackburn, Special Assistant for Counter-insurgency Activities (SACSA) for the Joint Chiefs of Staff, planned a raid to free the prisoners. Immediately, Colonel Bull Simons was put in command of Task Force Ivory Coast, a formation of fifty-six Special Forces troops from Fort Bragg, North Carolina and Fort Benning, Georgia. After training and rehearsing in the forests of North Carolina for three months, the task force deployed to Takhli, Thailand, on 18 November.[14]

At 2317 hours, 20 November, the Task Force boarded HH-3C 'Jolly Green Giant' helicopters, lifted off and headed across Thailand and into North Vietnam.[15] Shortly after crossing the border into North Vietnam, the Task Force mistakenly identified a North Vietnamese military school as their objective and all the helicopters opened fire with their mini-guns (7.62mm gatling guns). As they crossed directly over the compound, they realized their mistake and continued on to Son Tay, just a few miles to the north. The assault group leader, Captain Richard Meadows (who had been directly commissioned from his previous rank of Master Sergeant), provided this account:

We followed Apple 3 (the lead HH-3) who was already on its way to the true target. We were in good position directly behind Apple 3 for our approach. As we neared the compound, we crossed the small river and saw the tall trees along the West Wall which the aircraft had to hurdle, then began the landing procedures. All guns were firing. I saw the M-60 machinegun tracers hitting the Northwest tower with great accuracy. As we began to descend into the compound area, the props of the helicopter began chopping the limbs from the trees and near the ground a large tree in front of 5E [one of the buildings] was completely severed. Limbs and debris [from trees and brush chopped up by the whirling rotor blades] were falling even after the men dismounted the helicopter . . . The landing was an excellent performance by the HH-3 pilot and copilot.[16]

But several of the men in the assault group noticed that the compound was somewhat dilapidated – in fact appeared to be abandoned. This appearance was confirmed as Meadows' elements reported negative contact with any prisoners, although they killed some fifty NVA guards. The prisoners had been moved.

Meanwhile, Colonel Simons and his support group had inadvertently landed in an adjacent secondary-school compound which turned out to be teeming with Russian and Chinese soldiers. Simons and his team slaughtered literally hundreds of these soldiers before their helicopter returned and extracted them. They thus eliminated the principal threat to the assault group conducting operations at the prison. Both Meadows' and Simons' groups were extracted by helicopter with no casualties.

Although the raid at Son Tay failed to accomplish its principal objective of rescuing American prisoners-of-war, it clearly demonstrated to the North Vietnamese government that America was concerned for the welfare of her prisoners and would do what she could to assist them. A beneficial result of the raid was that treatment of American prisoners improved in the years afterwards.

A second result of the raid was that the United States clearly demonstrated that it would take violent, aggressive action against the forces of any foreign government found to be directly assisting North Vietnam. The slaughter of hundreds of Chinese and Russian soldiers in the secondary-school compound was clear testimony to this fact; no clearer signal could be sent.

Conclusions

The Vietnam War served as the crucible in which the capabilities of Army SOF were forged. In it, many concepts were tried; following the war, the ineffective concepts were identified and rejected while effective concepts were incorporated into emerging organizations and doctrine.

Much of the strategic and long-range reconnaissance organizations and techniques were incorporated into both conventional and special operations unit capabilities. The long-range surveillance detachments presently organic to US divisions had their genesis with the LRRP and Ranger units that operated in Vietnam.

American hostage rescue operations such as the Iran hostage rescue mission and the more successful operations in Panama had their origins in the Son Tay raid. Other nations took note – as the Israeli hostage rescue operation in Uganda soon followed in 1976. Moreover, the proliferation of specialized hostage rescue capabilities in the US Special Forces, British SAS, and the German GSG-9 can be attributed to a greater or lesser degree to the lessons learned at Son Tay.

Much of the Special Forces work with indigenous forces paved the way for highly successful civil affairs operations in Grenada, Panama, and Kuwait.

Although the overall impact of Vietnam was a tragedy of the first order, it did serve to develop special operations capabilities that would not only further American foreign policy aims, but also improve conditions for many oppressed peoples around the globe. Techniques developed in Vietnam have been employed in humanitarian interventions in the Philippines, Grenada, Panama, Kuwait, Iraq, Bangladesh, the former Soviet Union, and Somalia, to name a few.

NOTES

1. Shelby L. Stanton, *Green Berets at War; U.S. Army Special Forces in Southeast Asia 1956–1975* (Novato, California, Presidio, 1985 and London, Greenhill, 1986), p. 4.
2. Ibid.
3. Ibid, p. 36.
4. Ibid, pp. 74–5.
5. Ibid, pp. 75–6.
6. Ibid, p. 76.
7. Colonel Charlie A. Beckwith, USA (Ret) and Donald Knox, *Delta Force* (London, Arms and Armour, 1986), pp. 68–75.
8. Stanton, *Green Berets at War*, pp. 195–6.
9. Beckwith, *Delta Force*, pp. 68–75.
10. Captain Clyde J. Sincere, 'Operations of Mobile Guerilla Force 876, (Operation Blackjack 23), 5th Special Forces Group (Abn), 1st SF, on a Mobile Guerilla Operation in Support of the 1st Cavalry Division (Air Mobile) During the Period 5 March–3 April 1967 in Binh Dinh Province, Republic of Vietnam. (Personal Experience of a Mobile Guerilla Force Commander.),' Report prepared for US Army Infantry Officer Advanced Course Class Number 1–68.
11. Lt. Col L.H. 'Bucky' Burrus, US Army (Retired), *Mike Force* (New York, Pocket Books, 1989), pp. 12–18.
12. Shelby L. Stanton, *Rangers At War; Combat Recon in Vietnam* (New York, Orion, 1992), p. 78.
13. Nguyen Tuong Lai, 'Soldier of the Revolution,' in Al Santoli, *To Bear Any Burden: The Vietnam War and Its Aftermath in the Words of Americans and Southeast Asians* (New York: E.P. Dutton, 1985), p. 147.
14. Stanton, *Green Berets at War*, p. 272.
15. Captain Richard J. Meadows, 'Ivory Coast' After Trip Report, undated.
16. Ibid.

CHAPTER 4

Maritime Strike Force The Advent of Naval Special Warfare 1943–75

President Kennedy's insights on the Cold War led to the birth of SEAL (Sea, Air, Land) Team One in Coronado, California and SEAL Team Two in Little Creek, Virginia in January, 1962. These two units, initially manned by veterans of UDT operations in World War II, Korea and the late 1950s, were originally envisioned to be the Navy's counterpart to the Army's recently revitalized Special Forces, with the SEAL emphasis placed on training allies in maritime special operations. Like their counterparts in the Army, the SEALs would not only serve as trainers, but would continue the traditions of some of the other, more esoteric special warfare organizations as well. The Navy would merge the capabilities of the combat swimmers, divers, and underwater demolition teams to create this elite group of sailors known as SEALs.

UDT/Frogman Training, 1943–61

Since World War II, US Navy combat swimmer training has had a reputation for being some of the most physically and psychologically demanding special operations training in the world. Overcoming the forces of nature at sea and on the beach, and the enemy and basic human vulnerabilities, make combat swimmer missions some of the most challenging of all special operations. There is no room for men not fully in tune with their own, or their team-mates' capabilities when they undertake high-profile missions of strategic importance. Hence the combat swimmer and SEAL training is designed to enable men to realize their full physical and mental potential. It is also designed to 'wash out' those who cannot meet the challenge. Historically, drop-out rates for this training exceed sixty-five percent.

Paradoxically, few of the men who graduate from the six-month basic underwater demolition/SEAL (BUD/S) training course are physical giants or world-class sports competitors. However, each has repeatedly demonstrated the ability to give more than he ever thought he could give, persist under the most trying of circumstances and strive to complete the mission.

The BUD/S graduate is a proven, all-around athlete who can swim up to five nautical miles on the surface or two miles below it. He can run over four miles in full combat gear, negotiating forests, cliffs, swamps, and sandy beaches, en route to his destination. In addition to the physical training, the candidates must master a wide range of military hardware. Trainees become proficient with a wide variety of small arms and crew-served weapons, self-contained underwater breathing apparatus (SCUBA), explosives, communications equipment, and navigation devices.

The training exercises that candidates endure are designed to come as close as possible to simulating actual combat. Instructors strive to force their charges to deal with the unexpected and to persevere.

Specialized SEAL Training, From 1961

When it was established in 1961, SEAL Team One had an initial complement of ten officers and fifty enlisted personnel. Operationally assigned to Commander-in-Chief, Pacific theater (CINCPAC) the team prepared for operations in Southeast Asia. SEAL Team Two supported both Commander-in-Chief, Atlantic theater (CINCLANT) and Commander-in-Chief, Europe (CINCEUR) and prepared for operations in the Caribbean and Europe.

The SEAL 'plank owners,' the term for the original complement of a newly commissioned naval vessel or command, proved to be like pack rats as they collected any and everything that might be useful in future training and operations, even if these 'acquisitions' might not be strictly by the book. They adhered to the same practice as they began attending training that had previously been unavailable to frogmen. Such training included a variety of highly sensitive 'tradecraft' courses,[1] advanced High-Altitude Low-Opening (HALO) parachute, language, instructor, advanced demolition and crew-served weapons training. These courses were complemented with confidence-building courses such as army Ranger, hand-to-hand combat, close air support, rough terrain parachute and survival training.

Once team members had demonstrated proficiency in their newly acquired areas of expertise, unit training expanded and became more complex. What came to be known as SBI, or SEAL Basic Indoctrination, became the first internally administered training course for new assessions from the UDTs after selection for SEAL duty. Direct assignment of fresh BUD/S graduates to a SEAL Team would begin in the late 1960s. SBI would introduce previously waterbound frogmen to the new world of operations ashore using a wider variety of weapons, communications equipment, fieldcraft techniques, etc. Many hardcore frogmen could not make the transition and were returned to their no less demanding, but ever more dissimilar UDTs.

UDT/Frogman Operations, Circa 1965

The advent of SEAL Teams did not at all diminish the operational necessity for UDTs. Whereas SEALs began to orient more towards joint and combined operations, UDT 'frogmen' remained critical assets to amphibious force commanders. Each Amphibious Ready Group (ARG) had a UDT platoon assigned comprising one officer and twenty enlisted personnel. During the early stages of US involvement in the Vietnam conflict, UDT frogmen operating surface ships and special submarines reconnoitered every linear foot of South Vietnamese coastline with amphibious landing potential, recording their findings on meticulously hand-drawn charts.

A typical mid-1960s clandestine survey of a 2,000-yard stretch of beach would originate from a submarine like the USS *Tunney*. The USS *Tunney* was a World War II vintage 'Gato' class submarine that had been converted from a Regulus nuclear missile launch platform into an amphibious support ship. A hanger aft of the sail, originally meant to house the missile, was reconfigured to support the submerged or surface launch and recovery of UDT frogmen or US Marine Corps reconnaissance teams and their equipment.

After surfacing several miles off the coast, the UDT platoon would disembark just after dusk and paddle their inflatable boats to a point close to the $3\frac{1}{2}$ fathom or 21-foot point. The depth would be determined by sounding with a 'lead line' (a length of small gauge nylon line with knots every foot, attached to a small lead weight). Once a position was established on the right or left flank of the beach by either a radar vector from the submarine or by visual confirmation of recognizable features ashore, the swimmer line would begin to enter the water.

The swimmer line would consist of enough frogmen, usually spaced at twenty-five yard intervals, to form a line from an inflatable boat at the $3\frac{1}{2}$ fathom location to the high water mark on the beach. Distances would be maintained by using a flutterboard, a device consisting of a reel mechanism on which a length of thin gauge line with knots at each twenty-five yard increment was attached.

For this type of mission, called a combat parallel reconnaissance,[2] the flutterboard would remain in an inflatable boat. The 'bitter end man,' the one closest to the beach, would hold the bitter end of the flutterboard line. Each other swimmer would be spaced evenly to seaward, ending at the inflatable boat. Beaches with shallow gradients could require a large number of swimmers or a two-part effort, consisting of an inshore then an offshore series of soundings.[3] Once the swimmer line was lined up, all swimmers would take initial soundings with their leadlines and record the depth on a sanded piece of clear plastic attached to their arms with a pencil. Once the in-water officer-in-charge was satisfied that everyone had taken his sounding, a pre-rehearsed signal would prompt all swimmers to swim about twenty-five yards, with the direction of the prevailing current, toward the opposite flank of the beach. The process of taking soundings was repeated until the entire beach was covered. A 2000-yard reconnaissance would net eighty-one soundings recorded on each swimmer's slate.

If the mission required it, the team would make free dives to the seabed to look for any outcroppings, formations or other obstacles that could interfere with an amphibious landing. This part of a reconnaissance could become extremely dangerous if the prospect of underwater mines or other man-made obstacles faced the recon swimmers.

Also possible was the need to gain some amount of intelligence about the area immediately inland, normally referred to as the hinterland. If this type of information was required, two or three frogmen would go ashore to gather and record topographic and tactical data, perhaps taking photographs. During the early stages of the Vietnam conflict, the 'frogs' remaining in the inflatable boats offshore would be armed with older weapons such as M3A1 submachineguns, Browning Automatic Rifles of World War II vintage and maybe the occasional M-14 semiautomatic rifle. Not until the latter 1960s were the UDTs equipped with more widely used M-16 semiautomatic/automatic rifles, M-60 machineguns, and M-79 40mm grenade launchers. Personnel ashore would usually be armed with a blowback-type weapon such as the M3A1 or M-76 (Smith and Wesson) submachinegun. These types of guns proved more reliable after exposure to seawater, sand and other debris common in nearshore waters.

On return to the submarine, sometime before dawn, all recorded data and verbal debriefs to the UDT platoon's intelligence petty officer, a cartographer, would be transferred to a UDT beach chart. Most cartographers took great pride in their work. After hours, if not a day or two of tedious and painstaking effort, a work of art, supported by a photography collection, would be ready for submission to amphibious planners.

Indigenous Special Warfare Organizations

'Cry havoc and let loose the dogs of war'
William Shakespeare

This quote, used to describe warriors ranging from mercenaries to Vietnam 'River Rats', could have been written with SEALs in mind. Although brought into being to be a maritime equivalent of the Army's Special Forces, SEALs found themselves embroiled in direct action missions against the Viet Cong and North Vietnamese beginning in 1962, but as advisors, not pure all-American units.

The US established the Naval Special Warfare Training Center in Cam Ran Bay to provide UDT/SEAL training for the South Vietnamese Navy in the mid-1960s. It became part of a countrywide 'schoolhouse' oriented towards unconventional operations that would help complement the more conventional coastal and riverine capabilities that had their beginnings during the period when France dominated Indochina. From their birth, SEALs began to flourish preparing and advising South Vietnamese forces in exploiting techniques used against them by their adversaries. SEALs were associated with a wide variety of indigenous units from the mid-1960s.

LIEN DOC NGUOI NHIA (LDNN)

This unit was supposed to be the Vietnamese equivalent to the American SEALs. Personnel assigned to the LDNN (and the smaller Vietnamese equivalent to the UDT) were volunteers for the unique duties they were meant to perform within the boundaries of their own country. Basic training was derived from the American BUD/S curriculum. Few South Vietnamese officers and enlisted personnel actually attended training in California. The record of successful LDNN operational achievements was short, for although they were physically tough, the years of war, corruption and deprivation of a secure domestic life was evident in their widespread lack of motivation to succeed in action. Throughout Vietnam, SEAL detachments of one officer and three enlisted personnel provided guidance to their counterparts on mission planning, advanced tactics and equipment. They would also interface with supporting American units as necessary. During field operations the advisors would accompany the LDNNs as glorified radio operators, able to communicate with supporting artillery, air assets or naval gunfire platforms.

The LDNNs tended to behave in an arrogant manner because they knew they were supported by advisors (who knew how to use a radio) who were regarded as warriors by the US military, Vietnamese army and the enemy. The advisor detachments faced frustrating assignments that either kept them in their barracks due to inactivity by the Vietnamese or exposed them to risks for little more than the bounty the LDNNs would receive for captured VC/NVA equipment.[4]

PROVINCIAL RECONNAISSANCE UNITS (PRUS)

These were paramilitary units, generally of company or smaller size, comprising personnel indigenous to and supposedly very familiar with specific provinces. The PRU concept revolved around the theory that soldiers would fight harder and be more motivated when defending their own turf. PRUs almost exclusively conducted 'search and destroy' type missions. They were meant to augment conventional forces by locating, attacking and destroying any small enemy elements while conventional forces focused on larger units. Young enlisted men from the US Army, Navy (SEALs) and Marines were assigned as advisors to individual units. They were by no means specifically meant to provide leadership for their unit; rather they were there as a motivational presence and to provide a communications capability.

PRU advisors were required to live with their units, which often proved their greatest challenge to survival. Bases were primitive and support conditions were minimal by US standards. However, to establish rapport and, hopefully, instill a sense of purpose and aggressiveness in the combat behavior of the PRUs, the advisors had to immerse themselves fully. Several young SEALs were affected by this immersion in a less than positive manner.

The PRUs were usually not highly educated people and had questionable sophistication when it came to manners, health standards and the way they handled prisoners. In 1968, at least one experienced SEAL Team One petty officer was obliged to weather the experience of having the disembodied heads of recently deceased adversaries displayed on pikes at the entrance to his PRU compound.

On patrol, it was not uncommon to stop in a village for the Vietnamese equivalent of a soft drink, often dispensed in a clear plastic bag. On one occasion, after a minor engagement that left several hostiles dead, the afore-mentioned petty officer was offered a baggy of 'refreshment'. Combat being an activity that generates thirst, he accepted the offer, drinking the not so cool liquid through a straw. The taste was not totally foreign, but seemed more salty than sweet. His benefactor immediately shared with him that his strength would now be greater since he had drunk the blood of his enemy, fresh, as it turned out, since part of his adversary's freshly removed kidney was floating in the baggy.

The mercenary attitude of these troops and their less disciplined behavior standards did result in several noteworthy victories but, like the LDNNs, usually only when there was bounty involved.

KIT CARSON SCOUTS

Kit Carson gained fame in the mid-1800s as a guide and advance scout for army endeavors in unmapped areas of what was to become the western US. His exploits were envisioned as the type that could be conducted by a Vietnamese version of organized guides and scouts.

The designation 'Kit Carson Scouts' was given to small units consisting of ex-VC soldiers. These personnel, who came from the ranks of those referred to as *Hoi Chans*,[5] were recruited from detention centers. After being analyzed for sincerity, often through the use of a polygraph test, and potential for integration back into South Vietnamese society, those with experience of potential benefit to unconventional warfare operations were offered an opportunity to fight against their former brothers-in-arms. Knowledge of their former unit's capabilities, tactics, location and the terrain in which they operated was regarded as invaluable. SEALs, usually more senior (chief) petty officers, would advise small detachments, molding them in a manner that would make them acceptable to augment certain missions.

The Scouts were hard core warriors whose allegiance was always questionable. A Scout who slept in the same hut as his advisor may have been in the VC team that ambushed that advisor's platoon on a previous deployment.

The Scouts were also renowned for not taking what they perceived as unwarranted criticism from anyone. In 1971, one SEAL advisor in the Ca Mau peninsula fell into such disfavor with his Scouts that he had to be reassigned back to the US. A SEAL platoon was also assigned to the same base. Although the advisor's particular Scout detachment spontaneously disbanded itself, one disgruntled ex-member got the impression that a replacement officer joining the SEAL platoon was his detachment's previous advisor. The young officer, in Vietnam for the first time for no more than forty-eight hours, was unpacking his gear in the barracks when the sound of a nearby slamming door was followed by the noise of something weighty hitting the floor. The noise, upon investigation, was caused by a MK 138 demolition charge (20lb of C-4 explosive) hitting the wooden floor of the building. Initially believing this was part of some initiation prank by his fellow platoon members, the 'FNG'[6] ensign confronted the platoon chief. It was not a platoon prank. A short time fuse and an M-60 fuse igniter was attached to the assembly. The ex-Scout who had thrown it into the building had activated the igniter, but it had not ignited the fuse. The serial number on the charge assembly traced back to the now disbanded Scout unit. Luck prevailed that day (possibly complemented by poor attention by the Scout when he was trained to assemble a fuse igniter and time fuse).

The Scout units dissolved in the early 1970s, coincidental with heavy emphasis on the replacement of American with south Vietnamese units.

Sea Commandos

This name was given to those individuals, most with previous combat experience, that were under cognizance of MAC(V)SOG. They specialized in clandestine and often covert operations staged from Danang against primarily North Vietnamese targets. American advisors (primarily SEALs) provided planning, logistics support, tactical advice, intelligence and equipment to Vietnamese and other Asian mercenaries who conducted commando-like raids into the north and onto offshore islands. Normally inserted by indigenous craft (junks), Nasty class PTFs (Patrol Torpedo Boats, Fast) and, on rare occasion, American submarines, these personnel conducted true special operations. US personnel were restricted to a support role, not being officially sanctioned to go north themselves during the conduct of maritime operations, much to their disappointment. SEALs, although eager to do so, were never to conduct unilateral, American-only operations into the north.

Unilateral SEAL Operations, 1966–71

The initial advisory role envisioned for and assigned to small cadres of SEALs was finally complemented by the deployment of operational SEAL platoons beginning in 1966. Although the first SEAL Team One detachment most closely resembled a traditionally sized UDT platoon (two to three officers and over twenty enlisted personnel), this detachment size was too large for most assigned and anticipated ground operations. A SEAL platoon quickly stabilized at fourteen men.

SEALs found themselves amongst the diverse and sometimes surreal collection of military and paramilitary organizations that were beginning to crowd the military scene in South East Asia. The personalities of many of the men who populated naval special warfare in those days fitted well into this apocalyptic environment.

RIVERINE OPERATIONS

Primarily assigned to operational areas south and west of Saigon, in the military region referred to as IV Corps, SEAL actions were meant to clandestinely complement the overt military efforts in this area, focused on disrupting the opposition's ability to move freely in that part of the country. Although conventional military ground maneuvers were occasionally conducted in the predominant wetlands of IV Corps, they were rare due to the intense logistics burden necessary to move in terrain crisscrossed by thousands of streams, canals and rivers. This was the environment that would validate the operational capabilities and reputation of the 'Teams.'

The overt conventional actions that SEAL operations would complement were those meant to curtail the activities of VC and North Vietnamese regulars along the inland lines of communications – waterways – of southern South Vietnam. The military units involved in these activities were collectively grouped under the operational umbrellas of Task Force 115 – Coastal Surveillance Force (referred to as Operation MARKET TIME) and Task Force 116 – River Patrol Force (referred to as Operation GAME WARDEN). Operation MARKET TIME attempted to control offshore approaches to South Vietnam to reduce or eliminate the ability of North Vietnam or her allies to resupply the VC and North Vietnamese regulars operating in the south. GAME WARDEN was the attempt to control the inland waterways of South Vietnam, eliminating them as an option for troop movement and logistics resupply. These operations were predominantly accomplished through the use of a wide variety of US watercraft, most of which were eventually turned over to the Vietnamese navy.

During the conflict in Vietnam, the numerous small boat organizations, that also included Task Force 117 – River Assault Force, which were flourishing during Operations GAME WARDEN and MARKET TIME, were under conventional US Navy leadership. After the close of the Vietnam chapter, the units and assets that remained, primarily the riverine and patrol craft in the US Navy's inventory, were consolidated and absorbed by the naval special warfare community.

Two other units that were formed primarily to support the control of South Vietnam's waterways were the attack squadrons of the US Navy. The 'Seawolves' were the US Navy's Helicopter Light Attack Squadron Three and the 'Black Ponies' were Fixed Wing Light Attack Squadron Four. The Seawolves were equipped with 'Bravo' model UH-1 gunships and (unarmed) troop carriers ('slicks'). The Black Ponies operated OV-10A aircraft. The resources of the Seawolves were retained in the Naval Reserve after the Vietnam conflict. The Black Ponies were, regrettably, decommissioned in 1972.

Riverine Interdiction

The activities of the MARKET TIME and GAME WARDEN assets proved to be most effective in daylight hours. Although nighttime patrols offshore and on inland waterways were conducted, they proved relatively easy for the VC to avoid by their by use of smaller tributaries that the patrol craft could not negotiate and through the use of mining and ambushes that put allied activities on the defensive rather than the offensive during patrols. Into this domain the 'men with green faces'[7] were inserted.

SEALs quickly established their *modus operandi*. Using the best available intelligence, SEAL elements, usually seven-man squads or smaller three- to four-man fire teams, would depart from their base camp at dusk and proceed to a predetermined location on a waterway to establish an ambush position. Early in the involvement of SEALs, insertions were supported by GAME WARDEN and MARKET TIME craft such as thirty-two foot MK I and II Patrol Boats Riverine (PBRs), fifty-foot Patrol Craft Fast (PCFs or Swift Boats) or other available US military operated craft. As their involvement became more and more beneficial, specialized craft such as SEAL Tactical Assault Boats (STAB), Light SEAL Support Craft (LSSC) and Medium SEAL Support Craft (MSSC)[8] were introduced. The STAB was the forerunner of the LSSC, a twenty-four foot craft specially designed and built to support SEAL (squad-size) river operations. The MSSC was a thirty-six foot boat that was also specially built to support SEAL (platoon-size) river operations. These craft provided a dedicated asset pool that complemented the occasional use of indigenous craft of questionable reliability such as sampans and junks. As the conflict progressed, US Navy and US Army helicopters were used in both day and night operations.

Once SEAL platoons began to understand their operational areas, they would maximize the use of indigenous organizations that might increase the chances of success. South Vietnamese units such as the LDNNs, the local detachments of the Police Special Branch, 'Ruff Puffs' (regional/provincial [militia-like] forces), Kit Carson Scouts, PRUs, and selected individuals from Hoi Chan centers, were all exploited. A key factor proved to be the exploitation of the one or two interpreters that were hired by each platoon and were essential to mission success.

The nature of Vietnam, after years of war, presented a corrupted 'system' making vendettas and pay-backs commonplace. SEALs sometimes found themselves graced with 'hard intelligence' on VC activities that led to a successful interdiction or raid, only to find out later that they had been used to settle a score between two parties, the 'loser' a VC element, the other a South Vietnam official that had been 'on the take' until receiving a better offer. This did not really matter at the time to the operators who were most concerned with accomplishing their mission and completing their six month tour in one piece. It did come into play later in the conflict when the writing on the wall predicted a gradual withdrawal of all US support, Vietnamization of the complete war effort and the ultimate victory of the North Vietnamese.

An examination of a typical field operation by a representative SEAL platoon is necessary to understand what began to occur more and more often in 1969–71.

Fourteen-man SEAL platoons were typically based at Bien Thuy, Rac Soi, Rac Ghiang, Ben Luc, Dong Tam (Me Tho), Ben Tre and Solid Anchor. SEAL facilities usually consisted of Quonset huts, temporary wooden buildings, or the rare firm base facilities that were usually occupied by the advisors or conventional US military units. These facilities were usually arranged to provide areas for sleeping, briefing, weapons cleaning, ammo/ordnance storage and, if they were fortunate, a day room (really a bar).

Solid Anchor was the designator for a US Navy forward operating base in the Ca Mau peninsula, located on the Son (river) Cou Lon on the site of an old village named Nam Can. It was the shore-based successor to a concept developed by Admiral Zumwalt in the late 1960s called SEAFLOAT. This bastion consisted of a number of barges attached together, creating a man-made island from which allied operations could be staged in the southernmost area of IV Corps. Solid Anchor was in the middle of what was recognized as a highly active rear services area for the Viet Cong and North Vietnamese regulars. It served as a staging base for SEAL Team One operations until the last platoon departed in late 1971.

SEAL Team One, Oscar platoon, based at Solid Anchor in 1971, was typical of the SEAL platoons deployed to South Vietnam. It was initially commanded by an experienced lieutenant with a lieutenant (junior grade) as an assistant. The lieutenant rotated to the US two months into the deployment, allowing the lieutenant (junior grade) to take command, with a newly arrived ensign as his assistant. A platoon chief petty officer and a leading (first class) petty officer provided the irreplaceable, experienced senior enlisted leadership. Remaining personnel ranged from combat-seasoned petty officers to seamen fresh from SEAL Basic Indoctrination via Oscar platoon's pre-deployment training. Each member of the platoon had a specialist assignment, such as ordnance petty officer, air operations petty officer, diving petty officer, intelligence petty officer and engineering petty officer. One individual, the platoon's leading petty officer, was a US Navy hospital corpsman who had prior combat experience with the US Marines.

Each man also had a primary tactical patrol assignment such as pointman, radioman, automatic weaponsman or rear security. These assignments had been rehearsed during pre-deployment training and were, by this time, second nature. All personnel were capable of performing any tactical assignment, but specialization tended to ensure fewer errors in the field.

SEALs were then, and continue to be, strong believers in firepower. As a typical fourteen-man SEAL platoon of Vietnam vintage, Oscar platoon had the potential to lay down a base of small arms fire that exceeded the capabilities of an entire US Army or Marine rifle company of the day, but for only about thirty to forty-five seconds. At the end of that period, if the engagement had not been won, each man got the opportunity to demonstrate why physical fitness, especially the ability to run long distances quickly with heavy loads, was emphasized in naval special warfare training.

Although the platoon had numerous weapons available that would allow a patrol's configuration to match the anticipated situation, typical weapons carried during either squad- or platoon-size operations were as follows:

Pointman: Stoner 63A light machinegun (LMG), possibly augmented by an Ithaca 12 gauge shotgun, slung on the back, and/or a MK 23 9mm suppressed pistol, holstered or on a lanyard around the neck.

Patrol leader: M-16/M-203 Grenade Launcher, AK-47 or a Stoner (when the officers preferred to be flamboyant by shooting a lot rather than leading).

Radioman: M-16/M-203 (with lots of parachute flares).

Automatic weaponsman (two to three per seven-man squad): M-60 medium machinegun ('chopped' to reduce the weight from about twenty-three to about sixteen pounds).[9]

Rear security: Stoner or M-16/M-203 combination.

M-14s and Soviet AK-47s, when available, were preferred by some because of the heavier rounds they fired (especially beneficial in a heavily foliated area). Occasionally some carried suppressed 9mm submachineguns, usually M-76s or M-50 Karl Gustavs.

Typically, automatic weaponsmen would carry between 800 and 1,000 rounds of ammunition in boxes or bandoliers. Other platoon members would carry additional ammunition if the mission dictated. Personnel carrying magazine fed weapons would typically carry 300 to 600 rounds in twenty- or, preferably, thirty-round magazines. Grenade launcher equipped personnel would carry twenty-four to seventy-two rounds of 40mm ammunition; high explosive, canister, illumination, or tear gas in a vest or canteen pouches. A mix of fragmentation, smoke and concussion grenades would be carried by each man as well as pop-flares, pencil flares and other types of signalling devices. A particularly effective item was an M-14 smoke grenade canister filled with TIERRA, a solid substance that was a forerunner of Cyalume chemical light liquid. TIERRA could be used to mark landing zones or targets/flanks of friendly lines at night or in daylight if dispersed in a river, and was especially effective as an interrogation aid when applied to a prisoner's skin. Although harmless to touch, it lit up an unindoctrinated individual like a Christmas tree usually resulting in their delivery of more information than was requested. Like many other unique items available to special operation forces during war, it was no longer available after 1972.

Oscar platoon would plan missions based on information from many sources. These sources could consist of the local Naval Intelligence Liaison Officer (NILO), the South Vietnamese Police Special Branch (PSB), their host base Tactical Operations Center (TOC), headquarters in Saigon or platoon sources usually cultivated by the platoon's interpreter. During very slow periods of operational activity, dart board operations might be planned. This 'planning' consisted of actually throwing a dart at a map of the operations area and conducting a patrol into that area to see what was happening there. Not very sophisticated, but in areas of high VC activity, they often provided positive results.

After intelligence collection and examination, a standard mission would begin with a warning order. This would be followed by preparation of weapons, field gear and any specialized equipment. The patrol leader issued warnings, that the platoon chief checked for compliance, to avoid foods that would generate stomach gas, not to take showers with fragrant shampoo or soaps and to attend to coughs and colds. These warnings would attempt to minimize any tell-tales that could, albeit inadvertently, give away the patrol's presence in hostile territory; territory it was safe to assume the enemy usually knew better than did the SEALs.

To ensure higher authorities were kept apprised of sensitive operations, the platoon commander would provide written or transmitted indications of their intentions via a form called a UNODIR. This acronym stood for 'UNless Otherwise DIRected.' A UNODIR would generally outline the mission goals, location, and those involved, and could be used to request support.

Also, it was commonplace for the patrol leader to coordinate his intentions with other activities in a given area of operations. This was usually accomplished by blocking out several 1000m × 1000m areas on a situation map in the local Tactical Operations Center (TOC), indicating allied activity somewhere in that area. Rarely did the platoon officer identify the exact location of his intended mission to anyone outside the platoon. The larger number of Vietnamese that were beginning to replace US officers in operations centers especially bothered the men of Oscar platoon since their allegiance was not well confirmed and because they had easy access to radios. The frequency on a radio could be quickly changed to allow transmission of potentially compromising information, without alerting the senior watch officer. This proved to be the case for more than one SEAL platoon whose parent TOC was infiltrated by VC sympathizers. In 1970, SEAL Team One, X-ray platoon, operating from Ben Tre, lost its entire complement, some of its replacements, and its platoon commander because its individual mission details were compromised at the TOC level and reported to the enemy.

A standard format patrol leader's order would be given soon before mission 'kick off' covering the mission from enemy situation through how much water would be taken. Questions would be asked/answered about the brief. Rehearsal of any techniques considered appropriate would be conducted (ambush formations, seating arrangements in sampans, prisoner handling procedures, etc.). Mission gear would go through final preparation, with checks and cross-checks made to ensure none had any shiny objects showing, that nothing rattled or slapped when a man moved, etc. Riggers tape, also referred to as 'hundred-mile-an-hour' or green duct tape, was probably one of the most vital items a platoon had to stockpile.

Oscar platoon was deep into the southern extremities of South Vietnam where rivers and canals provide the only lines of communication. Riverine missions were the norm and would typically begin at dusk. One seven-man squad would leave base camp in their support craft, usually an MSSC, in a direction away from their actual area of operations. Once the support craft had circled around and reached the insertion location, it would be directed by the patrol leader to stop and drift to allow a period to listen for noises. If this technique was not considered necessary, a series of false insertions would be directed by the patrol leader, with the squad disembarking during one of the insertion attempts.

Once ashore, the squad would set a security perimeter according to the terrain and vegetation, and listen for about ten minutes. The support boat, in the meantime, would have proceeded to a location where it could use available dense vegetation for concealment until extraction was called for.

When the listening period was over, the patrol would proceed along the planned route. Intervals between men would be dictated by cover and ambient light. Spacing would recognize the potential of one man setting off a mine/booby-trap while being sufficiently separated from his teammates. Stops for water or to listen would occur roughly every twenty to thirty minutes. If someone had to heed the call of nature, they would usually wait until they could immerse themselves in a canal or some mud to cover the aroma of urine or other bodily wastes.

If the mission was to establish a listening post, the patrol leader and pointman would examine the selected site before placing the remainder of the squad in defensive positions. All men would be placed to maximize overlaps in fields of fire, while taking advantage of available cover. Claymore mines would be routinely placed to the rear and flanks of the position.

The boring part of this type of mission and the challenge to stay awake would begin. If the vegetation was not too thick, a Starlight scope would help to monitor the approaches to the hide site. If the site was on a river or canal, special attention would be paid for sounds of wood-on-wood, metal-on-wood, a cough, a whisper, anything alien to the environment. Well trained senses of smell would be prepared to register the aroma of the always-used Vietnamese fish sauce (*nuc moum*). Unless someone stumbled into the site, the patrol leader was responsible for identifying a potential target as enemy. Although a curfew was in effect during most of the Vietnam conflict, civilians would sometimes fish at night, unfortunately being very difficult to distinguish from a VC arms shipment moving down river.

If a potential target presented itself, the challenge was to classify it accurately as hostile or friendly. The outline of a weapon or a conversation with tell-tale VC jargon, usually detectable only by the fluent Vietnamese-speaking inter-preter, would be proof positive that engagement was justified. Once identity was confirmed, many things began to happen at once. The patrol leader might choose to have the interpreter, usually overriding his objections, hail the craft, especially in 1970–1 when the rules of engagement were made overly restric-tive.

Rules of engagement (ROE) were in effect during most of the Vietnam conflict. They became especially visible as the Vietnamese began to replace US-led efforts during the Vietnamization period from 1969–73. ROE briefs were given to all newly arriving personnel (including SEALs), who had to sign an acknowledgement of the training. In the field ROE could be so restrictive that operational forces were put at a severe disadvantage by having to challenge their adversaries, thus revealing their own presence. There does not appear to have been an equivalent requirement levied on the Viet Cong and North Vietnamese regulars.

If the patrol leader considered a challenge unnecessary, he would begin firing; this would signal the flank and rear security to detonate the Claymores. Fire would be brought to bear by the rest of the squad and the radioman would call for extraction. If return fire was received and considered serious, air support would be requested. Upon cessation of fire, a friendly head count would be taken and the residue of the target checked. Once the support craft arrived, the site would be vacated, ensuring very little, if anything of potential value to the enemy was left behind, such as claymore wires, pop flare canisters, magazines, etc. At the direction of the patrol leader, suppressive fire around the area with 12.7mm or 7.62mm machinegun, 40mm grenades or 60mm mortar rounds from a support craft might be delivered to discourage any enemy counter-attack.

Re-entry to home base would be followed by a debrief of all participants and preparation by the patrol leader of an after-action report. All gear and weapons would be cleaned, and a verbal report to the base commander offered. Any captured or recovered items would be cataloged and offered to the local intelligence officer for possible exploitation. Drafting and transmission of a Situation Report (SITREP), also called an after-action report, to higher authority would bring to a close a particular mission.

When hard, confirmed intelligence was available, direct action missions against VC strongholds were planned. Missions considered to have a higher probability of success in the daylight would probably be planned for insertion by helicopter.

POW Rescue Operation, 1972

The last operation of the war involving a SEAL platoon was attempted in June 1972. SEAL Team One, Alpha platoon, deployed to Naval Special Warfare, Detachment Western Pacific (Det WestPac), located in White Beach, Okinawa, to operate from the USS *Grayback*[10] in support of an embarked UDT Swimmer Delivery Vehicle (SDV) platoon. The SEAL/UDT mission would consist of surveillance activities from an island at the mouth of North Vietnam's Red River. The surveillance was part of an attempt to recover a number of US prisoners-of-war who had communicated details of an escape plan. The mission was conducted under the code name of Operation THUNDERHEAD.

An initial attempt to land two SEALs from an SDV onto an island failed when the SDV failed to negotiate against the prevailing currents before its electric motor batteries died. The SDV was sunk by machinegun fire from the helicopter that recovered the SEALs and the UDT/SDV crew. A link-up of these personnel with the *Grayback* was attempted two nights later. It was to be done under relatively administrative, unopposed conditions, except that the chosen method, helicopter cast, was to be done at night. The height of the helicopter, a Navy CH-46, was misjudged and the four men deplaned, not at the height they expected, ten to fifteen feet, but what debriefs determined was probably closer to seventy-five feet. The cast resulted in numerous minor injuries and one fatality, the platoon commander, who broke his neck on impact with the water.

These four men, who were now floating off the coast of North Vietnam, were joined during the night by four others who had attempted the mission with a second SDV that was onboard the *Grayback*. This attempt also failed due to a ballast imbalance in the SDV. This imbalance caused the SDV to head for the bottom as soon as it cleared the maindeck. En route, the *Grayback* took a roll and crushed the small, fiberglass skinned vessel. The crew successfully escaped from the craft, which was irrecoverable. The axiom 'one is none, two is one', proved one is none[11] twice in four days. A helicopter recovered the seven survivors and the dead officer's body the next morning.[12]

This mission was a poor finish to an otherwise highly successful chapter of naval special warfare.

Conclusions

During the '10,000 Day War' SEALs conducted hundreds of direct action missions to capture or eliminate VC cadre, destroy rear services areas, destroy small but annoying sabotage units, disrupt communications and attempt to rescue POWs. SEAL Team One Oscar platoon conducted over fifty such missions at a time when most US combat troops were heading home. Platoons deployed earlier in the conflict conducted as many as one hundred missions during a six month deployment.

Violence of action, playing by their own rules instead of the enemy's and giving more than they got, were the hallmarks of SEAL operations. Although not as particular about keeping accurate body count figures on enemy casualties as other American units, a conservative accounting shows about a fifty-to-one casualty ratio – SEALs versus the bad guys – as a result of SEAL platoon operations.

During the 'official' period of the Vietnam conflict, 1961–73, SEAL Team One lost thirty-four men, SEAL Team Two lost nine men and UDT losses were five. Of this total of forty-eight fatalities, fourteen died of non-hostile accidents and two due to friendly fire. Only thirty-two men died as a direct result of enemy action. Figures for the small boat operations during Vietnam are much larger than these, but are not discussed since the vast majority were not under naval special warfare control.

SEAL platoons were withdrawn from action in late 1971, leaving only a handful of advisors in the country until total withdrawal in late 1972.

NOTES

1. The term 'tradecraft' encompasses a wide variety of areas of skill usually associated with clandestine or covert operations. Tradecraft courses are usually offered only to selected military personnel with a strict 'need-to-know' requirement. They are normally taught by instructors assigned to non-military organizations.

2. The term 'parallel reconnaissance' refers to the direction a line of swimmers moves in relation to the beach, *ie* parallel to it. A 'perpendicular reconnaissance' is another technique in which a swimmer line would approach the beach in a perpendicular manner, although the line itself would be formed parallel to the waves/high water mark. The choice of technique takes into account the offshore drift (speed of any current), the potential of detection from enemy forces ashore, the ambient visibility, etc.

3. In the jargon of beach reconnaissance, the term 'inshore' is traditionally used to refer to the entire area of water and surface features landward of the five fathom (30 feet of depth) curve

76 Special Men and Special Missions

(as determined by a navigation chart). This was the traditional domain of UDT operations and remains such for SEALs. The term 'near shore' traditionally is used to refer to an area between the Mean Lower Low Water (MLLW) location on a beach and the five fathom curve. The term 'foreshore' is the area between the MLLW line and the High Water Line (HWL). The 'backshore' is the area between the HWL and the first line of permanent vegetation. 'Offshore' is a term used to refer to the area between the five fathom curve and the limit of territorial waters.

4. As an incentive to encourage South Vietnamese units to conduct operations (irrespective of those units' perceived 'elite' status) against the enemy, bounties were paid for certain types of equipment (weapons, explosives, ammunition, etc.) that confirmed actual engagements had occurred.

5. The term 'hoi chan' referred to ex-Viet Cong who had surrendered to the South Vietnamese government, usually bringing with them a highly prized weapon or other indicator of 'sincerity.'

6. 'FNG' means 'Fucking New Guy'.

7. A translation of a Vietnamese term coined by the Viet Cong in reference to the SEAL units that proved to be such a thorn in their sides.

8. The family of combatant craft that was specifically oriented to support SEAL operations evolved due to a series of lessons that were learned through the employment of other riverine craft employed in Vietnam. The need for quick acceleration (to help break contact), high top speed (to leave a hostile area or to get casualties to a safe haven quickly), armor (to defeat, at least, small arms if not rockets), high onboard firepower potential (to gain the tactical advantage quickly) and stealth (in the form of low noise, if not completely silent engines) were determined to be essential for the clandestine operations engaged in by SEALs.

9. The term 'chopped M-60' was used to describe a machinegun that had been modified at the unit level to be lighter in weight. All extraneous attachments that contributed to its intended use as a crew-served weapon were removed and it was reconfigured to be a personal weapon. Modification techniques varied, but usually a standard 23lb M-60 lost 7lb during its transformation. It often gained a stronger recoil spring and feed mechanism springs that could increase its cyclic rate of fire to about 1,000 rounds per minute. It was slung over the shoulder, sometimes by a guitar strap, had a pistol grip affixed to the barrel assembly and had a 100-round box affixed or 100 rounds of loose ammunition loaded. For some missions, a backpack could be carried with over 1,000 rounds at the ready, being fed to the weapon through flex-guide, used primarily in aircraft applications of the weapon. A typical SEAL automatic weaponsman would carry about 800 rounds on a mission and most everyone else would carry 100 to 200 rounds bandolier-style as back-up.

10. The USS *Grayback*, SSG-574 ('Grayback' class), was a mid-1950s vintage amphibious warfare-configured submarine, originally intended to be an attack submarine capable of launching Regulus missiles. It was converted in 1967–8 into a transport submarine (and redesignated LPSS 574). Two hangars on the forward maindeck, intended to accept a missile each, were reconfigured to support, launch and recover SDVs or mass swimmer lockouts. It remained in service until the late 1970s.

11. The phrase 'one is none, two is one' is used to describe what is normally the situation when only one of a given item of equipment is taken on a mission. Having one of something critical to mission success can, by itself, doom the mission to failure especially if that one item has a very good chance of being rendered (or rendering itself) unusable prior to when it is needed due to environmental influences. The wise technique of carrying backup critical items supports the part of the phrase '... two is one.' This is especially true when dealing with SDVs, combatant craft, electronics equipment, or anything that is not easily repairable in the field.

12. Orr Kelly, *Brave Men Dark Waters*, (Novato, California, Presidio, 1992).

CHAPTER 5

Fire from the Sky
The Genesis of Air Force
Special Operations 1961–75

The potential of nuclear warfare revolutionized the way America envisioned future military conflict and the new Air Force reoriented its focus to being the principal combatant. Resources and funds were poured into follow-on generations of nuclear bombers and the development of precision, inter-continental ballistic missiles.

It was not until President Kennedy's administration addressed the issue of low-intensity-conflict that air force planners began to re-examine the issue of tactical, battlefield, air support. Consequently the first post-World War II special operations units commenced operations with upgraded, but nevertheless vintage, World War II aircraft.

Jungle Jim, 1961

In response to President Kennedy's initiatives to reinvigorate special operations, the air force created its first special operations unit since World War II, the 4400th Combat Crew Training Squadron (CCTS), code named 'Jungle Jim,' at Hurlburt Field, Florida. The 4400th CCTS was specially created to deal with the demands of the new low-intensity-conflict doctrine. Manned entirely by volunteers, the unit began service in April 1961 with sixteen C-47 Dakotas ('Gooney Birds'), eight Douglas RB-26 Counter-Invader fighter-bombers, and eight T-28 Nomad trainer aircraft, and bore a striking resemblance to the 1st Air Commandos of the old China–Burma–India theater.[1] By modifying the T-28s with .50 caliber machineguns, 2.75 inch rocket pods, bomb racks and armor plating, these trainers were transformed from rickety old training planes to lethal close-air-support aircraft. The new squadron had the mission of training for and executing special operations strike, reconnaissance, and airlift missions.

As the American involvement in Vietnam escalated, the 4400th would expand, becoming the seed of the 1st Special Operations Wing.

4400 CCTS conducted its first operational deployment in August 1961 when Detachment 1 deployed to Mali, West Africa, to begin Operation SANDY BEACH I. SANDY BEACH I was an airlift exercise with Mali

77

paratroopers that demonstrated aircraft capabilities for the President of Mali, Modiba Keita, in an effort to woo him into the American sphere of influence. The microcosm of the 'Cold War' was most evident here as Detachment 1 shared the airfield with Czechoslovakian and Soviet aircraft and crews showing their wares.

While SANDY BEACH was taking place, Detachment 2 packed out for Bien Hoa, Vietnam on 6 November to train the Vietnamese Air Force (VNAF) in operations and tactics developed by the 4400th. Colonel Benjamin H. King, who commanded the 4400th CCTS, deployed in command of Operation FARMGATE with a detachment consisting of four RB-26s, four C-47s, and eight of the modified T-28s.

The early FARMGATE missions consisted of close-air and resupply support to Vietnamese and Special Forces units. The RB-26s and T-28s provided the close-air support. A routine patrol on 23 November 1962 provided an excellent example of the skill of the pilots who flew these antiquated aircraft.

Intelligence reported that a large building adjacent to a canal south of Can Tho, South Vietnam, was the scene of significant enemy activity, but the precise nature of the activity was unclear. The RB-26, flown by Lieutenant Colonel Phillip O'Dwyer and Major Robert P. Guertz, rolled in on the target, unloading its payload of bombs directly on target. During the pass the RB-26 received ground small arms fire from the bank of the canal that was obscured by overhanging foliage. Making several more passes, the RB-26 raked the bank with strafing fire. Shortly after the mission, Army of the Republic of Vietnam (ARVN) troops moved in to secure the area.[2] They found it completely undefended.

They also found the fifteen survivors of a 296-man Viet Cong (VC) battalion. They had been securing an arms factory that had been housed in the target structure. The friendly troops also found twenty wrecked motorized sampans and smaller boats.

In a typical week, FARMGATE C-47s would fly sixty to seventy cargo sorties, delivering 60,00 to 70,000 lb of cargo and personnel. The T-28 Nomads would fly up to one hundred sorties, finding and engaging the enemy sixty percent of the time.

Fixed-wing Gunships, 1961–75

The first aircraft truly unique to air force special operations was the fixed-wing gunship. These highly accurate and devastatingly lethal aircraft are superbly suited to special operations in a LIC environment. The fire support provided by the fixed-wing gunships has become as essential to special operations as artillery and air support are to the conventional commander. Their capabilities are uniquely suited not only to pure air force special operations, but also to integration with Army Special Forces and Navy SEAL operations.

Responding to President Kennedy's emphasis on counter-insurgency, Ralph E. Flexman of Bell Aerosystems and Gilmore Craig McDonald of Ames, Iowa, developed and proposed a concept for a laterally firing fixed-wing gunship. Two years later, Captain John C. Simons initiated a fixed-wing gunship test program at Wright–Patterson Air Force Base code named Project Tailchaser. Project Tailchaser testing indicated that the new C-131 cargo aircraft was ideally suited for the gunship mission, but its complete development cycle would require several years.

AC-47 'Spooky'

It was Captain Ronald W. Terry who took over Tailchaser from Simons, testing an alternative concept that involved installing three gatling guns in the side of a C-47. This aircraft, along with trained crews, was already in the inventory. It had plenty of cargo space for ammunition, was capable of extended operations, and could loiter over the target for damage assessment. Its only vulnerability was to ground fire. Therefore, on 2 May 1964, Terry and Lieutenant Edwin Sasaki proposed to the Air Force Chief of Staff, General Curtis LeMay, that a team go to Vietnam, modify an existing FARMGATE C-47, from the 4400th CCTS, and test it in combat.

By 15 December, Captain Terry and his team had completed the modification of the first two FC-47 (later designated AC-47) gunships. Each aircraft was armed with three SUU-11A, 7.62mm gatling guns (called mini-guns) and carried a crew of seven air force personnel and one Vietnamese observer. The pilot fired the guns while flying the aircraft as the copilot monitored the instruments and supervised the crew. A mechanic monitored the various systems on board while the navigator plotted aircraft position and worked in concert with the Vietnamese observer to identify targets.

In the first daylight missions, Captain Terry and his crew shot up enemy sampans, buildings, trails, and staging areas. In one sortie, they attacked a large hut into which some fourteen Viet Cong had run. Friendly ground troops who cleared the area found some twenty-one bodies and a building that looked 'like a sieve.'[3]

The first night operation was in support of a South Vietnamese outpost at Thanh Yend (near the Mekong River Delta) which was under heavy attack. The defenders reported that the VC offensive broke off with the first burst of gunfire from the sky. Dropping magnesium flares to illuminate the target area, tracer ammunition was used in the mini-guns to spot where rounds were hitting. With each gun firing 6,000 rounds per minute, the planes appeared to be spewing forth tongues of fire into the night sky accompanied by a sound that roughly resembled a chain-saw rending sheet metal. It was this appearance that earned the early gunships the nicknames of 'dragonship,' 'Spooky,' and 'Puff, the Magic Dragon.' Clearly the tests were enormously successful.

On 8 February 1965, a gunship supported a major US Military Assistance Command (Vietnam) (MACV) operation in the central highlands. In the course of the operation, a South Vietnamese sergeant was captured. After his escape, he told of tremendous confusion and carnage on the VC side when the gunship went into action. He had personally helped to carry some eighty to ninety bodies out of the approximately 250 killed by the gunship. The VC had been confused by the source of the attack, not being sure if their numbers were being wiped out by a new type of gun or a vicious ground attack.

As increasing numbers of Spookies were delivered or modified in Vietnam, the Air Force established the 4th Special Operations Squadron (SOS).

Gunship Support to Special Forces Border Camps, 1965–6

The forte of the AC-47 was hamlet and outpost defense. In one operation, four gunships supported a 32-man South Vietnamese outpost that was under attack by a VC company. The VC had just announced by loudspeaker that 'we are not afraid of your firepower,' when the AC-47s dropped some seventy-five flares and opened fire. After expending some 48,800 rounds, two F-100 jet aircraft rolled in low and flash-fried the enemy positions with napalm. The VC attack stopped instantly.

As effective as they were, the gunships were unable to prevent the fall of the Special Forces Camp A Shau, in March 1966 (the actions of Army Special Forces in this battle are detailed in Chapter Three). On 9 March an AC-47 was dispatched to support the friendly defense of the camp when Army Special Forces Captain John D. Blair reported his outpost was in imminent danger of being overrun. The gunship, flown by Captain Willard Collins, tried to get in under the 400 foot cloud ceiling to provide support.

After two tries, on his third attempt, Collins was able to make a successful firing pass at the attackers. On his next pass, ground fire ripped his right engine completely from its mount and silenced the other engine. Collins crash-landed the gunship into a mountainside; one crewmember was injured. Some fifteen minutes after the crash the VC attacked. Although the crew fended off one probe, a second assault killed Captain Collins and the wounded airman.

As an HH-43 rescue helicopter dropped through the clouds, Collins' copilot, Lieutenant Delbert Peterson, single-handedly assaulted an enemy machinegun with his .38 pistol and M-16 rifle to cover the extraction of the remainder of the gunship crew. Unfortunately, only three of the crew got into the helicopter before heavy enemy fire forced it to take off again. Peterson and the rest of his crew were lost to enemy action.

Air Force Support to MAC(V)SOG

It was not long before the MAC(V) Studies and Observation Group (SOG) leadership recognized the utility of the gunships for interdiction missions along the Ho Chi Minh Trail. US ambassador to Laos William H. Sullivan requested the commitment of gunships against the Trail, and on 10 January 1966 two gunships deployed to Udorn Royal Thai Air Force Base in Thailand. The gunships performed two types of missions along the trail: armed reconnaissance and forward air control for air strikes by other types of aircraft. A typical armed reconnaissance mission was performed by Captain William Pratt and his crew on the night of 23 February. During the conduct of their patrol, Captain Pratt observed a truck convoy halted by a bomb crater on a trail. Working in a valley with steep cliffs, the Spooky began its firing orbit and struck the last truck in the convoy, setting it afire and trapping the remainder of the trucks. Panicked for their lives, the enemy soldiers manning the trucks responded with heavy gunfire. Using what was known as an 'orbiting strike maneuver', the Spooky systematically destroyed eleven more trucks and damaged numerous others before disengaging.

The 'Spookies' saw their last action in Vietnam in 1969. On 2 March, Colonel Conrad S. Allman, commander of the 14th Special Operations Wing, flew an AC-47 on the Wing's 150,000th combat mission. On 30 November 1969, Lieutenant Colonel Adam Swigler, Jr., commander of the 4th Special Operations Squadron, flew the last Spooky mission of the war. Under the Military Assistance Program, the Spookies were then distributed to the Thai, South Vietnamese and Laotian Air Forces.

AC-130 Spectre

Even as the first Spooky was being tested in 1963, Captain Simons was examining the potential for more sophisticated gunships. A true visionary, Simons anticipated inclusion of infrared and laser technology to enhance the night/limited visibility potential of the gunship. Two test programs began looking at a follow-on for the AC-47: Project Little Brother looked at mounting gatling guns in a twin engine Cessna while Project Gunboat (later called Gunship II) examined the potential of the C-130 as the firing platform. Eventually, Project Little Brother fell victim to budget cuts while Gunship II eventually produced the formidable AC-130A Spectre Gunship.

Ultimately, it was the broadening US involvement in Southeast Asia that brought emphasis to the problems endemic to night air operations. The VC were now conducting tactical and logistics operations primarily at night, to exploit the American lack of night-vision capability.

The first C-130 under the Gunboat program would have a starlight image intensification system working in concert with a fire control system. An infrared illuminator and beacon detector completed the prototype's target acquisition capability. This extensive combination of targeting systems would be used to provide firing data to two M-61 20mm gatling guns and two mini-guns. Gunship II required a crew of eleven.

After initial flight testing in the United States, the first combat trials of Gunship II began in South Vietnam on 21 September 1967. During the period September to December, the AC-130 spotted ninety-four trucks and destroyed thirty-eight. In fact, by the end of the evaluation, Gunship II had proven three times more effective than Spooky.[4] General Westmoreland was so impressed with its performance that he would not permit its return to the US for refurbishment until the commander of the 7th Air Force, General William Momyer, assured him that the new gunship would be back in Vietnam by February 1968.

Upon its return, Gunship II flew from February until November 1968, with splendid results: 1,000 trucks sighted, 228 destroyed, 133 damaged. It also managed to destroy or damage seventeen of the thirty-two enemy sampans it sighted. By the time the prototype returned to the US, it had been replaced with six production AC-130s.

As the first AC-130s entered operations in Southeast Asia, the North Vietnamese were getting wise to their tactics. Taking advantage of President Johnson's decision to reduce bombing in North Vietnam, the NVA repositioned hundreds of 37mm anti-aircraft guns along the Trail in Cambodia and Laos. To counter this, the Spectres began conducting interdiction operations in tandem with F-4 Phantom jet fighters. When the Spectres were fired on by anti-aircraft guns, they called in the F-4s to silence them. This made the NVA practice of firing on gunships a costly one indeed. An account from a mission flown on 30 December 1968 from Ubon Air Base, Thailand, provides an excellent example of a typical Spectre/F4 Phantom mission:

Ubon ground crews readied aircraft 1629 for the evening's flight. They put aboard Mk-24 and Mk-6 flares and 6,000 rounds of 20-mm ammunition. Meantime the crew studied the night's armed reconnaissance mission. The aircraft lifted off before dusk (at 1705) and while still over Ubon a checkout of equipment commenced. Operators aligned and prepared for operation the night observation device and other sensors. Gunners loaded and checked the weapons. Within 10 minutes the gunship was 'crossing the fence' [Mekong River separating Thailand and Laos] and making radio contact with Moonbeam, the ABCCC [Airborne Command, Control, and Communications aircraft] operating over southern Laos. Using current intelligence information the ABCCC assigned the AC-130 to a specific operating area whereupon the gunship's navigator assumed a key role as he plotted coordinates. The Gunship II's radio call sign was Spectre 01.

Spectre 01 reported 'on-station' at 1720. For the next 55 minutes it practiced intercepts with F-4 flights in case their help was needed to suppress AA fire. At 1815 gunship sensor operators probed infiltration route 922 working a 15-mile road segment until 2035. At 1840 four eastbound 'movers' were detected. The sensor inputs fed the fire control computer and the information reflected in the pilot's gunsight as he turned into a left orbit at 4,500 feet AGL (above ground level). Selecting the lead truck to stall traffic, the pilot pushed the trigger button as the movable and fixed target reticles superimposed in his gunsight. The 1,000 rounds of 20-mm fired in a 4 minute attack damaged 1 truck.

At 1855 Spectre 01 detected target 2 – 1 mover – and in a 2-minute attack orbit fired another 1,000 rounds of 20mm damaging 1 truck. Farther down the road the gunship discovered three stationary trucks and a suspected truck park. While marking the area with flares Spectre 01 met with 37-mm AA fire. From 1902 to 1925 the pilot squeezed off 1,000 more rounds of 20-mm on both the suspected truck park and the 37-mm site. An explosion and fire told of the AA emplacements's destruction.

Two more stationary trucks became target 4. Spectre 01 attacked from 2002 to 2006 and damaged both of them. Two F-4 flights – call signs Schlitz and Combine – worked AA sites together with Spectre strikes and claimed two sites destroyed. From 2021 to 2026, Spectre 01 once more fired 1,000 20-mm rounds upon return to the scene of the suspected truck park of target 3. No visual results were obtained of this final attack. Spectre 01 left the target area at 2035 after an elapsed time of 3 hours and 15 minutes with 6,000 rounds of 20-mm ammunition and 15 Mk-6 flares expended. The night's work totaled four trucks damaged, one 37-mm antiaircraft site destroyed, and one 37-mm AA site silenced. Spectre 01 recrossed the fence and touched down at Ubon at 2115. Total mission time stood at four hours and ten minutes.[5]

Unfortunately, this technique for neutralizing anti-aircraft fire required the enemy gunner to give away his position by firing. If he got the Spectre with his first burst, the consequences were tragic. Such was the case for Aircraft 1629 on 3 March 1969:

Aircraft 1629 reached its Laotian target at 1935 local time and was joined by a fighter escort. Spectre made a firing pass 5 minutes later at a moving truck. It then flew to a road intersection and began a 120 degree turn to reconnoiter the new route. As the turn was completed, illuminator operator SSgt. Jack W. Troglen reported antiaircraft fire at 6 o'clock and accurate. Ten 37mm rounds were seen – four on each side, one striking the gunship's tail section and hitting an undetermined spot on the fuselage.

The wounded Spectre turned westward toward home base. Its utility hydraulic system was out followed by the booster hydraulic system a few seconds later – leaving the aircraft temporarily out of control. The aircraft commander and copilot brought the gunship out of a nearly uncontrollable climb by bracing the control column to full forward position and by bringing all crew members to the flight deck.

Further aircraft checks disclosed Sergeant Troglen wounded and dying and the rudder, elevator trim, and autopilot inoperative. The gunship was nursed back toward Ubon by use of aileron trim and engine power. Near the base the aircraft commander ordered non-essential crewmembers to bail out. Left aboard were pilot/aircraft commander Lt. Col. William Schwehm and copilot Maj. Gerald H. Piehl (to control the aircraft), flight engineer SSgt. Cecil F. Taylor (to manually lower the gear), and a navigator sensor operator who wanted to stay.

As Colonel Schwehm slightly reduced power the aircraft's nose dropped hard on the runway. The gunship bounced and hit heavily on the landing gear. An attempt to reverse engines was futile. Some 2,000 feet down the runway the gunship veered to the right, despite application of more power to number 3 and 4 engines (nose wheel steering was inoperative). The right wing sheared off. The gunship burst into flames and the pilot, copilot, and navigator sensor operator safely evacuated. The body of Sergeant Troglen and that of flight engineer Taylor were lost in the billowing flames and explosions of burning ammunition. All crew members who bailed out were rescued.[6]

For the most part, Spectre missions were quite successful; the most successful mission flown by one of the early A model gunships was flown on 7 April 1969 by aircraft 627, which achieved a one hundred percent kill ratio.

The AC-130, call sign 'Schlitz' for this mission, began its pylon turn shortly after 1900 hours over one of the most heavily defended areas of Laos: Route 911, just south of the Mu Gia pass. Over a trail lined by sheer cliffs, a thick barrage of 37mm anti-aircraft fire snaked up toward the lone Spectre. Undaunted, the crew identified a total of twenty-five trucks and attacked them. All were destroyed. The Spectre returned home safely.[7]

A highly unusual first for a gunship occurred on 8 May 1969 when the night observation device (NOD) operator of aircraft 629 (call sign Bennet) spotted an object moving over the jungle canopy at 1,000 feet altitude. Suspecting it to be a North Vietnamese helicopter, the navigator computed the coordinates and called the ABCCC for permission to fire. While awaiting clearance, the NOD and Forward-looking Infrared (FLIR) operators tracked the helicopter to a clearing. Twenty minutes after requesting permission, Bennet was authorized to fire, and did so. Several 20mm bursts hit the perimeter of the clearing and set off explosions. Five rounds hit the helicopter, causing it to explode. Bennet's was the first gunship successfully to destroy a helicopter.

The AC-130As originally deployed to Vietnam underwent several upgrade programs before they flew their final missions in 1972. Before the end of the war, Spectres had been outfitted with laser designation systems, improved low-light television target acquisition systems, improved 40mm ammunition, and finally, a 105mm howitzer. These improvements all served to improve the survivability of the aircraft and multiply its lethality.

AC-119G/K Shadow/Stinger

Through a tremendously convoluted path of logic that proceeded from a combination of politics and economics, Secretary of the Air Force Harold

Brown, in 1967, decided that in addition to the C-130 follow-on to the Spookies, the air force would also deploy C-119 Flying Boxcars modified as gunships. In flight trials, the AC-119G Shadow proved inferior to the AC-47 in terms of flight performance, and had to be significantly modified to meet air force standards. The explanation for this strange initiative lay in the fact that there were numerous C-119s in the mothball inventory and Brown wanted to avoid sacrificing the airlift capabilities of the new C-130s in a gunship role.

So, in January 1969, the AC-119 Shadow began combat evaluations and proved valuable in armed reconnaissance and base defense missions. Tactics for these missions were essentially the same as those used by the Spookies and Spectres, but a Shadow flew a highly unusual mission in early 1969.

During a VC attack, a friendly outpost had its generator disabled as a doctor was performing surgery on a wounded South Vietnamese soldier. 71st Special Operations Squadron dispatched a Shadow to assist. Orbiting the compound, the Shadow illuminated its one-million-candlepower search lamp, providing the visibility necessary for the doctor to complete his operation. The soldier lived.

Psychological Operations (PSYOPS)

The air force activated the 5th Air Commando Squadron (code named 'Quick Speak'), their first Psyops squadron in Vietnam, in August 1965. This squadron consisted of four C-47s and ten U-10 Courier light observation planes equipped with loudspeakers. Unfortunately, due to the power of their speakers, the early missions were subjected to heavy groundfire, although no aircraft were lost. In conjunction with the broadcast missions, Quick Speak aircraft dropped literally millions of propaganda leaflets.

Special Operations Outside Vietnam, 1961–6

I consider the civic action role of the Air Commandos to be one of our most important undertakings. We have made a beginning during 1963 and plan to continue. If we can train allied air forces to use tactical air power as a nation building or civic action vehicle, we may never have to train them to drop bombs or fire rockets and machineguns. I firmly believe that, through civic actions and given enough time, Communist subversion can be stopped before it gets to the shooting stage.

Brigadier General G.L. Pritchard
Commander, Special Air Warfare Center

As evidenced by the early deployment of special operations aircraft to Mali, in 1961, the air force participated in extensive special operations in the third world in order to promote democratic ideals and provide humanitarian relief to destitute peoples and nations. Many of these exercises were highly unusual, but quite beneficial to those they assisted.

The earliest such operation was conducted during exercise BOLD VENTURE. One of the primary objectives of the exercises was to examine the viability of the airstrip at Nargana, Panama. In conjunction with the operation, a crew flying a U-10 carried in 200 lb of school books for the school children in the village. During Operation BOOKS the crew got to practice touch and go landings and made a quantum improvement in the quality of education in the local community.

In the latter half of 1963, the 1st Air Commando Wing at Hurlburt Field, Florida, deployed mobile training teams (MTT) to six Latin American countries to train indigenous air force personnel in various civic action skills. Military from Bolivia, the Dominican Republic, Guatemala, Honduras, Equador, and Paraguay received training in many facets of preventive medicine. Travelling in a Cessna aircraft, Air Commandos provided training in water and milk testing, tooth extraction, veterinary medicine, cooking, and inoculations. In areas inaccessible by aircraft, the crew would use a loudspeaker to provide directions to the local populace on how to construct an airstrip. In August 1963, when an outbreak of hemorrhagic fever broke out in Bolivia, Air Commandos flew doctors and 20,000 lb of medical supplies to the village of San Joaquin.

In the latter part of 1966, the Air Commandos engaged in a massive civic action effort in Laos and Thailand. Medical teams of one doctor and several medics worked closely with military and political authorities in remote areas besieged by Communist terrorists. With the assistance of 50,000 lb of medical supplies donated by the World Medical Relief Association, Air Commandos treated malaria, typhoid fever, dysentery, tuberculosis and vitamin deficiencies.

In Laos, the teams primarily treated wounded from across the Mekong River in Vietnam at a one-hundred-bed hospital. The US Agency for International Development (USAID) built the hospital and Dr Robert E. Jackson, an Air Commando medic, and a Laotian Army doctor trained the staff of twenty-five villagers in basic medical care. The numerous casualties from mines resulted in a high number of amputations causing Dr Jackson to establish a blood bank. This significantly reduced the mortality rate for the wounded. In six months, the Air Commando effort treated almost 8,000 patients.

Conclusions

The early years of air force special operations demonstrated the clear dichotomy in their nature that would continue throughout their history. Special operations were characterized by the lethal, devastating slaughter wrought by the gunships on the one hand and the idealistic, compassionate mercy demonstrated by the civic action teams on the other. The seeming paradox is that attack aircraft, gunship and civic action crews all were Air Commandos.

The gunship techniques and hardware developed in Vietnam have proven extremely durable. The AC-130 would continue in service until well into the 1990s. Techniques and lessons learned in Vietnam would be applied with ever greater effect in Cambodia, Grenada, Panama and the Persian Gulf.

The air force was the first service to bring civic action and Psyops under the umbrella of special operations. Although the Army civic action and Psyops personnel worked closely with Special Forces, it was not until the latter half of the 1980s that the Army incorporated those two functions into their special operations doctrine and organizations. Clearly, the air force concept of using civic action in peacetime to forestall crisis and conflict was visionary. It was not until the early 1990s that US military doctrine would recognize the need for military operations short of war.

NOTES

1. Herbert H. Kissling, *An Air Commando and Special Operations Chronology 1961–1991* (Hurlburt Field, Florida, First Special Operations Wing, Air Force Special Operations Command, United States Air Force), p. 4.
2. Ibid, p. 17.
3. Jack S. Ballard, *Development and Employment of Fixed-Wing Gunships 1962–1972* (Washington, Office of Air Force History), p. 20.
4. Ibid, p. 89.
5. AC-130 Mission Report, Mission 1316/17 Detachment 2, 14th Air Combat Wing, 30 December 1968.
6. Message, 8th Tactical Fighter Wing to 13th Air Force, 251041Z May 6, Subject: AC-130 Battle Damage Accident, May 24, 1969; AC-130 Mission Report, 16th Special Operations Squadron, 24 May 1969.
7. *History of the 8th Tactical Fighter Wing, Apr–Jun 1969*, volume III, part 12.

Hardening the Steel Transition and Evolution 1975–86

Battles of Influence American Special Operations in Transition 1975–86

Reeling from the backlash of a humiliating withdrawal from Southeast Asia and the resignation of President Richard Nixon in the wake of the Watergate scandal, President Gerald Ford was confronted with an entirely new set of foreign policy and domestic issues. The ethics of United States foreign and military initiatives, including some special operations, were spotlighted in the retrospective glare of national media and the US Congress. The institution of the United States military seemed to be selected to atone for the shame of Vietnam.

A sickness of the spirit pervaded America in the 1970s and government corruption and cynicism were at the heart of that malaise. The Congressional action that prevented President Ford from intervening militarily to assist the Saigon government signified a fundamental shift toward isolationism in American foreign policy; America did not want any more of her sons and daughters dying in foreign involvements. Unfortunately, the twentieth century had not seen the end of pirates and brigands. America's attempt at isolation only encouraged outlaw activity against her interests overseas and placed her interests and people in peril.

Harbinger of the Future: Assault on the *Mayaguez*, 1975

Two weeks after the fall of Saigon, on 12 May 1975, the new Communist Khmer government of Cambodia ordered its Navy to seize the SS *Mayaguez*, an American cargo ship crossing the Gulf of Siam bound for Singapore. The Khmer government was enforcing a ninety-mile territorial limit it had announced four days before. At 1418 hours, the *Mayaguez* reported by radio to the Delta Exploration Company in Jakarta that she had been fired upon and that she was being towed toward an unknown Cambodian Port. The first crisis in the post-Vietnam era was underway.

Within a week, the *Mayaguez* and her crew were returned, principally as a result of diplomatic efforts, but not before fifteen American marines and airmen lost their lives in an abortive rescue attempt. The *Mayaguez* incident was a warning of things to come; America's international interests and citizens abroad were now fair game.

The Presidency of Jimmy Carter, 1977–81

Jimmy Carter succeeded Gerald Ford to the presidency of the United States, elected by a difference in the popular vote of four percent on the appeal of being a Washington 'outsider' and having a fresh perspective. He immediately proceeded radically to change America's foreign policy, and as a consequence put many of America's citizens abroad, business interests and allies at risk. There were three pillars to his foreign policy.

The first pillar was to make the first move in reducing tensions with those nations that were traditional Cold War enemies, such as the Soviet Union and Korea. The second involved building the trust of his fellow world leaders, and conversely eliminating the seeds of distrust. One of these seeds was the American intelligence community, and so he severely restricted their activities because of some of their perceived excesses of the past several years. The third pillar was to link all aid to foreign countries to their human rights policies.

The net effect of this well-meaning new foreign policy was to leave America like a boxer standing blindfolded in the ring with hands and feet tied, waiting for his opponent to tell him when and where the next punch was coming. The test came two years later.

Iran, 1979–80

In November 1979, radical Iranian military students took over the United States Embassy in Tehran, seizing some fifty-three hostages in the process. America was powerless to react effectively, either politically or militarily.

Although since 1977 the army had been unilaterally developing a Special Forces hostage rescue capability, the other services failed to follow suit. Consequently, when the Pentagon began to plan the Iran hostage rescue mission, the air force, navy and marines had to organize and equip provisional special operations units. For an operation as extensive as a surprise rescue of fifty-three hostages held in a fortified compound in the capitol of a country half-way around the world from America, air force and naval support was essential; a joint service hostage rescue team was needed, but did not exist.

When Operation EAGLE CLAW commenced in April 1979, under the command of Army Major General James B. Vaught, the Pentagon and service planners had done the best they could in only five months. An effective special operations force must be able to operate as a team, and five months is not sufficient time to recruit, organize, equip, train and rehearse a large team for such a complex mission. Further, the Chairman of the Joint Chiefs of Staff, Air Force General David Jones, had succumbed to inter-service politics by authorizing all services to participate, violating the principles of simplicity and unity of command.

The factors mitigating against a successful mission were insurmountable. The mission failed, and failed in a highly visible manner.

Public outcries in Congress and the press forced the administration to conduct a detailed investigation. The report, entitled simply *Report on Rescue Mission*,[1] provided detailed findings and recommendations that would eventually revolutionize the way the United States military would handle joint special operations.

Although all members of the investigating panel originally believed that both planning and execution phases were poorly handled, by the time the inquiry concluded they had all developed admiration for the men who had planned and attempted to execute the operation. The report concluded that although the mission had a sixty to seventy percent chance of success, its failure was brought on largely by bad luck. It was a high-risk operation that depended on its personnel and equipment operating to extreme limits of their capabilities. Essentially, there was little or no margin for error and somewhere along the line, inevitably, error occurs.

The panel found that Major General Vaught and the planners had established and used a new, untried, command and control system rather than modify the existing Joint Chiefs of Staff (JCS) system. Although emergency contingency plans for Iran existed, Vaught chose to build a plan from scratch. Operational security was the rationale for both these actions, although the panel believed that existing organizations and command and control systems could have been used without compromise.

Because of terrain requirements and logistics, the task force had to train at sites scattered throughout the United States and Vaught chose to supervise personally the training rather than delegate training supervision to a staff officer. Consequently, because of all the other demands on his time, Vaught was unable to provide adequate training supervision. Further, again using the security rationale, the units from the various services involved in the operation were isolated from each other, degrading the coordination necessary to build the team effectively. Finally, Vaught decided against integrating the training in a full dress rehearsal, concerned that this might telegraph America's plans and intentions.

The report made two major recommendations: that the Defense Department establish a counter-terrorist task force and that it establish a special operations advisory panel. Both of these actions would be undertaken by the next presidential administration.

On 20 January 1981, the hostages were freed and Ronald Reagan was inaugurated fortieth president of the United States. The two actions were not coincidental. Following Reagan's landslide victory, he made it clear that he would take whatever action was necessary – by implication full military – against Iran to free the hostages.

Rebuilding Special Operations Forces, 1981–3

Immediately following his inauguration, Reagan went to work on the three major themes of his campaign: the economy, foreign policy, and the military, rebuilding America's former strength as a world power, and, perhaps more importantly, her self-image.

The Pentagon and Congress continued to identify the lessons learned from Operation EAGLE CLAW, and began immediately to take corrective action. At Fort Bragg, North Carolina, the Joint Special Operations Center, or JSOC, was established to study the special operations requirements and techniques of all the services to ensure standardization.[2] Each of the services began to revitalize their special operations programs. The United States was rebuilding the might necessary to pursue and enforce her foreign policies.

Privately Funded Special Operations, 1984

As soon as he took office, Reagan acted against the Communist Sandinista government in Nicaragua. Using special operations forces and privately contracted military experts, the United States began providing covert backing to the budding anti-Communist Contra movement in Nicaragua.

The Contras were a large group of guerillas, under the leadership of men like Adolpho Calero and Eden Pastora, who believed that the Sandinistas had stolen the revolution from the people of Nicaragua and replaced the fascist tyranny of Somoza with the Communist tyranny of the Ortega brothers. As the Sandinistas began receiving massive shipments of Soviet aid and vowed to export their revolution, the US began providing aid to the Contra insurgency.

A constitutional crisis between President Reagan and the Congress resulted in a new wrinkle on special operations. Congress, in opposition to Reagan's policies enacted the Boland Amendment in 1984, prohibiting governmental aid to the Contra insurgents fighting the Sandinista government in Nicaragua.

The Contra movement deteriorated to the verge of collapse when a private organization called the World Anti-Communist League (WACL), led by retired Army Major General John Singlaub, began a project to privately resupply and train Contra fighters. Singlaub travelled the world soliciting funding from private individuals and governments sympathetic to the Contra cause. He recruited ex-military and medical personnel to train Contra units. As other US government aid efforts succumbed to scandal and corruption, Singlaub breathed new life into the democratic movement in Nicaragua.

Singlaub undertook this effort for altruistic reasons: he believed that Americans should stand behind their commitments, that the despotism and excesses that were Communism should be destroyed wherever they manifested themselves, and that the Sandinistas as Soviet surrogates intended to export revolution throughout the Americas.

LEBANON, 1982–4

Turmoil in the Middle East prompted Lebanon's president, Amin Gemayel, to request deployment of a multi-national force to his country to restore order in 1982. In response to this request the United States deployed 24th Marine Amphibious Unit (MAU), consisting of 1st Battalion, 8th Marines (Battalion Landing Team or BLT 1/8), Marine Helicopter Squadron 162 (HMM-162), and Marine Service Support Group 24 (MSSG 24) to Beirut airport.

Unfortunately, United Nations and US objectives for this deployment were unclear and the Marines found themselves in a most difficult predicament: confronting invading Israelis, Syrians, a myriad of different armed militias and backing up a highly unreliable Lebanese Army. Eventually, the Marine battalion deployment became a static defense of the Beirut Airport. For the next fourteen months the Marines were targets, being subjected to increasingly violent episodes of harassment fire and sniping attacks from Israelis and various ethnic militias. Finally it all came to a head in October 1983 when the radical Shi'ite splinter group Islamic Hezballah Amal decided to get even with the marines for killing four of their members in an anti-sniper operation.[3]

On 19 October, the group attempted to kill the commander of the 24th MAU, Colonel Timothy J. Geraghty, when they ambushed a supply convoy carrying him to a conference. Although the vehicles were blown to bits, no one was killed.

So the Hezballah tried again, and succeeded. On 23 October 1983, a member of the Hezballah drove a five-ton truck filled with explosive through the gate of the Marine compound at the airport and into the four-storey marine barracks. 1,200 pounds of explosives detonated, demolishing the building and killing 218 marines, eighteen sailors, three soldiers, a French paratrooper, and a Lebanese civilian.

This single but devastating act publicly demonstrated the bankruptcy of UN and US policy in Lebanon. By February 1984, the Marines and the remainder of the Multi-national Force had been withdrawn.

Grenada, 1983

As the Marines in Lebanon were taking stock of their casualties from the truck bombing, Navy SEALs were beginning the first of a number of special operations in support of a major US intervention on the island of Grenada in the Caribbean. This intervention would clearly demonstrate to the world that as far as Ronald Reagan was concerned, the Monroe Doctrine was back in force.[4]

Grenada had been under Communist rule since 1979, when the fascist government of Sir Eric Gairy was ousted in a virtually bloodless coup led by opposition leader Maurice Bishop, who headed the New Jewel Movement (NJM). Immediately, Grenada moved into the Soviet/Cuban sphere of influence. Cuba began constructing a military airfield on the island and the Soviet Union provided massive supplies of military hardware and training to Grenada's Peoples Revolutionary Armed Forces (PRAF).

But since its rise to power in 1979, a power struggle had been brewing in inner circles of the NJM. This struggle ended in a singularly bloody coup on Wednesday 19 October 1983, when the ousted deputy party leader, Bernard Coard, seized control of the Army and stormed Fort Rupert where Bishop and his supporters had run for protection. The Army killed between thirty and forty people (many of whom were unarmed women and children) in the initial assault. Upon seizure of the fort, they then executed Bishop and eight of his supporters by firing squad.

Bishop had been a charismatic and popular leader, and the resultant popular outcry prompted the new junta to impose a 24-hour curfew.

Reagan decided to intervene: six hundred American students attending Saint Georges University were at risk and the new Grenadan regime was also inclined toward an even more direct alignment with the Soviets.

The new JSOC played a major role in planning the employment of special operations forces in Grenada. Unfortunately little time, only four days, was available to plan the operation and this lack of prior planning manifested itself in flawed execution. Nevertheless, the special operations forces of the army, navy and air force each played important parts in the operation to intervene in Grenada. Air force special operations aircraft brought in army Rangers on the initial assault and provided their fire support. SEALs rescued the British governor-general and his family. The real value of the action, from the perspective of the special operations community, was that it yielded valuable lessons that would increase the effectiveness and precision of special warfare in later operations.

A Unified Command For Special Operations, 1986

The problems encountered with special operations during Operations EAGLE CLAW (Iran hostage rescue) and URGENT FURY had not gone unnoticed. Not satisfied that the Pentagon had created an effective framework and structure for the command, control, and provision of special operations forces, Congress held a series of hearings beginning in 1983. The result of those hearings was the Fiscal Year 1987 National Defense Authorization Bill which directed a reorganization of SOF; and specifically the creation of 'a unified combatant command with responsibility for providing operationally ready special operations, psychological operations, and civil affairs forces to theater unified commands and for conducting special operations missions when directed by the national command authority.'[5] United States Special

Major General Robert C. Kingston began his special operations career during the Korean War. A true 'Mustang', Kingston enlisted as a private and retired as a General. He was behind a number of Special Forces initiatives, most significantly the development of the Special Forces hostage rescue capability. (*USA JFK Special Warfare Center and School*)

General Carl Stiner, Commander-in chief, US Special Operations Command (CINCSOC), 1990 until 1993. During his tenure of command, Stiner effectively consolidated America's special operations units under one umbrella, building a solid, formidable special operations team. (*USSOCOM photo*)

Mission accomplished; a Navy SEAL patrol reboards their inflatable boat after a mission. These boats are constantly used in special warfare operations and SEALs are introduced to them during their initial training. (*USSOCOM photo*)

Ready for almost anything, this patrol of SEALs silently approaches a coast. Note SEAL in the fore is armed with an M203 grenade launcher/automatic rifle. This weapon puts the devastating firepower of an automatic rifle and a 40mm grenade launcher in the hands of one man. (*USSOCOM photo*)

Ready to go! An F470 Zodiac boat idles toward the beach during a SEAL mission. The Zodiac is light-weight, can be powered by electric and gasoline engines, and is suitable for open ocean transits of up to fifty nautical miles. (*USSOCOM photo*)

A Special Boat Unit readies its craft. These special boats plied the coastal waters of both Saudi Arabia and Kuwait harassing Iraqi coastal units and shipping (*USSOCOM photo*)

Navy Special Boat Unit twenty-eight-foot high-speed cigarette boat zooms along the Saudi Coast near Dhahran during Operation DESERT SHIELD in 1991. These boats were used to support raids and clandestine reconnaissance. (*USSOCOM photo*)

Seafox Special Warfare Craft, Light (SWCL). This craft carries up to ten SEALs or UDT swimmers and was designed to support over-the-horizon deployments from ships at sea. It is powered by two 425 horsepower Detroit Deisel engines. (*USSOCOM photo*)

Naval Special Warfare Mark III (Spectre Class) Patrol Boat. Note the deck mounted 40mm and 20mm cannon, which were prevalent on later versions of the craft. These are extraordinarily powerful craft: each has three 625 horsepower Detroit Diesel engines. This is the type of craft used to insert Navy SEALs over the beach for reconnaissance in Grenada in support of Operation URGENT FURY in October 1983 (*USSOCOM photo*)

Naval Special Warfare Scorpion and Fountain high-speed boats (HSB) preparing for a mission during Operation DESERT STORM. These craft were used to disrupt Iraqi shipping and coastal operations in occupied Kuwait. (*USSOCOM photo*)

Mission: Son Tay. Special Forces soldiers head out to the helicopters that will transport them into North Vietnam to liberate the Son Tay Prisoner-of-War Camp near Hanoi in 1970. Although they found no prisoners, these grim-faced commandos did manage to kill a large number of enemy soldiers. (*US Army Special Forces Museum, Fort Bragg photo*)

Calisthenics, five-mile swims and seemingly endless runs characterize basic underwater demolition/SEAL training. Note the instructor at the left, rear of this formation correcting an errant trainee. (*USSOCOM photo*)

Jubilant basic underwater demolition/SEAL trainees exercise on the 'Mud Flats'. Although hiding their elation, these trainees know that they are nearing the end of the initial phase of their training. (*USSOCOM photo*)

DESERT STORM psychological operations (Psyops) leaflets. Thousands of these were printed by American special operations psyops units and dropped by MC-130 Combat Talons on Iraqi troops. They were used to warn Iraqi troops to stay away from their equipment when coalition air strikes were imminent. They were also effectively used to encourage surrenders. (*US Army Special Operations Command photo*)

5th Special Forces Group (Airborne) soldiers engage in an after-action review with their Arab counterparts during Operation DESERT SHIELD/DESERT STORM. 5th Group soldiers performed advisor/liaison/communications functions with Arab coalition forces, providing status reports on their units to General Schwarzkopf. (*US Army Special Operations Command photo*)

(Left) US Special Forces personnel deliver humanitarian relief supplies to Kurds in northern Iraq during Operation PROVIDE COMFORT 1991. Because of Saddam Hussein's continued threats against his Kurdish population, this operation continues as this book goes to press. (*USSOCOM photo*)

(Below) Before the ground war began, teams from the 5th Special Forces Group (Airborne) manned outposts along the Saudi frontier. These outposts collected and reported information on Iraqi movements and served as a 'tripwire' in the event of an Iraqi raid or incursion. Note the soldier on the right wearing laser resistant goggles. (*USSOCOM photo*)

On alert, an MH-53 Pave Low stands by for a combat search and rescue (CSAR) mission into Iraq. These helicopters and their crews were on alert almost twenty-four hours a day during the Desert Storm air campaign. Their mission: to rescue downed coalition pilots. (*US Air Force Special Operation Command photo*)

Known as 'Puff the Magic Dragon' and 'Dragon Ship' to the Vietnamese, this AC-130 Spectre Gunship cuts loose with its 20mm gatling gun. With pinpoint accuracy and a rate of fire of 6,000 rounds per minute, these guns rapidly broke North Vietnamese assaults against US protected South Vietnamese villages. (*US Air Force Special Operations Command photo*)

Helocasting. A member of a Navy SEAL team enters the water on a mission. The helocasting technique is used to drop off SEALs embarking on a mission or link them up with submarines or special boats already under way. At this point, the real work begins for this SEAL as he may have to swim up to five miles to a hostile shore. (*USSOCOM photo*)

Special Forces Mike (Mobile Strike) Force in Nha Trang preparing for a mission in 1968. The Mike Force was a heliborne quick response force that reinforced Special Forces border camps when they came under concerted VC or North Vietnamese attack. Special Forces were teamed with indigenous Nung tribesmen, whom they had trained and armed. (*US Army Special Forces Museum, Fort Bragg photo*)

Four Special Forces soldiers being extracted from the jungle by a STABO rig. The rig is first dangled from a hovering helicopter into heavy foliated areas, where the troops climb into the harnesses. When they are ready, they signal the helicopter and away they go. This extraction method was used extensively by Special Forces and long-range patrollers in Vietnam. (*USSOCOM photo*)

US Air Force Special Operations Weather Team (SOWT) member measures wind velocity. These personnel are trained to deploy into potentially hostile target areas, monitor and report weather conditions that could impact on planned special operations. (*USSOCOM photo*)

The big brother of the Pave Hawk, the MH-53 Pave Low has an extremely sophisticated navigational suite combined with the awesome firepower of two 7.62mm gatling guns. Here a Pave Low crew winches in a fellow special operator at the conclusion of a mission. (*USSOCOM photo*)

Although similar to the US Army Blackhawk helicopters, the Air Force special operations Pave Hawks are equipped with the in-flight refuelling capability and are designed for longer range infiltration and extraction missions. They are especially well suited for combat search and rescue operations. (*USSOCOM photo*)

Three MH-6 Little Bird helicopters on a mission. Carrying 7.62mm gatling guns or 2.75in rockets, these aircraft were used extensively in Grenada and Panama. (*USSOCOM photo*)

AC-130H Spectre Gunship in operation over the American southwest. Spectre gunships first saw service in Vietnam and have participated in every major American conflict since. Note the two 20mm gatling guns forward of the wings and the 40mm Bofors cannon and 105mm howitzer aft. The aircraft fires its weaponry from a pylon turn with deadly accuracy, using a variety of sophisticated sensors working in concert with a fire control computer. (*Lockheed-Ontario*)

US Army MH-47E Special Operations Chinook. These helicopters were fielded recently to provide long-range special operations resupply capability. (*Boeing*)

MH-53 Pave Low moving in for refueling. Note the drogue refueling pod on the lower right-hand corner. These aircraft are designed for clandestine infiltration and exfiltration missions and have a sophisticated navigation suite, and pack a tremendous amount of firepower with 7.62mm gatling guns mounted in the doors during missions.

Operations Command (USSOCOM) would become the headquarters of all army, navy and air force special operations forces. The legislation also created an Assistant Secretary of Defense for Special Operations and Low-Intensity Conflict (ASD-SOLIC) and a coordinating body within the National Security Council to advise the President on matters involving SOF and Low-Intensity Conflict (LIC) policies.

The establishment of these two powerful new entities paved the way for the brilliant special operations successes of the 1990s.

NOTES

1. *Report on Rescue Mission*, commissioned by General Jones and prepared by Admiral James L. Holloway III and a board of six officers of flag rank, all with special operations experience. Subsequently referred to as the 'Holloway Investigation.'
2. *United States Special Operations Command*, pamphlet published by the US Special Operations Command Public Affairs Office, MacDill Air Force Base, Florida.
3. Daniel P. Bolger, *Americans at War 1975–1986; An Era of Violent Peace* (Novato, California, Presidio, 1988) p. 225.
4. President James Monroe first articulated what would become known as the 'Monroe Doctrine' on 2 December 1823 in his annual message to the US Congress. In that address, he made three points that would become cardinal doctrine in American foreign policy: (1) that the American continents were not to be considered subjects for future colonization by European powers; (2) that any attempt by the nations of Europe to colonize any portion of the Americas was a manifest threat to peace and US safety; and (3) that America would not involve itself in wars between European powers. Although the third point would be permanently abrogated with US involvement in World War I, points one and two have been more or less in force since they were first espoused.
5. US Special Operations Command Public Affairs Office Memorandum to the author, with enclosures, Subject: Security Review of Manuscript, dated 9 September 1993.

CHAPTER 7

Battles of Influence
Army Special Operations in
Transition 1975–86

The backlash from Vietnam struck army special operations forces harder than the other services. Because the army had the largest presence in Vietnam its actions were better known and more carefully scrutinized. Special Forces endured much criticism for their role in the Phoenix program, the objectives of which had been severely misreported in the American media. Special Forces had taken on an image of being cruel, ruthless, amoral cowboys who undertook clandestine violence. Essentially, Vietnam and the press had destroyed virtually any pride that America had in her fighting men.

As a consequence of this, during the Carter administration, army special operators found themselves fighting for the very existence of the capability they represented. As the army was being reduced, so was its SOF. Further, as a consequence of its image problems, the army was forced to lower its recruiting standards in order to maintain its numbers. This had a deleterious effect on the quality of men SOF were getting; forcing both Special Forces and Rangers to lower minimum standards for physical fitness and rank.

The degeneration of army SOF was not complete, however, thanks to the efforts of some far-sighted individuals. These men foresaw the potential consequences of America's new direction in foreign policy and began to build a military capability to deal with its consequences.

Hostage Rescue, 1975–9

America's Special Forces hostage rescue capability began in October 1975 when Major General Robert C. Kingston went to Fort Bragg, North Carolina, to take command of the John F. Kennedy Center for Military Assistance and the US Army Institute for Military Assistance. Nicknamed 'War Lord' and 'Barbed Wire Bob,' Kingston was a tough, seasoned veteran of special operations in Korea and Southeast Asia.

Terrorism was becoming more and more popular to radical fringe causes. The Black September attack on the Israeli athletes at the 1972 Munich Olympic Games had catapulted the plight of the Palestinians to international attention. It was foreseen that sooner or later, terrorism would become a tool for some faction seeking international attention to use against America. Kingston had seen the Munich massacre and the *Mayaguez* action as harbingers of things to come, and with the new trend toward isolationism and disarmament, Americans overseas would become more and more vulnerable to terrorism.

Kingston had met Lieutenant Colonel (then Captain) Charlie Beckwith in June 1962 in England, as Kingston was finishing up his exchange tour with the Parachute Regiment. This was a one-year exchange assignment and Beckwith was replacing Kingston; but he was not going to the Paras. Beckwith would be assigned to 22 Special Air Service Regiment, or the SAS.[1] When he returned to the US in 1963 Beckwith would be positively fired with enthusiasm for the SAS, its unique mission and organization, and the capabilities it represented. Over the years, he conveyed this enthusiasm for the SAS to his friend and mentor, 'Barbed Wire' Bob Kingston.

As a result, it was Kingston's concern about America's vulnerability to international terrorism that prompted him to contact Beckwith and direct him to develop a concept for an elite hostage rescue unit. Although Special Forces and Rangers were well equipped to deal with a number of high-profile missions, Kingston and Beckwith both felt that a force dedicated to hostage rescue was essential to deal with professional, well-trained terrorists. By May 1977, Kingston and Beckwith had sold the concept to most of the senior leadership. In June 1977, Kingston and Beckwith got the approval of the Army Chief of Staff, General Bernard Rogers, to form the unit. In November, the unit was activated, under Beckwith's command.[2]

The key to special units has and always will be the selection of special men to fill them. Such was the case with the Special Forces hostage rescue team. It would take Beckwith two years to select and train his team. In the interim, the 7th Special Forces Group at Fort Bragg would handle any crises that might arise.

Beckwith required that his men be able to pass a rigorous physical fitness test comprising push-ups, sit-ups, a two-mile run and a 100-meter swim in full combat gear. Following that, each candidate had to complete an eighteen-mile forced march over rough terrain, wearing a fifty-five pound rucksack. Each event had to be completed in a limited amount of time. Those that completed the physical requirements were subjected to psychological evaluations to determine if they could live up to the mental and emotional demands of the elite unit.

Finally, in April 1978, enough volunteers had been assessed to begin specialized training. This nineteen-week course consisted of specialized marksmanship training, command and control procedures, communications, fire and movement techniques, forcible entry, hostage management, first-aid, airborne and airmobile techniques, hostage protection, hand-to-hand combat and numerous other techniques essential to hostage rescue operations.

From individual training, teams would be formed and team training would be conducted. Soldiers would practice clearing buildings and aircraft, and killing terrorists but not harming hostages. Explosive handling in a variety of situations would then be practiced along with a numerous other arcane skills.[3]

Early in 1979 the Special Forces hostage rescue capability validated in a highly realistic exercise.

The scenario was that a team of terrorists had seized American hostages in Canada. Although the Royal Canadian Mounted Police (RCMP) were en route, the Canadians had requested US assistance. Beckwith assembled a team of his Special Forces soldiers for the mission, put them aboard an aircraft, and deployed them. None knew that this was only an exercise. They had live ammunition and explosives.

The team was en route to a rural part of North Carolina to a place called Camp Smokey, although air traffic chatter was introduced on-board the aircraft via the intercom to convince them their destination was actually in Canada. Upon arrival, near midnight, the men were met by role-players dressed as Canadian and American police and diplomatic officials, with the Canadians speaking with authentic accents. These 'officials' briefed the team that three terrorists had taken hostages, two of whom were American, and the Canadians could not handle the operation. They were holed up in a secluded house.

As the soldiers reconnoitered the house, role-player terrorists, who had been standing guard, entered it. They then left the facility through a trap door in the floor. Inside the house, a complex system of mannequins moved about. The soldiers moved into their assault positions, loaded their weapons, and waited for the order to attack. They believed they were in Canada and in a real-life situation.

Beckwith gave the authority and the operation was over in eight seconds. The terrorist mannequins had all been shot. The hostage mannequins were unharmed and Beckwith's men were extremely angry at the charade.[4] But they were ready.

The Iran Hostage Rescue Mission, 1979–80

On Monday 5 November 1979, Beckwith dispatched a liaison officer to the Pentagon to begin contingency planning for the Iran hostage rescue mission. The hostages had been seized the previous day. On 11 November 1979, the Special Forces hostage rescue team went into isolation at Camp Smokey, to begin working out how they could carry out a rescue mission.

Detailed intelligence began to flow in. From it, the operators constructed a detailed model of the embassy compound and attempted to determine precisely where the hostages were. For this type of operation, highly detailed intelligence was necessary; where were entrances and exits, what was the size, disposition, and equipment of the guard force, which way did doors open or close? Slowly but surely, the team obtained the information. Six weeks later, the team had sufficient information to formulate a detailed plan.

Then the rehearsals began. A mockup of the embassy compound was built at Yuma Army Airfield in Southern Arizona. This enabled the soldiers to rehearse with their helicopter and fixed-wing (C-130) support. The compound was some twenty-seven acres in size with fourteen separate buildings surrounded by a wall. The team numbered almost one hundred personnel and was organized into Red, White, and Blue elements.

Red element was the largest and would seize and secure the southwest corner of the compound. Blue element would seize the Ambassador's and Deputy Chief of Mission's residences and a warehouse. White element would support the assault by securing the streets outside the compound.

President Carter was briefed on 16 April 1980 on the plan for Operation EAGLE CLAW, the hostage rescue mission. He approved it *in toto*. The plan for the ground assault force, Beckwith's hostage rescue team, was as follows:

Staging at dusk, the troops would deploy aboard MC-130 Combat Talon Transports to the site known as Desert One, in the Dasht E' Kavir desert. The transports would be accompanied by three EC-130 aircraft hauling fuel. From the aircraft carrier USS Nimitz, eight RH-53D helicopters would fly into Iran and rendezvous with the task force at Desert One, thirty minutes after the trail MC-130 had landed. On arrival, the RH-53s would refuel and Beckwith's men would transfer from the MC-130s onto the helicopters. A mission abort would be called if less than six helicopters were operational after the flight to Desert One.

As the MC-130s departed Desert One the helicopters, with Beckwith's force aboard, would proceed to Desert Two, a hide-site some sixty-five miles southeast of Tehran. The helicopters would drop off the force and fly to their hide-site some fifteen miles away, where they would be hidden under camouflage for the day.

At Desert Two, the assault force would be met by two US Department of Defense (DOD) agents who would be deployed to Tehran a few days in advance of the operation to reconnoiter and make preparations. These agents would lead the men five miles overland to a dry stream bed, or wadi, where they would hide throughout the day.

That night, just after dark, the agents would return to the wadi and would transport a team of drivers and translators to a warehouse in Tehran. Beckwith would reconnoiter the route to the embassy before returning to the hide-site.

At about 2030 hours, Red, White and Blue elements would begin their journey to Tehran. A thirteen-man Special Forces team would go to the Iranian Foreign Ministry Building to rescue three hostages being held there. Along the route, the Red, White and Blue elements would pass a two-man checkpoint. If they were stopped, they would take action to neutralize the checkpoint.

At 2300 hours, a small element would approach the front of the embassy compound, on Roosevelt Avenue. Using silenced .22 caliber pistols, they would take down the two guard posts and the walking guards. The assault force would then go down the street and when opposite the embassy, enter the embassy compound silently, using ladders. Red Element would secure the western sector of the compound, freeing any hostages it might find. Blue element would secure the residences, a warehouse and the chancellery. White element would monitor Roosevelt Avenue and cover the withdrawal of the two assault elements to the soccer stadium across the street.

Once all elements were in position, the embassy wall would be blown open and the assault would begin. Any Iranian guards would be killed; all hostages would be freed. The operation up to this point would take approximately forty-five minutes.

As the assault was taking place, the helicopters would be orbiting at a point north of the city. Upon completion of the assault, and once the grounds were clear of any obstructions, two helicopters would be brought in and the hostages would be loaded on them. Medical personnel accompanying the assault team would make sure all hostages were accounted for.

Once the hostages were lifted out, Red and Blue elements, covered by the White element, would exit through the opening in the compound wall and proceed across the street into the soccer stadium, with White element acting as rear guard. The remaining helicopters would land inside the stadium and airlift out the rest of the assault force. One of the helicopters would then proceed to the foreign ministry building to retrieve the thirteen-man assault team there, along with their three hostages.

As the embassy operation was going on, a company of Airborne Rangers would land at an airfield thirty-five miles south of Tehran, at Manzariyeh. They would hold the field and await arrival of the helicopters carrying the hostages and assault force and a flight of C-141 Starlifter cargo aircraft. Once all the hostages, assault personnel, and DOD agents were assembled at Manzariyeh, they would be flown out on the Starlifters. The Rangers would be flown out at the conclusion of the operation.

If insufficient helicopters were available to lift the assault force from the stadium, the force would establish defensive positions and helicopters would shuttle them to Manzariyeh. If necessary, the force was prepared to disband and escape across the desert.

The assault team left Fort Bragg, North Carolina on 20 April, landing at their staging area the next day. Simultaneously, an army civilian named Dick Meadows (who as an Army Captain had planned the Son Tay Raid), arrived in Tehran heading a team of four DOD agents. As the assault force prepared for the mission, Meadows and his team reconnoitered the embassy, and procured and staged the vehicles that would be used by the assault force. On Wednesday

23 April, the team received an intelligence report indicating that all the hostages were in the chancellery. Beckwith modified the plan accordingly. On 24 April, the team flew to the jump-off point for their journey into Iran.

By 1630 hours, the team was dressed for the mission: Levi blue jeans, unpolished combat boots, black field jackets, dark blue knit Navy watch caps. An American flag was sewn on the shoulder of the jackets and covered with tape.

At 1800 hours, the pathfinder MC-130 was in the air. The remaining aircraft, carrying the assault team and fuel, would leave an hour later. At 2200 hours, the pathfinder, carrying Beckwith and the Desert One security team, landed.

The team deployed on motorcycles and began setting up security. Before the team was actually in position, though, a large Mercedes bus, with forty-four Iranians aboard, approached the site. Warning shots were fired, the bus stopped, and its passengers corralled. These would be flown out aboard the C-130s. Shortly after this, a gasoline tanker approached and was set ablaze by a Light Anti-tank Weapon (LAW). Unfortunately, a second vehicle, trailing the truck, pulled up next to it, picked up the terrified driver of the blazing tanker, and fled.

The remaining aircraft then landed and waited. Forty-five minutes late, the first of the helicopters arrived, having been delayed in a severe dust storm; by the time the last arrived, the operation was ninety minutes behind schedule. Further, only six helicopters had made the trip. One had made a forced landing in the storm and the other picked up its crew and returned to the *Nimitz*. It was highly unlikely at this point that the assault team could reach Desert Two before first light.

The situation at Desert One was like a scene from Dante's *Inferno*. All aircraft engines were running as the helicopters moved into position behind the C-130 fuelers. Then one of the helicopters developed hydraulic problems, rendering it incapable of continuing the mission. After reviewing his airlift requirements to continue the mission, Beckwith confirmed that he could not complete the mission with only five helicopters and notified Vaught that he was aborting.[5]

One of the members of the ground assault force provided this account of what followed after Beckwith aborted the mission:

> I was a member of the assault element tasked to rescue fifty-three American hostages held prisoner in Tehran, Iran. My team's mission was to secure the American Ambassador's residence and rescue any hostages that may have been held there. The ground rescue element had been training together for two years for this kind of mission, but the complete rescue task force had only recently been assembled. Even in training we recognized we were likely to have problems with our aviation support. Long-range navigation, climatic conditions, refueling difficulties, were all potential problem areas. Nevertheless, we had complete

confidence in our ability to rescue the hostages if we could get to the US Embassy. We were prepared, if necessary, to escape and evade out of Iran. I was on the first C-130 to land at Desert One. After landing, an Iranian bus wandered into the area and we were forced to detain forty-four men, women and children. We remained at the desert refuel site for several hours trying to round up the complete elements of the force. Finally the word came to abort the mission, so we loaded in a C-130 that had been used for refueling. We were all set to depart when an RH-53 helicopter crashed into the left side of our cockpit. Instantly there was flames everywhere. The only door we could use was the right, rear, paratrooper door. I was near the front, so I was nearly one of the last ones to evacuate. I did not think that it was possible to get out alive. Although there was considerable confusion, there was no panic. The helicopter crews left their aircraft and joined the ground force to file onto the remaining fixed-wing aircraft. I found room on another C-130 and made my way out of the Desert.[6]

A helicopter had crashed into the side of one of the C-130s, killing five airmen and three marines, destroying a C-130 and forcing the helicopters to be abandoned at Desert One. Had Beckwith's people been able to get past Desert One, the mission would have had a high probability of success. Unfortunately, such was not the case. Thus, the last special operation of the Carter administration ended in ignominious tragedy, with eight American servicemen dead on the ground.

In the ensuing storm of publicity and investigations, blame has been thrown at Beckwith, Vaught and Carter, and there is surely plenty of blame to go around. But the bottom line is that when the army activated its hostage rescue force in 1977, the Pentagon, in a leadership failure, neglected to require a supporting special operations capability in the other services. The fact of the matter is that when the hostages have been taken, it is too late to create the capability to rescue them.

On the brighter side, however, America would learn its lesson from this experience and build a first rate, joint service, hostage rescue capability.

Rebuilding the Capability, 1981–3

With President Ronald Reagan's initiatives to revitalize America's special operations forces, the Army immediately moved to energize its own. Their force structure began to expand and along with that, manpower increased; by 1985 their numbers had increased from some 4,000 to just over 6,000. Their activities expanded accordingly.

By August 1981, Special Forces teams were heavily active in Honduras, which shares its southern border with Nicaragua and El Salvador. These teams advised the Honduran army in border operations: a critical function since leftist insurgents in El Salvador were using Honduras as a conduit for supplies and a refuge from Salvadoran government forces. Sealing the Honduran–Salvadoran border was vital to American and Salvadoran government efforts to foster and develop democracy in El Salvador.[7]

In response to stepped up guerilla activity in El Salvador, additional Special Forces troops were deployed there to train one of El Salvador's battalions in counter-insurgency operations. Ultimately, this battalion would be the spear-point of a governmental initiative to re-take the countryside from the Communists. The Special Forces instruction was geared to enable the government forces to gain the moral high-ground by instituting rural civic-action programs and safeguarding the rural population from guerilla strong-arm tactics.

Although these soldiers were technically deployed as a Mobile Training Team (MTT), they were definitely in a combat environment. The embassy attempted to restrict their armament to .45 caliber pistols, but their leadership made sure they were properly armed to defend themselves against the threats they faced. Consequently, the Americans carried M-16s, M-60 machineguns, and M-79s, as required by the situation. Communists and right-wing fanatics regularly shot at them at any time, day or night.[8]

Grenada, 1983

All Army special operations forces, which now included the Rangers, 160th Special Operations Aviation Regiment and Special Forces were consolidated under the 1st Special Operations Command (Airborne) at Fort Bragg, North Carolina, on 1 October 1983. Less than a month later, the Grenada intervention would clearly demonstrate that Army SOF had come a long way in overcoming the neglect they experienced after Vietnam.

The intervention in Grenada has been characterized in numerous media and literary sources as a bungled operation that succeeded only because of the overwhelming force exercised by the United States. From the operational perspective, at the theater command level, this characterization is fairly accurate. With only a few days to plan and execute the operation, the plan was hurried and incomplete. Insufficient intelligence led to flawed tactical plans and insufficient time prevented effective coordination between the services.

Another problem was that the conventional planners at the joint task force level had little experience or training in the effective employment of SOF. Consequently, SOF were assigned inappropriate missions for which they were ill-prepared, but which they accomplished using savvy and determination. Nevertheless, cunning, strength and stamina could not overcome all the dis-advantages of inadequate planning and some missions failed.

RANGERS

In 1974, the Rangers were consolidated into the 75th Ranger Regiment, headquartered at Fort Stewart, Georgia. 1st Ranger Battalion was located at

Fort Stewart while the 2d Ranger Battalion was organized at Fort Lewis, Washington. In the aftermath of URGENT FURY, the regimental headquarters and 3d Ranger Battalion were activated. With the exception of a minor role in the Iran hostage rescue mission, the Rangers had been perfecting Ranger unit training and doctrine since their formation. By the time of the Grenada intervention, the role of the US Army Rangers had changed radically since Vietnam; they had become shock troops – elite infantry. Their role was to seize the critical high-profile targets, such as airfields and military garrisons. Rangers were employed in critical, high-profile missions, when a tough, determined fight was anticipated.

The training at the US Army Ranger School, Fort Benning is nine weeks of hell. With an extremely high failure rate, the soldier who completes the course demonstrates unusual determination to persevere in the face of compounded adversity. Ranger training is heavy on physical endurance, sleep deprivation, prolonged exposure to the elements and rough terrain, teamwork, leadership, common sense, and fieldcraft.

The initial Ranger objective for the Grenada intervention was the airfield at Point Salines. It was garrisoned by a force of some 650 Cuban armed construction workers: a formidable threat if they chose to fight. This was probably the only objective assigned a SOF unit that fitted its unique capabilities. Their second objective was the Saint Georges University True Blue campus, where they would rescue American medical students. Two battalions would assault the airfield; the 1st Battalion, from Fort Stewart and the 2d Battalion, from Fort Lewis. 3d Battalion would remain at Stewart.

2d Battalion flew to Hunter Army Airfield at Fort Stewart on 22 October, where it linked up with the 1st Battalion under the cover of an exercise. Because of airlift constraints, both battalions had to deploy understrength, taking only their best men. For the next two days, the Rangers zeroed their weapons and rehearsed their actions on the objective.

The plan was to drop the battalions on the east and west ends of the airfield, adjacent to the Cuban construction camp. Although fairly good information was available on the layout of the airfield there was almost no intelligence on the disposition of Cuban and Grenadan defenders, anti-aircraft positions, or the condition of the airfield. The first two aircraft carried Company A, 1st Battalion, who would parachute to the runway and clear the obstructions. The rest of the battalion would land.

The 1st Battalion rushed to load its six C-130 aircraft two hours ahead of schedule after they learned that their flight schedules were not synchronized with the 1st Special Operations Wing, which owned the aircraft. After loading gun jeeps, MH-6 Little Bird helicopters, motorcycles, medical supplies, ammunition, food and the Rangers, the aircraft took off at 2130 hours, 24 October 1983; only twenty-five minutes behind schedule.[9]

The first unit scheduled to hit the runway was Company A. Company A would attempt to clear the runway so that the aircraft carrying the rest of the Rangers could land. Unfortunately, a reconnaissance AC-130 reported heavy vehicles blocking the runway – it was unlikely that Company A could clear it in time to land the rest of the battalion. So, one hour prior to H-hour (terminology for the exact time an operation is to begin) Lieutenant Colonel Wesley Taylor directed the rest of his battalion to rig for paradrop: no easy task in the confines of an airplane loaded with equipment and troops. To compound the problem, because of a communications foul-up the last three planes had been told to de-rig. By the time it was straightened out, the planes were forced to orbit until their Rangers were ready to jump. A drop that should have taken five minutes took over an hour-and-a-half to complete.[10]

Although the Cubans held their fire, the Grenadans opened up on the aircraft with 23mm anti-aircraft guns. This fire prompted the commanders to reduce their drop altitude to five hundred feet, well below normal, to get below the flak. The lead aircraft dropped Taylor and his battalion headquarters at 0534 hours (H-hour had been delayed), but heavy anti-aircraft fire caused the next aircraft to abort its approach. Consequently, Taylor and his headquarters found themselves alone on the airfield for twenty minutes before Company A arrived. Fortunately, the Cubans held their fire.[11]

Taylor called in an AC-130 to suppress the anti-aircraft fire and at 0552 hours the next MC-130 arrived and dropped most of its men. With a dozen gunships, transports, and an EC-130 command and control aircraft over Salines, confusion reigned. It was not until 0634 hours that the rest of Company A landed and the entire battalion did not arrive on the ground until 0705. In contrast the second battalion was out in thirty seconds; the drop was complete at 0710. No Rangers were killed in the jump.

At 0730, Company A assaulted Cuban positions in the village of Calliste across the runway from them and, after a brief exchange of gunfire, silenced them. During the assault, one Ranger was killed. One platoon seized the True Blue campus in about fifteen minutes, its Grenadan guard detail fleeing into the hills. No students or Rangers were hurt. Jubilation erupted from the students.

On the runway, B Company assaulted the Cuban camp and after a brief firefight the Cubans fled and the company occupied the high ground overlooking the Cuban headquarters. Using a captured machinegun, the Rangers effectively suppressed two mortar positions in the headquarters compound. One Cuban was killed and twenty-two surrendered in the course of this operation.

By 1000 hours, the Rangers appeared to have their initial and follow-on objectives well in hand when Company A was taken under fire from a 90mm recoilless gun. The Company was forced to withdraw from its exposed positions and call in helicopter gunship support. After initial delays caused by confusion over maps and radio frequencies, the US Marine Cobra gunships rolled in over the gun position. The air controller with the Rangers directed the gunships on target and one opened up with 20mm cannon fire while the other fired a TOW (Tracked-optically, wire guided) missile into the building where the gun had been located, destroying the building. Three Cubans then tried to run for a truck, only to see it explode from another TOW shot.

Other action occurred when two Ranger motorcyclists were gunned down by the Cubans in the middle of the runway. Fortunately, they were not mortally wounded because the Rangers could not get to them in their exposed location. Protecting them by sniper fire, the Rangers were able to rescue their comrades during a lull in the fighting.[12]

Here is one Ranger's first-hand account of the battle for Point Salines:

On 25 October 1983, I was a member of the 1st Ranger Battalion during Operation Urgent Fury. The battalion's mission was to conduct a night combat parachute assault to secure Point Salines Airfield and surrounding terrain so follow-on forces could air–land. Approximately two hours from drop time we were told that the runway was clear, so we de-rigged our parachute equipment and prepared for air–land assault. When we were about twenty minutes from time-on-target, we were told that the runway was, in fact, not clear and so we would have to conduct a parachute insertion. Immediately all the Rangers began helping each other rig their equipment to include conducting parachute equipment checks ... We jumped without reserve parachutes and most of the Rangers held their rucksacks in their hands as we did not have time to re-rig them prior to the jump. On my plane, some of the Rangers had to hook up their static lines as they exited the plane. The aircraft approached the drop zone at 100 feet above the water and, as the green jump light came on, the aircraft popped up to 500 feet. With the delay in the jump, we ended up conducting a daylight parachute assault instead of the night drop we had planned for. Immediately upon landing I de-rigged my parachute equipment and began to follow other Rangers to the company assembly area. While we were moving we started receiving small arms fire from the surrounding hillsides. While some Rangers removed debris from the runway, others laid down suppressive fire. Upon reaching the assembly area, I linked up with my squad and we waited for our vehicle to be air–landed. When we linked up with our gun-jeep, we moved to our primary position, which was north of the runway. While we were moving along the base of the hillside, we started receiving small arms fire from two enemy positions. The squad deployed and began to fire and maneuver on both the positions, clearing them one at a time. We then moved to the road junction that was in our sector and established our blocking position. At about 1800 hours, a company from the 82d Airborne Division moved into our sector and relieved us. Rangers lead the way![13]

At 1045 hours, the first elements of the Caribbean Defense Forces, composed of Jamaican, Barbadian, and Antiguan troops, arrived at the airfield. By 1405, the first elements of the 82d Airborne Division began arriving in C-141 Starlifters to relieve the Rangers.

As the linkup between the 82d and the Rangers was taking place, Grenadan forces launched a counter-attack with three BTR-60PB wheeled armored personnel carriers against Company A positions. The 14.5mm machineguns raked the Ranger positions as mortar rounds exploded around them.

Armed with 90mm recoilless guns, the Ranger anti-tank teams responded immediately, slamming a missile into the side of the lead BTR. Simultaneously, Ranger machinegun fire raked the enemy crew and riflemen attempting to flee the vehicle. A second 90mm round blasted the second vehicle which skidded to a halt, trailing hunks of metal, as its crew tried to flee amid a hail of accurate, Ranger machinegun fire. The third BTR fled for the jungle, only to be destroyed by a Spectre gunship which had arrived overhead.

The counter-attack having failed, the airfield was now secure.[14]

HOSTAGE RESCUE

As part of the Reagan initiative to reinvigorate SOF and create a SOF airlift capability, the army established Task Force 160, the forerunner of 160th Special Operations Aviation Regiment at Fort Campbell, Kentucky. In January 1985, this unit was officially reassigned from the 101st Airborne Division to 1st Special Operations Command (the forerunner of Army Special Operations Command) in 1985, redesignated the 160th Special Operations Group in 1986, and officially activated as the 160th Special Operations Aviation Regiment in May of 1990.[15]

The primary mission of the 160th is to provide dedicated, rotary-wing support to all Army Special Operations Forces.[16] When the Grenada intervention took place in 1983, the 160th figured prominently in a special operation to liberate political prisoners from Richmond Hill Prison. Intelligence reported that opposition would be light.

The 160th was equipped with MH-60 Blackhawk, CH-47 Chinook, and MH-6 Little Bird special operations helicopters. The Blackhawks and Chinooks provided an aerial insertion and resupply capability, while the MH-6s provided accurate, rapid response firepower, with rockets and machineguns.

Transportation delays in getting the helicopters staged in Barbados caused the mission to take off at 0530 hours, the time that the team of Special Forces troops and Rangers were supposed to be on the ground, assaulting. As the five helicopters carrying the rescue team were lifting off, the two Ranger battalions were assaulting Point Salines and the enemy alarm had already been sounded.[17]

At 0615 hours, the five Blackhawks and two Little Birds roared in low over the jungle toward Richmond Hill Prison. Immediately, the lead Blackhawk, flown by Captain Keith Lucas, met with a hail of bullets as the Grenadan defenders opened up with machinegun, small arms and 23mm cannon fire. The landing zone that they had expected to use was non-existent – the intelligence on the prison was inaccurate – so, as the pilots searched in vain, the enemy concentrated their fire. Lucas was hit in the right arm and another pilot's leg was smashed. Under the withering fire, the Blackhawks broke off and flew out to sea to regroup. Incredibly, all five were still flying.

At 0630, the formation took another run at the prison. This time, Lucas' Blackhawk took five direct hits, which killed Lucas. Lucas' copilot, whose head was grazed, guided the crippled helicopter out to sea where it was hit again, causing the controls to lock. The helicopter burned into a hillside, killing several of the occupants. But, incredibly, the copilot and crew chief escaped.

The mission was aborted. Yet another hostage rescue mission had ended in failure.

Conclusions

A lot of mistakes and terrible tragedies occurred as army SOF attempted to rise from the ashes of their post-Vietnam decline. Nevertheless, these failures were caused by errors of commission as opposed to omission. New concepts were being tested, accepted and rejected as these men were thrown into the crucibles of Iran and Grenada. The new capabilities were not yet mature and errors were to be expected.

But, to paraphrase Nietzsche, that which does not destroy us makes us stronger, and this axiom was clearly applicable to army SOF as it continued to mature in the latter half of the 1980s. The army now understood the value of lessons learned, and had dedicated part of one of its institutions, the Command and General Staff College, at Fort Leavenworth, to the study of combat experience. The service schools, particularly the John F. Kennedy Special Warfare Center and School at Fort Bragg, were also examining combat experiences with a fine-tooth comb to identify the future requirements of SOF in terms of training, doctrine and organization.

These efforts would bear fruit in the later 1980s, when army SOF would play critical roles in two major campaigns, as well as several American foreign policy initiatives in underdeveloped nations.

NOTES

1. Interview with General Robert C. Kingston, US Army (Retired), 21 September 1992.
2. Colonel Charlie A. Beckwith, USA (Ret) and Donald Knox, *Delta Force* (London; Arms and Armour, 1983), pp. 90–106.
3. Ibid, pp. 137–9.
4. Ibid, pp. 164–7.
5. Daniel P. Bolger, *Americans at War 1975–1986; an Era of Violent Peace* (Novato, California, Presidio, 1988), pp. 117–18.

6. US Special Operations Command Presentation, Association of the United States Army (AUSA) Convention, Washington, DC, 13 October 1992.

7. Raymond Bonner, 'Green Berets Step Up Honduras Role,' *The New York Times* (August 9, 1981).

8. Dave Morris, 'Salvador's Unsung Heroes; SF Advisers Fight for Recognition,' *Soldier of Fortune* (July 1992), pp. 30–1.

9. Mark Adkin, *Urgent Fury; The Battle for Grenada* (London, Leo Cooper, 1989), p. 201.

10. Ibid, p. 208.

11. Ibid, p. 212.

12. Ibid, pp. 214–18.

13. U.S. Special Operations Command Presentation, Association of the United States Army (AUSA) Convention, Washington, DC, 13 October 1992.

14. Bolger, *Americans at War 1975–1986*, pp. 310–20.

15. US Special Operations Command Public Affairs Office Memorandum to the author, with enclosures, Subject: Security Review of Manuscript, dated 9 September 1993.

16. Ibid.

17. Mark Adkin, *Urgent Fury*, pp. 179–80.

CHAPTER 8

Battles of Influence Naval Special Warfare in Transition 1975–86

The period following the end of active Naval Special Warfare (NSW) involvement in the Vietnam conflict was one of transition. The previous ten-year period had required only a relatively narrow operational focus and mind-set. The coming years were to bring with them the challenge not only to justify the very existence and need for such a specialized organization, but also to align its capabilities with a military that was trying to reorient toward a more global, peacekeeping role.

Coastal Piracy: The *Mayaguez* Operation, 1975

When the *Mayaguez* was seized by the Communist Khmer Rouge Navy off the coast of Cambodia on 12 May 1975, the US immediately began to plan a rescue attempt. Unfortunately, with little time to plan, and without the knowledge to employ effectively the specialized naval assets available to them, Pacific Command planners put together a flawed plan whose execution proved tremendously costly. The result: on a beach at Koh Tang, an island off the Cambodian coast, fifteen marines, navy corpsmen and air force helicopter crewmen died, three Marines were declared missing and presumed dead, fifty personnel were wounded by hostile fire and thirteen of fifteen CH-53 helicopters involved in the mission were shot down or severely damaged. All this occurred during a fourteen-hour period on 15 May 1975 during an attempt rescue the *Mayaguez* crew, who were elsewhere, with conventional forces and inadequate reconnaissance.

Delta Platoon, SEAL Team One was alerted to support the operation – they were to proceed to one of the three beach helicopter landing zones, unarmed, and recover three bodies of fallen marines detected by aerial reconnaissance. This, after the *Mayaguez* was boarded from alongside by another group of marines and passively retaken, and as the ship's crew were being transported to sea from the mainland on an American-built and provided Swift Boat. The ill-advised SEAL body recovery mission and all other offensive missions being planned were aborted late on that day by President Ford's wise decision to cease all further action in this matter.

Had a SEAL option to reconnoiter Koh Tang been exploited earlier and in a manner consistent with the doctrine in effect and operational capabilities available at the time, US casualties might have been less than they were or avoided altogether. It was a statement of the times that the naval special warfare option was not to be seriously considered until too late, if at all, for over ten years after operational withdrawal from Vietnam.

The Transition of Naval Special Warfare, 1975–83

During the Vietnam involvement, SEALs had established a well-deserved and earned reputation as hard-core, success-oriented night fighters with little aversion to inflicting enemy casualties. They also had a well-deserved reputation, primarily among the senior officer corps, as being essentially incorrigible when not in the field. With Vietnam over, these tendencies put them in the category of being kept in a glass dome with a sign attached that read 'in case of war, break glass.'

As with their counterparts in the army and air force, funding for force structure, new equipment and research was reduced. Good and effective, but non-standard equipment that was produced for SEALs during the war became less available and eventually disappeared from inventories. A few of the more forward-thinking senior naval special warfare officers began a search to find a place in the new military order for SEALs, 'Frogs' and the 'Boat People.' The lack of ability or desire of the military in general, and the navy in particular, immediately to redirect the vast energy available in special operations forces was to prevail until the early 1980s.

The nature of naval special warfare missions and the environment in which they take place speak well for individuals involved in this profession who are personally motivated and constantly looking for a challenge. When challenges in a combat environment are not offered, such men must be challenged in other ways. Soon after Vietnam many sought their personal challenges in the civilian community. This movement took with it much of the combat experience that would be essential in preparing the next generation of 'webfooted warriors' and 'boat people' for their battles. Those veterans that did remain in the service began to engage in a wide variety of activities, ranging from 'adventure' training, with few obvious benefits to military disciplines, to speciality training that had been deferred during the Vietnam era.

Adventure training, regarded by some as inappropriate for military personnel while in a duty status, was folded into naval special warfare training and took the form of several activities that civilians pay quite a lot to enjoy. Attacking white water rapids on rivers such as the Colorado, the Rogue and the Golley in the always-reliable inflatable boat not only sustained the attention of those involved, but also of the those civilians out for a leisurely vacation who came across to watch the spectacle. More often than not, SEALs attempted to set records in negotiating stretches of water and entered, rather than more wisely avoiding, the more treacherous areas of turbulence. No one was ever seriously hurt in these endeavors, but all emerged with a greater respect for the power and danger of America's rivers.

Other forms of adventure training included assaulting mountains such as Whitney in California and McKinley in Alaska, competing in team and individual athletic events such as rugby, boxing and outrigger canoeing, and helping to pioneer the first Hawaiian 'Iron Man' competition. While these and other activities offered a physical challenge and required a degree of planning, ultimate benefit for a group of warriors required to develop and sustain capabilities in a vast number of subspeciality skills remained questionable. The main contribution such activities made to naval special warfare was to retain a level of interest and enthusiasm among the younger sailors during a period of operational doldrums.

Toward the end of the 1970s numerous areas of specialization that could not (and need not) be sustained during involvement in Vietnam began to receive serious attention.

Air Operations

During the Vietnam era, the skills of military freefall and HALO (High-Altitude Low-Opening) parachuting were acquired by a very small number of SEALs. The army conducted this type of training and it was normally provided to a SEAL as a reward for a successful combat tour. In the mid-1970s entire SEAL platoons began to go through the requisite training at both SEAL Teams One and Two. Platoons with this basic training could then fine tune their skills in preparation for potential operational employment.

An enhancement over static-line parachuting while attached to an inflatable boat evolved in the late 1970s, and became known as the 'rubber duck' technique. Using this procedure, a fire team or squad of SEALs would parachute from a C-130 after pushing out a palletized package containing the inflatable boat with the outboard motor, fuel and most mission-essential equipment secured inside it.

This technique, once perfected, permitted SEALs to parachute at sea and, in a motorized craft, proceed to a target area or rendezvous at ranges in excess of fifty nautical miles. Growing pains saw 'ducks' impact the water without benefit of a completely inflated parachute and, at least once, in a manner that ignited the on-board gasoline, resulting in an undesirable technique known thereafter as 'duck flambe.' Once these pains were suffered and improvements made, the technique became a cornerstone for rapid employment of naval special warfare combat swimmers, and the forerunner to more complex paradrops of higher performance, mono-hull craft.

An additional capability, albeit one that would take over a decade to institutionalize, was the certification and design upgrade to the C-2 aircraft. Although a capable airframe, the C-2 was not initially designed to support loads exiting its ramp while in flight. Simple kits, installed to strengthen the ramp, coupled with an enhanced roller system for the deck and a specially configured 'duck' platform, have allowed this aircraft to evolve into one capable of supporting special operations when required.

Combat Swimming

Combat swimming, long regarded as the primary dominion of Frogmen, was only given cursory attention during the Vietnam era, although all graduates of Basic Underwater Demolition/SEAL (BUD/S) training were qualified in a variety of SCUBA equipment. Through the 1960s and most of the 1970s this equipment included a variety of different sizes of open circuit (air) tanks, the MK VI semi-closed circuit (mixed gas) underwater breathing apparatus (UBA) and the Emerson closed-circuit (oxygen) UBA.

Open circuit equipment has little tactical value because of the tell-tale bubbles it emits. It was, and is, used for entry level training and for administrative or ship-support diving. The MK VI used a mixture of oxygen and nitrogen that could be preset before operations depending on the depth and duration planned for a given dive. This apparatus gave off bubbles usually only during ascent, but was not highly regarded or widely used by all in naval special warfare. The Emerson closed-circuit UBA, which had replaced a series of post-World War II apparatus of European design, was an oxygen rebreather with the oxygen tank and carbon dioxide (CO_2) scrubber assembly mounted on the back and a set of breathing bags over each shoulder. This is the type of apparatus necessary when tactically conducting clandestine underwater approaches to maritime targets. The Emerson was replaced by the more advanced, German Dragar Lar V.

Complementing the advanced training were other equipment improvements, such as the limpet backpack. This is a packframe that enables a swimmer to carry a standard MK I limpet assembly (consisting of the explosive charge, a detonator, a timing device and an anti-removal device), the buoyancy of which has been neutralized. The chest-mounted configuration of the Lar V made this arrangement very efficient and a vast improvement over the towing technique required when using the Emerson.

An example of the relative complexity but effectiveness of a true clandestine combat swimmer mission was demonstrated several times during the annual Flintlock special operations exercises in Europe. A favorite combined operation was one involving the German Kampfschwimmers and combat swimmers from SEAL Team Two. A typical mission began from a German (diesel electric) submarine that had approached a targeted harbor and bottomed some distance from the entrance. A combined assault team would lock out of the submarine while it remained submerged via the forward torpedo tubes. Each swim pair, their diving gear and their equipment would be locked out together. The twenty-one inch diameter of the tubes required the swimmers to face each other while inside them, breathing from their UBAs, which were positioned to their front. When ready, a 'slug' of air, similar to that which would push a torpedo clear of the tube (but much less powerful) would 'assist' the dive pair in extracting themselves from the tube. Once clear of the outer doors, the swimmers would don their equipment properly, get their bearings and proceed with their assigned navigation profile. Approaches to designated targets could be as much as 4000 yards or more. Once their ordnance was delivered, a return swim to the mother ship or to a location ashore for alternate extraction would culminate with, in the case of a totally submerged mission, a rendezvous with the submarine and a reverse of the lock out procedure. Such a mission was not for those prone to claustrophobia or a worry of getting grease on their gear (as would be the case inside the torpedo tube).

Swimmer Delivery Vehicles

While the majority of the community was improving its combat swimmer capabilities, a smaller, but more technically oriented component of naval special warfare was improving on the techniques that the operators of the ill-fated *Grayback* mission were obliged to follow. By the late 1970s, SEAL and UDT operators of Swimmer Delivery Vehicles (SDVs) began using newer models that had replaced the older MK VII Mod 6 craft. Two specialized craft, the MK VIII SDV, which was a 'people mover,' and the MK IX, which was meant for reconnaissance and surgical underwater missions, had been introduced. Both craft were still powered by electric motors. The MK VIII, billed as a six-man craft, usually was restricted to the pilot/navigator crew and no more than three passengers in the rear of the craft (four if all were very small).

An example of the operational potential offered by a SDV/combat swimmer direct action profile was demonstrated during a bi-annual east coast OCEAN VENTURE exercise in 1983. A SEAL detachment was staged aboard a US Coast Guard buoy tender operating in southern Florida waters. The detachment was comprised of a SEAL squad from SEAL Team four and a MK VIII SDV from SDV Team Two. They received a mission directive to penetrate the harbor defenses at Truman Annex (Key West, Florida) and destroy (with simulated demolitions) a number of small craft berthed there. After a planning and rehearsal period, the SDV, carrying four passengers (of relatively small stature), launched from the Coast Guard vessel nearly twenty miles offshore.

The transit to the mouth of the small harbor proved uneventful, if not boring. About 100 yards outside the mouth of the harbor, the four SEAL passengers, equipped with their demolition charges, disembarked from the now bottomed SDV and, in two swimmer pairs, entered the harbor. They successfully located their targets, planted their charges and returned to the waiting SDV. The return transit to a rendezvous with the tender also proved uneventful.

This mission profile tends to be less than impressive unless the entire scenario is brought into focus. Unlike a real-world mission, which the operators would insist should occur at night, this mission had to be done during hours of daylight for safety reasons. Also, the opposing force, ostensibly to gain maximum training benefit for the defenders, knew generally that they were to experience an attack sometime within a twenty-four hour period, so they were expecting a combat swimmer approach.

The defending force comprised over 100 personnel on various foot and offshore small boat patrols. They were augmented by an MIUW (Mobile Inshore Undersea Warfare) unit located ashore that was radar-equipped and monitored an offshore grid of sonabuoys. Inside the small harbor there was an experimental 360 degree sonar in place backed up by a marine mammal defensive system consisting of specially trained dolphins.

Around and through all of this alert defensive force, the SDV and swimmers were able to accomplish their mission undetected. Needless to say the senior officer in charge of defense cried foul, and made sure the next scheduled SDV mission against his facility a few days later was so constrained that it was inevitably compromised. If executed properly by trained, equipped and, most importantly, motivated individuals, combat swimmer operations can be the most effective maritime special operations option available to a commander.

Surface Operations

In addition to maintaining the ability to function over and under the water, NSW forces spend a considerable amount of time on the water. Small boat operations have remained a key capability since the early days of World War II. During Vietnam most of the vast number of small boat operations offshore and on inland waterways were under the control of surface warfare officer, not special warfare officer leadership. This was to change dramatically in the early 1970s, and in earnest in 1979 when SEAL officers began to assume command of the successors of the various coastal/riverine forces of the Vietnam era, the Special Boat Units.

The mainstay surface craft, organic to a UDT or SEAL platoon for well over two decades, was the venerable seven-man inflatable boat. This craft, originally meant to be a life raft, functioned as a means to aid the overside cast and recovery of swimmers from various surface craft, to being the craft of choice for submarine lockout operations. Its use is second-nature to all Frogs and SEALs as it is introduced on the first day of Basic UDT/SEAL training. This craft remains in limited use today, but has been replaced by a more capable inflatable, the F-470 (signifying 4.7 meters in length) built by Zodiak. This craft began to gain favor in 1982.

The features of the F-470, its construction, ruggedness and seaworthiness led it to be the inflatable craft of choice in the community. It is not uncommon for over-the-horizon transits from a submarine, surface vessel, or paradrop location, to exceed fifty miles, to a beach landing site through heavy seas exceeding four on the Beaufort scale.

Several engines have been (and are today) used for propulsion, but the most novel is referred to as the MARS (Marine Amphibious Reconnaissance System) engine. This modified 35hp Evinrude engine is equipped with a dewatering valve that allows it to be fully submerged in salt water, then retrieved, started and used. The engine, if properly maintained and operated, offered certain operational advantages over its commercial counterparts, especially during submarine lock-out operations.

Other inflatable craft with unique characteristics used by SEALs were the Zodiak K-40 and its larger brother, the K-50. The '40' and '50' coding indicated four and five meter lengths, and the 'K' denoted Kevlar as the main construction material. When first exposed to the American market in 1980, these craft were revolutionary for the simple reason that they weighed about $\frac{2}{3}$ to $\frac{3}{4}$ less than any other comparably sized craft. This was due to the Kevlar material replacing the standard canvas or other heavy fabric to which some type of rubber, latex or PVC compound was bonded. Operators instantly liked the craft because of their light weight, ease of handling and resulting performance increase with a standard 30–35hp engine. Also, the craft's ability to be tightly rolled in a manner that permitted it to fit easily through the hatches of a submarine's forward escape trunks was a vast improvement over any other available craft. But it too was doomed to a short service life due to the tendency of the boats to delaminate.

Because of the inability of navy designers to provide an acceptable craft to meet SEAL requirements the submarine community cooperated in providing space in forward line lockers, external to the pressure hull, which could accommodate F-470s, thus minimizing the need for a trunk-compatible boat.

Combatant Craft

Another major area of evolution in NSW was in the combatant craft inventory. After Vietnam, the navy all but totally disestablished its small boat capability, reminiscent of the immediate aftermath of World War II. NSW retained a small capability, primarily residual from those craft dedicated to SEAL support in Vietnam, within commands called Boat Support Units (BSU). The craft that were retained included several thirty-six foot MSSCs (Medium SEAL Support Craft), a small number of thirty-two foot MK II PBRs (Patrol Boat Riverine) and an even smaller number of eighty-foot PTFs (Patrol Torpedo Fast of the Norwegian Nasty and American Osprey and Trumpy classes).

The sixty-five foot MK III Spectre class patrol boat (MK III PB) was meant to be a replacement for the Vietnam era fifty-foot PCF (Patrol Coastal Fast or 'Swift Boat'). It did, in fact replace these craft, most of which were left in South Vietnam because of their transfer to that nation's navy during the Vietnamization era. The MK III was made of aluminum and configured to accept up to seven minor calibre gun mounts.

Unfortunately, adding weapons to small boats quickly loses priority when no conflict is raging, so the MK IIIs did not begin to receive adult weapons, such as 40mm and 20mm guns, until the late 1970s. Until that point, their weapons suites were composed of 7.62mm and 12.7mm machineguns and the MK 2 81mm (naval) mortar. Fortunately, they were not required to go into harm's way during this period. The MK IIIs were powered by triple (Turbocharged, Aftercooled) Detroit Diesel engines, which could generate about 625 hp each. Lightly loaded (when new) they were capable of burst speeds in excess of thirty-five knots. As time progressed and their weight grew (because of increases in crew size, weapons, etc.), the craft became a twenty-five knot non-high performance craft. Although not especially well regarded in its early days, as a class of craft it began to gain favor in the late 1980s.

The Special Warfare Craft Light (SWCL), commonly referred to as the SEAFOX, was developed to replace the various models of LCPLs (Landing Craft Personnel Light) that had been in service since World War II. The SWCL was conceptualized and designed to overcome these shortfalls. A fiberglass hulled craft powered by twin Detroit Diesel engines generating 425 hp each, a SWCL was able to carry ten fully equipped personnel. It was primarily meant to support UDT and SEAL squads during amphibious operations after being launched from ships over the horizon.

It looked the part, but its appearance was deceiving. Although fitted with a capable communications and navigation suite, and possessing a radar warning detector and an IFF (Identification Friend or Foe) system, it proved to be less successful than expected. Due to a displacement in excess of eleven tons, its speed and range were never what was anticipated. It also demonstrated a tendency to bow plunge unexpectedly and to beat itself, its crew and any passengers to a pulp in moderate to heavy seas. Although better equipped than the LCPL, the SWCL generally did not live up to expectation or requirements.

Although adequate for peacetime assignments, each of these craft was, for the most part, effectively obsolete when introduced, and they were regarded as appropriate only for use in low threat environments. This notwithstanding, these craft brought with them the need to revisit and refine tactics and operational techniques.

Operations in the colder extremes found in the northern European theater brought with them lessons that could only be learned through experience. One such lesson was the inability of a fiberglass boat (SWCL) to negotiate an ice-bound fiord without being severely damaged.[1] Steel-hulled MK 4 LCPLs assigned to some amphibious support ships as ships boats, albeit lesser performance capable, demonstrated the toughness needed in this extreme (being able to break through the ice rather than being broken by it).

In counterpoint to these design/system shortfalls, the personnel that crewed these craft overcame limitations and fulfilled, if not exceeded, operational expectations when called upon to perform in a hostile environment. This is a tribute to those 'brown water sailors' who for many years, without due recognition, struggled against the tide to fix what was broke and satisfy mission requirements.

EVOLUTION

In May 1983, the NSW community went through the first major organizational evolution since the establishment of SEAL Teams One and Two in 1962. To eliminate the confusion of having competent personnel with identical qualifications regarded and employed differently, a reorganization took place. The navy retired Underwater Demolition Team unit designations and NSW unit tables of organization, personnel and equipment authorizations were standardized. This eliminated confusion when allocating funds, planning training and operations, and simplified the command and control structure of the NSW community.

While the Special Boat Units struggled to make obsolete boats, categorized as high performance, perform at all, and while the reorganization was challenging those who develop logos for command coffee cups, the NSW community was preparing for involvement in the first application of force of arms in the early 1980s.

Grenada, 1983

On 17 October 1983, planners on the staff of the Atlantic Command (USLANTCOM) asked for some help from Naval Special Warfare Group Two (NSWG Two) to assist in a contingency plan. The two planners who responded developed the initial concepts for NSW involvement should a Presidential decision be made to liberate US citizens on the island of Grenada.[2]

A year prior to this, as luck would have it, the readiness of selected NSWG Two (SEAL) platoons had been assessed during a series of no-notice command post exercises (CPXs). One of these CPXs, for which an entire intelligence package had been assembled, used the island of Grenada as an objective. The planners used that intelligence package as the basis for their preliminary planning session at CINCLANT. The package contained the most recent overhead imagery, order-of-battle data and charts available on Grenada.

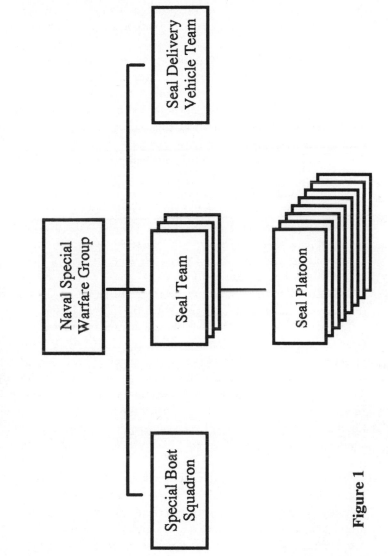

Naval Special Warfare Group
Organization 1983

Naval Special Warfare Group

Special Boat Squadron

Seal Delivery Vehicle Team

Seal Team

Seal Platoon

Figure 1

Upon assessing this data and receiving updates on weather patterns, nearby allies who could provide support, then clarifying the needs for NSW capabilities, the planners developed the following plan:

A SEAL platoon, then stationed at NSWU Four (Naval Special Warfare Unit Four), Roosevelt Roads, Puerto Rico, would get underway onboard a destroyer.[3] The destroyer would proceed toward Grenada at best possible speed, putting it within range of the platoon's organic inflatables inside thirty hours.

Upon receiving execution authorization, the SEAL platoon would proceed to Glover Island. This island is a small, uninhabited speck approximately 2000 yards south of Point Salines. From there, the SEALs could easily cross to the island proper, under cover of darkness, and conduct a surveillance of areas of interest, reporting back findings via the destroyer, which would remain over the horizon.[4] Grenada had no surface search radar or air assets, but did possess four small coast guard craft that could conceivably patrol from their home port of St George's harbor.

The SEALs would also be able actually to enter the True Blue medical campus location at the east end of the Point Salines runway, thought to be the residence for all students on the island.[5] Through discussions with the staff/ students, they could have determined the status of the Americans on the island, thus providing the decision-makers with a better idea of the conditions that might be faced by a large rescue force.

This plan was then shelved pending a US National Command Authority (Presidential) decision on how to resolve the Grenada issue.

Four days later, on 21 October, President Reagan had decided to intervene in Grenada, and the SEAL planners returned to CINCLANT to execute their plan to get eyes on the ground at the earliest possible time. The planners decided that the accelerated timetable demanded an at-sea rendezvous, by paradrop, with a destroyer, the USS *Clifton Sprague*, which was then leaving a port call in St Vincent. The NSW assets tasked with the mission of delivering an air force Combat Control Team (AFCCT) to the beach after the rendezvous were equipped with a high performance mono-hulled craft and were experienced in parachuting with them.

The NSW planners had to modify the initial plan, almost beyond recognition, to accelerate the schedule before the NSW force began their mission on 23 October. A series of delays resulted in the first of two C-141s, which would each drop a boat and an eight-man squad, arriving at the open ocean drop zone just before dusk instead of that afternoon as planned. The jump proceeded with disastrous results. The parachute release mechanism on the first boat failed and it was overturned by its parachute which remained inflated by the twenty-knot winds, well above the safety standard for water jumps. Of the eight jumpers, three were lost at sea. The survivors counted themselves as lucky that they were not also swept away by the strong winds and heaving seas. An exhaustive search by the destroyer proved fruitless.

The second C-141 arrived in the vicinity of the drop zone after darkness fell. Releasing jumpers over what the aircraft's navigator believed to be the destroyer, the SEALs and their boat contacted the water. The boat's release mechanism functioned properly, but one jumper was unable to make his way to it and was lost. The vessel believed to be the destroyer was actually a passing merchantman. The destroyer was several miles distant from the second drop. When closure was made between the surviving high performance craft and the ship, the realization that four good men had been lost hit their team-mates. To the credit of the survivors, many of whom were injured, the single boat made off towards Point Salines to deliver the AFCCT, which had previously flown into St Vincent and linked with the destroyer. The entire team could not rendezvous with the destroyer in this manner because of the perceived need for the rigid hulled boats in this and subsequent missions, the restrictive runway facilities in St Vincent and the need for security.

This phase of the mission was equally doomed. Under strict orders to avoid contact with anyone who could alert the Grenadan and Cuban forces on the island, the mission was aborted when it appeared the lone craft was about to encounter what was believed to be a Grenadan patrol boat. The SEALs and their air force charges limped back to the destroyer to await the drop of another boat the following day.[6] This drop, which did not include personnel, was successful.

The mission was attempted a second time on the night of 24 October, but was again aborted when the senior (non-SEAL) military officer on scene, ignoring the ability of the SEALs to deal with the prevailing conditions, assessed the seas as too rough to allow a successful beach crossing.[7] Within sight of the beach and the runway that would see elements of the 75th Rangers and 82d Airborne paradrop from 500 feet the next morning, the boats turned away and returned to the destroyer. This particular force saw no further action during URGENT FURY.

On 25 October, after having been diverted from its cross-Atlantic course towards the Mediterranean and Lebanon, Amphibious Squadron Four, commanded by Captain Carl Erie, proceeded to a location east of Grenada and prepared for amphibious landings in support of the now designated Commander, Joint Task Force 120, Vice Admiral Joseph Metcalf. The embarked platoon from SEAL Team Four, with a detachment from SDV Team Two and two SBU 20 detachments, one comprising two SEAFOXes, the other with two MK III PBs, prepared to support the landing of marines as did their UDT forefathers 40 years earlier in the Pacific.

After an abbreviated period of time to plan and brief, a SEAL squad proceeded to the beach in two F-470s, after launching from a SWCL. Initially intending to conduct a perpendicular beach reconnaissance, the SEAL platoon commander quickly assessed the surf as being too high to support LVT (Landing Vehicle Tracked) and LCM/LCU (Landing Craft Mechanized/Landing Craft Utility) operations. He and his men proceeded through the surf at the end of Pearls airfield and relayed their recommendation against an amphibious landing through the SWCL to CATF (Commander Amphibious Task Force) and his Marine counterpart CLF (Commander Landing Force). The SEAL squad's advice was heeded and a Marine force took Pearls airfield that morning by vertical envelopment, without any friendly cr Grenadan casualties.

Naval special warfare forces supported the remainder of Operation URGENT FURY by conducting a variety of other missions.

Subsequent to the initial landings at Pearls, a fathometer survey of St George's harbor was conducted from the SWCLs to support a landing by marines. This survey was done during daylight hours in order to identify enemy emplacements by drawing their fire as well as to monitor a residential area ashore.

A NSW contingent was tasked to secure the Governor General, Sir Paul Scoon, at his residence in St George's. An element, delivered by helicopter from Barbados, now the hub of much activity involving heli-borne SOF, fast roped into the Governor General's residence. They were to prepare a helicopter landing zone (HLZ) for a subsequent helicopter that had more SEALs as well as state department personnel who would function as liaison with the leadership of the island. The second helicopter received heavy fire from Grenadan/Cuban guards that wounded several occupants and damaged the aircraft, requiring it to break off its attack and return to the deck of the USS *Guam*, near the shore. The original SEAL element protected the Governor General and his family until relieved over twenty-four hours later by a marine unit. They received some fire during this period, but successfully destroyed two attacking BTR-60PB armored personnel carriers with a light anti-tank weapon and directing in fire from an overhead AC-130H to suppress other opposition forces.

One NSW element, that also originated from Barbados, made an uneventful helicopter insertion near a facility believed to be the island's radio station. They secured their objective, encountering no immediate opposition. The original plan envisioned that the Governor General, once rescued by the SEALs, would be escorted by a contingent of Rangers from Point Salines, to the radio station where he would tell his fellow islanders not to resist the American and Organization of Eastern Caribbean States (OECS) forces. The Rangers, however, were delayed at Salines past the intended timeline and the NSW force was too busy providing security.

It turned out that the plan was fouled for another reason – the facility was not the radio station, but a radio transmitter site. The SEALs remained in place for nearly twenty-four hours during which they engaged numerous enemy forces, inflicting several casualties. The officer-in-charge withdrew the group when communications could not be established with higher authority and it became evident that relief was delayed. During the withdrawal toward the anticipated comfort of the nearby water, the officer-in-charge was painfully wounded in the arm. He and his men were to spend that night evading enemy probes by positioning themselves in the dense vegetation on a cliff above the water. Several men made it to the water, and eventually made it offshore, linking with the USS *Caron* that sent its ship's boat to the beach for the remainder of the force.

Another night beach reconnaissance was conducted north of Point Salines in anticipation of the potential need to land marines there to support the Airborne forces that, for a short period of time, encountered stiff opposition on the airfield. A 'blue on blue' situation developed when a Ranger patrol that, unbeknownst to the SEALs in the water, had occupied that part of the peninsula took them under fire. The SEALs completed their mission and withdrew. A Marine landing was not needed.

The final significant SEAL operation during URGENT FURY took place on Carriacou island, about twenty miles northeast of Grenada. The mission was to determine activity on a small airstrip on the island suspected of providing a means of escape for some Cuban officials and precede a Marine landing to secure the entire island. There were also rumors that North Korean advisors were using the island for training.[8] The SEALs infiltrated over-the-beach and almost immediately encountered thick vegetation that hindered their progress toward the airstrip. Encountering a barking dog and a woodcutter who appeared to be its master, and being under orders to avoid encounters, the SEALs withdrew, leaving the dog barking, but giving the woodcutter the opportunity to log a SWCL ride.

During the entire operation, offshore control of the waters was a prime concern of Vice Admiral Metcalf. He was concerned that no one escape the island and that possible reinforcements did not approach unnoticed. The task force was transporting two MK III PBs which had been intended to support offshore security around Beirut. They were considered ideal for the task at hand. Once off-loaded, the PBs commenced barrier patrols. Unfortunately, one ran aground on an uncharted coral reef severely damaging its rudders and screws, since the best navigation chart available for these waters was dated 1936. The other PB continued operations and was the staging platform for what could have been the brightest action of all the NSW involvements, the capture of General Hudson Austin, the leader of the Cuban-backed People's Revolutionary Army.

Austin was believed to be hiding in a boat basin at the northern end of the island preparing to make good his escape. The officer-in-charge from the SEAL platoon, now aboard the remaining MK III, requested permission to attempt a capture. While this request was being coordinated, and debated over a common satellite link,[9] Austin was captured by a marine detachment that arrived on scene in LVTs.

Operation URGENT FURY can be regarded as the end of the post-Vietnam era for the military in general and NSW in particular. It was the first major action since 1971 that involved operational SEAL elements and combatant craft. Certain command and control techniques and problems were carried-over from the 1960s and seventies, but the era of short, fast-paced low-intensity conflicts had arrived. During the previous decade an evolution had occurred within NSW that was mostly invisible to outsiders. A new generation of warrior was blooded and exposed to a form of conflict that would become the rule rather than the exception.

Lebanon, 1983–4

The Naval Special Warfare Task Unit (NSWTU) involved in URGENT FURY continued its six-month deployment to the Mediterranean immediately after its eight-day battle in the Caribbean.[10] Similar to the decades-old UDT deployments aboard the Amphibious Ready Group (ARG) in the Western Pacific, Marine Amphibious Ready Group (MARG) deployments also required the capabilities of an embarked NSWTU. It should be borne in mind that the NSWTU assigned to MARG 1-84, which participated in URGENT FURY, was composed of a sixteen-man SEAL platoon, a ten-man SEAL Delivery Vehicle Platoon, and two Special Boat Detachments; a seven-man, two-craft SEAFOX detachment and a twenty-four man, two-craft Mark III Patrol Boat detachment. The deployment of MARG 1-84 provided the first introduction of Mark III PBs into the Mediterranean. Their deployment had been requested by Commander, Sixth Fleet (COMSIXTHFLT) to provide security for American ships at anchor off the coast of Lebanon.[11]

In the early 1980s, on orders from President Reagan, Commander-in-Chief Europe (CINCEUR) positioned US forces ashore in Lebanon to support the Multinational Peacekeeping Force, whose mission it was to minimize the confrontation between rival armed factions in and around Beirut. On 23 October 1983, one day prior to the commencement of Operation URGENT FURY, a suicide truck bomb had been driven in to the facility which housed the Battalion Landing Team (BLT) assigned to MARG 2-83 (1st Battalion, 8th marines, 1/8).[12] The bomb detonated just underneath the entrance to the building that provided headquarters and barracks for the marines. The explosion killed 241 peacekeepers and effectively signaled the end of the US peacekeeping efforts ashore.

But prior to this incident, the NSWTU assigned to MARG 2-83, had moved ashore to take advantage of training opportunities not possible afloat and, most importantly, to be in a better location to participate in peacekeeping or other contingency operations. Before deploying ashore from their support ship, the assigned SEAL platoon from newly designated SEAL Team Four (formerly UDT Twenty-One) had conducted numerous day and night patrols of the area offshore from Beirut aboard SEAFOXes and reconfirmed beach gradients at a location near downtown Beirut, called Black Beach. They did this in support of planning for possible amphibious landings by the marines who remained afloat. The SEAL platoon moved quickly ashore and began operations in support of the Marine Battalion.

Initially the SEALs augmented Marine security patrols in downtown Beirut allowing them to re-familiarize themselves with squad-size patrolling techniques and build on their pre-deployment training in urban operations. Fully appreciating the hazards endemic to their mission, the SEALs took their operations seriously. Their patrols were characterized by the use of leap-frogging techniques to cover one another and minimize individual exposure and using available cover and concealment rather than overtly patrolling single file down a street or alley. Their training and instinct to survive, while not playing by a potential enemy's rules, differed substantially from the more conservative techniques for urban patrols used by the marines in those days.

While ashore, the platoon enjoyed one of the many pleasures of being situated in a hostile environment with an ill-defined, but varied threat. That was the opportunity to receive mortar fire from Druze militia, the Hezbollah faction and just about anyone else who needed to expend their daily ammunition allocation in the direction of peacekeeping units.[13] While no SEAL was injured by the usually ineffective fire, the experience contributed to the rapid maturing of the younger, less experienced members of the platoon.

When not staging an act of terrorism such as that perpetrated at the Marine barracks in 1983, the hostile factions in Beirut engaged each other, the innocent civilian populace, and their perceived American adversaries from afar. Artillery, heavy caliber guns, rockets and mortars were favored weapons. But on occasion, several extremists – who must have had an inflated opinion of their own marksmanship skills – attempted to deliver sniper fire over ranges of several hundred to over a thousand yards with small caliber, usually 7.62mm, weapons. This action, while more of a nuisance than effective application of firepower, was soon answered by SEAL counter-sniper activities. A dedicated surveillance of likely firing positions usually resulted in visual confirmation of movement or the smoke-discharge from a weapon. Once pinpointed, a spotter in the SEAL sniper team would direct his shooter's fire down on the enemy position. No SEALs were killed or injured by snipers in Beirut; the opposition could not make the same claim.

Earlier in the 1980s, a Mobile Training Team (MTT) from SEAL Team Two had been sent to Beirut, primarily to train the marines ashore in the use of a most effective weapon which was only in the inventory of naval special warfare.[14] This was the .50 caliber (12.7mm) Special Application Sniper Rifle (SASR) produced for the navy by the ordnance firm of Haskins. Most aptly described (especially by those on the receiving end of its capabilities) as a small cannon, this original SASR was a single shot, bolt action weapon that fired a variety of both standard ball and specialized rounds. In the hands of a well trained sniper it could deliver accurate and effective fire at ranges well in excess of 1,000 yards with devastating results. This capability proved to be a significant augmentation to the standard 7.62mm M-21 (modified M-14s) and M-24 (Remington 700) sniper rifles also used for this purpose, the ranges of which were effectively limited to less than 750 yards. It was the use of this family of weapons that helped deter the sniper threat in Beirut.

The MARG 2-83 SEAL platoon, situated on the beach near the Marine Barracks, became actively and quickly engaged in casualty assistance and removal of live ordnance from the debris that had been the barracks building immediately following the blast that demolished it. The former was not a pleasant task and the latter was not a mission that had received any attention during pre-deployment training. The SEAL presence ashore in Lebanon also ended after this incident.

The veterans of URGENT FURY were destined to remain aboard ship for most of their deployment. But it was this platoon that was to be most instrumental in helping to advise the Amphibious Task Force Commander on potential terrorist threats. This advice quickly resulted in stateside pre-deployment training for all deploying navy ships and development of techniques to counter threats such as high speed boats, surface and subsurface swimmers, low-slow aircraft, etc. Due to the damage incurred by one of the two MARG 1-84 MK III patrol boats in Grenada, it had to go into overhaul for several months. But the one undamaged patrol boat proved its worth immediately because of its ability to remain underway for lengthy periods and its relatively heavy firepower. The ships anchored off Beirut were never engaged by a surface threat while the PBs provided security support.

The NSW participation in action ashore and off the coast of Beirut was indicative of the employment possibilities that faced and continue to confront an embarked NSWTU. Missions present themselves for which detailed planning, pre-deployment training and rehearsals may not have occurred. While outside the operational 'comfort zone' of the involved personnel, the NSW track record of achievement under these unpredictable and fluid employment conditions is essentially flawless.

Latin America, 1981–6

In the early 1980s NSW activity in Central and South America began to increase. SEALs augmented MTTs supporting Military Advisory Group activities in El Salvador. Although less than four SEALs were ever stationed there at the same time, they were continually involved in advising the El Salvadoran Marine (equivalents) and naval forces on subjects ranging from maintenance of outboard engine powered 'Piranha' (25-foot Boston Whaler) assault craft, to the use of Claymore mines in an inland interdiction situation.

The rules of engagement (ROE) in El Salvador were highly restrictive, prohibiting US forces from going on field operations or live fire missions with their counterparts. Unfortunately, the Communist insurgents did not abide by the same ROE and advisors were regularly exposed to hostile fire. Raids against their compound at La Union, on the Gulf of Fonseca, and other places they frequented, although not continuous, did put the NSW contingent on a combat footing. The senior NSW advisor in the country in 1983 paid the ultimate price for participation in this type of military advisory endeavor when he was murdered in downtown San Salvador, the capital city, in what appeared to be a pre-meditated and well-planned action.

While the established MTT in El Salvador continued for nearly a decade, similar support, but on a less regular basis, was being provided in Honduras. The Honduran navy initially requested assistance from the United States to assess and possibly improve their capabilities to conduct the Central American version of maritime special operations. This request resulted in a low key, in-country effort to assess their existing standards and capabilities and recommend improvements considered potentially beneficial. That nation's need for a SEAL-like capability was not exceptionally great. What they did need was a strong and capable coastal patrol force to protect their Atlantic and Pacific coastlines. However, they needed little assistance in this type of endeavor from a US Navy that had not engaged in such activities for over ten years. The Hondurans had operational experience both against the El Salvadoran Navy during the 'Soccer War' in 1973 and against the Nicaraguans since 1980. The US Navy, especially the Special Boat Squadrons, actually learned more than they imparted by observing counterparts' combat-tried techniques and studying their successes.

The low visibility attempts to establish a linkage with the Honduran Navy were overshadowed by the more aggressive NSW involvement in Joint Training Exercises (JTX) and civic action tasks. A series of JTXs began in Honduras in the early 1980s. These yearly exercises were preceded by a series of administrative site surveys in areas never before used for military training. Isolated and primarily populated by Misquito Indians, who are of mixed Spanish and English blood, these areas, such as Laguna de Caratasca on the Caribbean coast near the Nicaraguan border, were ripe for realistic and challenging training as well as meaningful civic action. One difficult assignment given to SEAL Team Four, a command beginning to specialize in Central and South American operations, was to help clear an extensive log jam that had for years precluded small craft movement down the Rio Patuca in northern Honduras. Tons of explosives were used by small contingents of SEALS to break the jam and turn the waterway once again into a useful thoroughfare for the locals.[15]

For a short period of time in the mid-1980s SEALs were also employed from a unique, but short-lived offshore asset, the USS *Sphinx*. This ship, a 1944 vintage 'Achelous' class Small Repair Ship[16] that had seen duty in Vietnam as a riverboat repair tender, was recommissioned from the mothball fleet in Bremerton, Washington, to sustain a presence off the Pacific coast of El Salvador. Its primary mission was to maintain surveillance of the offshore approaches to coastal landing locations suspected of being receiving points for weapons and supplies being provided by the Sandinista regime in Nicaragua to the Popular Forces of Liberation (FPL) and Farabundo Marti National Liberation Front (FMLN) rebels in El Salvador. Four-man SEAL elements were assigned to the ship for potential contingencies requiring their specialized skills. An opportunity to employ these skills never materialized and the afloat personnel from SEAL Team Four kept busy instructing ship's company in the use of small arms and the very few installed crew-served weapons.

The increased activity in Central America was a natural evolution of the continuous participation by SEALs and UDTs in the annual Commander-in-Chief, Atlantic Fleet (CINCLANTFLEET) UNITAS and WATC (West Africa Training Cruise) deployments. UNITAS was a four-month series of exercises by a small flotilla of surface ships, which usually included at least one amphibious ship. This flotilla's capability was complemented by a SEAL squad and Special Boat Unit (SBU) detachment. The primary objective of these exercises was and remains the conduct of combined training and exercises with counterparts in the southern hemisphere. Activities with elements from the navies of Colombia, Ecuador, Peru, Chile, Brazil, Uruguay, and Venezuela provided training, area familiarization and what many considered the best deployment opportunity open to the East Coast NSW community. The extent of NSW involvement in this area and the reorganization thrust within the community at that time eventually led to the establishment of naval special warfare Unit Eight, located in the Panama Canal Zone. This unit would quickly become the most heavily employed advance NSW headquarters due to its responsibility for all planning and employment of NSW forces in Central and South America.

Conclusions

A number of operational lessons were relearned immediately as a result of URGENT FURY and subsequent combats, which would form the foundation of the naval special warfare community that was to evolve from that point on.

○ *Train the way you intend to fight.* Use the best available and trained force for the mission.

○ *Don't underestimate the enemy or the environment.* Old maps must be regarded with caution. Always remain aware that when fighting in someone else's own back yard, he doesn't need a map!

o *Be continually aware of the potential for receiving friendly fire.* Particularly in Joint operations, plan in detail and coordinate. Don't assume others know your intentions.

o *Be prepared.* It's better to have a capability that you thought you might need and not use it, than need a capability you don't have.

o *Simplicity* in planning and action usually translates into success.

o *If at all possible get eyes on the ground early.* Even in the age of sophisticated imagery and intelligence collection assets, the only truly reliable information is that collected by the military unit that will use it.

o *Be aware of the Rules of Engagement.* In Low-Intensity Conflicts free fire zones probably won't exist.

Probably the single, most grievous problem experienced in naval special warfare operations was operational planning. It was the conventional planners at the joint staff level, ignorant of the capabilities and limitations of special operators, who often pitted them against difficult or impossible missions. A lack of standardized considerations for special warfare assets contributed to the flawed planning. But the actions of the early 1980s would provide the basis for standardizing special warfare planning.

The single, most important strength of naval special warfare was its operators. Several operations went well in spite of bad planning, due to the skill and resourcefulness of the special operators on the scene. The men of naval special warfare were up to any task they were assigned, their leadership need only direct them at the right target, at the right time, in the right circumstances, and these sailors would ensure success.

NOTES

1. E. Tilford Jr., *Search and Rescue in Southeast Asia* (Washington, DC, Office of USAF History, 1980).

2. This account of URGENT FURY is based in part on an interview with one of the initial SEAL planners who is still a serving member and desires to remain unnamed.

3. Previous publications addressing URGENT FURY refering to interviews with senior SEAL officers have indicated that the SEAL Team Four platoon in Puerto Rico in October 1983 was eliminated from consideration as an advance reconnaissance option because only a submarine was available for an insertion vessel, and they were not fully trained for submarine operations. In fact, a submarine insertion was considered by the SEAL planners but was discounted because the nearest submarine was in Guantanamo Bay, Cuba, while a destroyer was in port at Roosevelt Roads, Puerto Rico, and was considered a more responsive asset. Had a submarine been in Puerto Rico when initially planning occurred, it would have been a more competitive option because it was faster. The SEAL Team Four platoon would have conducted a dry deck (surface) launch from a submarine, not a submerged lock-out (because there was no serious threat around Grenada that demanded this complex technique). The

platoon was experienced in surface launches from submarines. This explanation comes from individuals who were in senior leadership positions at SEAL Team Four at the time.

4. Mark Adkin, *Urgent Fury* (Massachussetts, Lexington Books, 1989).

5. Ibid.

6. The Boston Whalers in service at the time were powered by twin high-performance outboard motors. In a following sea, the potential of being overtaken by a large wave or swell is always possible. This happened to the SEAL support craft, causing one of the engines to flood and stall in a manner that could not be fixed at the time.

7. This decision by an air force officer, albeit one who was senior to the SEAL officer present, was not popular among either the SEALs involved or their team-mates. After losing four men and aborting a previous attempt to land ashore, aborting a second attempt because of high seas was considered unnecessarily cautious. The SEALs were more than capable of negotiating the prevailing surf conditions. The CCT personnel, who continually train across the spectrum of insertion possibilities, should have been selected for this mission with full understanding that high seas/surf conditions could be encountered in the mid-latitudes in late fall.

8. From an interview with a senior enlisted petty officer who was in the SEAL platoon that planned and executed the mission.

9. From an account by a SEAL officer, now retired, who was present in the CINCLANT Tactical Operations Center when this conversation took place and was piped in over a loudspeaker.

10. R. Rowan, *The Four Days of Mayaquez* (New York: W.W. Norton & Co, 1975).

11. Personal knowledge of the author.

12. B. Frank, *U.S. Marines in Lebanon* (Washington, D.C., History and Museums Division, HQ, USMC, 1987).

13. Interview with the SEAL officer in charge of the platoon on the beach.

14. Interview with the officer in charge of the MTT.

15. Interview with the commanding officer of SEAL Team FOUR at the time.

16. *Jane's Fighting Ships, 1985–6*.

CHAPTER 9

Battles of Influence
Air Force Special Operations
in Transition 1975–86

As with the other services, the post-Vietnam period saw a rapid decline in the air force special operations capability. In order to mitigate the effects of President Carter's initiatives to shrink America's military capability, the air force chose to focus its efforts on trying to preserve what it could of its conventional force, at the expense of its special operations forces (SOF). The fiasco at Desert One clearly and publicly pointed out the deficiencies of air force special operations and was the turning point in their decline. The years of the Reagan presidency then saw quantum improvement in SOF force structure and equipment.

Mayaguez, 1975

The AC 130 Spectre gunships of the 16th Special Operations Squadron, still based in Thailand, were the first SOF elements to feel the heat of battle after the fall of Vietnam. With the *Mayaguez* rescue operation, two weeks after the last Americans pulled out of Saigon Spectres were again in action: first in a reconnaissance role, then in an Airborne Command, Control and Communications (ABCCC) role, and then in their precision fire support role.

Throughout the 1980s and into the 90s, the AC-130H model gunship was the principal gunship in use. It was armed with two 20mm M-61 gatling type guns, a 40mm Bofors and a 105mm automatic cannon. Unlike the older A model gunships with their fixed cannons, the cannons on the H model were trainable and slaved to a sensor suite composed of Low-Level TV (LLTV) and infrared sensors. Sensor operators had a laser illuminator available for operating in complete darkness as well as the Black Crow sensor, which detected and tracked truck ignition systems and hand-held radio beacons carried by friendly ground troops. The existence of the Black Crow was initially published in *Aviation Week* magazine and prompted the Soviets to shield their ignition systems more effectively.[1]

The two sensor operators and the electronic warfare officer work in a booth behind the gun stations. They identify targets to the fire control officer (FCO), who sits beside the navigator. The FCO in turn determines which targets to engage, selects the armament to service them, and passes them to the gunners of the specific gun systems. All guns cannot be fired simultaneously, since the recoil of the 105 causes the entire plane to fishtail and makes it impossible to track with other guns.

Following the *Mayaguez* seizure, American intelligence believed that the crew had been taken to Koh Tang, an island off the coast of Cambodia in close proximity to where the ship had been moored. On 13 May 1975, at nightfall of the day following the seizure, a Spectre relieved the conventional aircraft that had been patrolling over Koh Tang. Its mission was to use its robust night-vision capabilities to attempt to locate the *Mayaguez* crew.

Braving a fusillade of heavy machinegun fire with each low pass, the Spectre accurately reported troop movements on the island, as well as the presence of additional personnel; possibly the ship's crew. Its passive infrared sensors were picking up the body heat of the crewmembers and their Cambodian captors.

On the night of 13–14 May, a Spectre controlled an aerial show-of-force over the island as F111 fighter-bombers and A7 Corsair fighters made mock strafing runs. At 0715 hours, 15 May, a Cambodian PCF Swift Boat and a fishing trawler left Koh Tang. Intent upon keeping the island isolated and to discourage movement of the *Mayaguez* crew, the Spectre directed the conventional aircraft to bomb the path of the PCF to make it turn back, but to no avail. The only reaction occurred when the Spectre fired its gatling guns in the boat's path – the feisty Cambodians returned fire and pressed onward. Finally, the Spectre directed an A-7D Corsair to destroy the boat with 20mm cannon fire. The boat sank almost immediately.

As the aircraft moved in for a closer inspection of the trawler, they reported seeing thirty to forty Caucasians on board. The Cambodians were transferring the *Mayaguez* crew to the port city of Kompong Som; the problem was that American intelligence wrongly estimated that only a fraction of the crew was aboard the vessel. Consequently, the subsequent mission to rescue the crew was directed against Koh Tang island, which was garrisoned by a well-trained, reinforced infantry company who were busily constructing fortifications in light of the aerial show of force happening over their heads. Since there were only two small beaches, on either side of the island, the Cambodians concentrated their defenses on them.

The *Mayaguez* crew was not to be at the place where their rescue operation would take place. Nevertheless, the Cambodian infantry on the island had prepared a reception.

At 0607 hours on 15 May, the first huge CH-53 helicopters from Thailand began attempting to disembark US Marines on the two beaches amid a hail of withering gunfire. One helicopter, on the east beach, took a direct hit through the windscreen from a rocket propelled grenade (RPG), starting a fire that killed ten marines and three of the flyers aboard. Those marines and crew that survived swam to deep water, where they were eventually rescued. This incident prompted the marines to abort the landing on east beach and concentrate on west beach.

West beach was no picnic either. Although they had not taken any RPG rounds, the big helicopters were being raked by accurate small arms and machinegun fire. One helicopter was damaged so badly that it crashed as it attempted to return to its home base in Thailand.

This was the environment the Spectre flew into when it arrived on station at 0730 hours; Marines were either pinned down on the beach or locked in close combat with Cambodian infantry. Majestically, Spectre began its trademark pylon turn and raked the tree line with gatling gun and 40mm cannon fire. The forward air controller (FAC) knew his business and was placing the fire scant meters from friendly positions. The marines then identified the location of the anti-aircraft positions, right in the middle of the encampment in which they suspected the *Mayaguez* crew was being detained. The FAC called for 105mm howitzer fire and got it; the site was destroyed with no collateral damage. This business done, the Spectre continued to rake the tree line with its smaller weaponry. Unfortunately, although the Spectre fire did force the Cambodians to keep their heads down, they were well dug in, and suffered few casualties.

The *Mayaguez* crew were released from Kompong Som, through diplomatic efforts, at 0949 hours. By 1155 hours, the Joint Chiefs had ordered all offensive action to cease, but the marines at Koh Tang remained pinned down by the Cambodians until 1945 hours, when another Spectre arrived over Koh Tang. Behind the curtain of fire it provided, the big CH-53 helicopters returned and extracted the remaining marines.[2]

It would be four years before the air force supported another special operation.

Iran Hostage Rescue Mission, 1979–80

When the US Embassy in Tehran was overrun on 4 November 1979, Pentagon planners immediately set to work formulating a plan for a hostage rescue. Air force planning was initiated by veterans of some of the Vietnam special operations units, such as Major Lee Hess, Lieutenant Colonel Bob Horton and Colonel James H. Kyle. Kyle was recalled from an assignment at Kirtland Air Force Base, New Mexico, to do the detailed planning for the operation and act as an air deputy to Major General Vaught.

The 1st Special Operations Wing (SOW), at Hurlburt Field, Florida, was the headquarters for all air force special operations aircraft. Its inventory held MC-130 Combat Talons special operations transports, AC-130 gunships, and some special operations helicopters. 1st SOW had taken its licks in the post-Vietnam drawdown, reduced to some 3,000 personnel and twenty-eight aircraft from its former glory of 10,000 personnel and 550 aircraft in Vietnam. Further, its fleet of aircraft were now almost twenty-five years old. In this era of austere resources, the planners had kept the special operations capability at the bottom of the priority list.[3]

By 15 November, Kyle and his planners, in coordination with Colonel Charlie Beckwith of the Special Forces, had formulated the general concepts for inserting the ground assault force, providing their fire support during the assault on the embassy, and extracting the hostages and their rescuers. The rescue would take two nights. At dusk on the first night, MC-130 refuelers would fly south around Saudi Arabia to a refueling site inside Iran. This would be accomplished by MC-130 Combat Talons and a mid-air refueling would be required. Simultaneously, conventional RH-53 Sea Stallion helicopters, carrying the Special Forces ground assault force, would depart from an aircraft carrier in the Indian Ocean, en route to the refueling site. Having taken on fuel, the RH-53s would transport the rescue team to the vicinity of Tehran, where they would remain for the day. The next night, Rangers would fly into Iran on MC-130s and seize an airfield outside Tehran, as the ground assault force rescued the hostages. AC-130s would provide fire support to the ground assault force. The MC-130s, accompanied by 'slick' C-130s, would extract the entire force, hostages and rescuers, conducting a mid-air refueling on the way out.[4] All aviation operations would be conducted in total blackout conditions.

THE MC-130 COMBAT TALON

A far cry from the B-24s and C-47s of World War II, the MC-130E Combat Talons were designed for long-range infiltration, resupply and extraction using both conventional and unconventional methods. Within the aircraft, one of the cargo pallet positions was replaced with a communications and electronic warfare center. The radio operator station is equipped with state-of-the-art, secure Ultra-High Frequency (UHF), Very-High-Frequency/Frequency Modulated (VHF/FM), High-Frequency (HF) and specialized jam resistant VHF radios. Additionally, the aircraft has a satellite communications capability. Sitting adjacent the radio operator is the electronic warfare officer, with a rear-aspect infrared set, jamming pods, chaff, and flare dispensers under his control.

Forward, at the rear of the cockpit, two navigators sit before a sophisticated instrument panel. The combination of a terrain-following radar, forward-looking infrared (FLIR), a Doppler navigation radar, a precision ground mapping (PGM) radar, and an Inertial Navigation System (INS) give the plane a Night Low-Level, Terrain Following (NLLTF) capability. The complexity of this system requires the two navigators, but they never get lost.

The pilot and copilot simply fly the plane, watch the instruments, and visually check for obstacles through the windshield. Standard flight altitude for this aircraft is 250 feet, or about seventy-five meters, at night. Consequently, both the pilot and copilot wear night-vision goggles (NVG) when in flight and when landing in unlighted areas.

In addition to the high-speed electronics gear, the aircraft has an unusual cargo unloading system. The High-Speed Low-Level Aerial Delivery System (HSLLADS) allows for up to 2,200 pounds or 1,000 kilograms of cargo to be dropped while the aircraft flies at speeds of 250 knots. The advantage of this is that the aircraft need not climb or slow down to make a drop, making it near impossible for enemy radar operators to determine if a load has been jettisoned.

HSLLADS is a low-tech solution to a high-tech problem: it is a giant slingshot. HSLLADS pallets are slung down two rails and out of the rear of the aircraft by sets of huge 'industrial strength' elastic or 'bungee' cords.[5] Additionally, there is provision for a loadmaster, rigged in safety harness, to dangle off the rear ramp and drop small loads on command from the navigator.

One method of extracting personnel is to land in very short spaces, pick up the passengers, and take off in equally short spaces; something the C-130 is well equipped for. But the Combat Talon is equipped with the Fulton STAR (surface-to-air-recovery) system; a remarkable, but extremely dangerous device that enables the aircraft to extract personnel without landing. It works as follows: the aircraft arrives in the pick-up zone and drops a bundle of extraction equipment to the person or team being extracted. The 'extractees' don special protective body suits attached to a cable. A helium balloon is inflated, attached to the cable, and pulls the cable aloft. The MC-130, equipped with a special V-shaped device on the nose, approaches and snatches the cable. The troops are then yanked off the ground and, if necessary, dragged through any trees in the flight path. Meanwhile, the cable is attached to a rotating anchor plate while a crewman crawls out of a hatch in the top of the plane and snips off the balloon. The trail end of the cable is snatched by a loadmaster with a parahook, similar to a shepherd's crook, and connected to a winch, which begins to haul in the extractees. As the troops approach the aircraft, the loadmaster pulls them in through a door. One soldier who went through the extraction described the experience as the 'ride from hell.' Among special operators, this is considered the extraction method of last resort; to be used only under the most dire of circumstances.

THE RH-53 HELICOPTERS

The Joint Chiefs of Staff (JCS) determined that Navy and Marine pilots would operate the helicopters since they would be staging from a carrier. This put these men at a distinct disadvantage for two reasons. First, they had little experience operating over land, in a desert environment, and had no experience operating with night-vision goggles (NVG). Secondly, none of the pilots had any special operations experience. The air force had a number of special operations veterans with experience in Southeast Asia. However these veterans had no experience with carrier operations.

The Pentagon planners selected marine pilots to fly the helicopters, probably because they would deploy from an aircraft carrier. However, as these pilots worked their way through training, problems were identified that would contribute significantly to the failure of the mission. Marine pilots are trained to support maritime and over-the-beach operations, primarily. In the hostage rescue mission, they would be required to traverse almost a thousand miles of desert, at night. The ability to fly at night, in deserts, is an acquired skill considerably different from the skills necessary for maritime operations; dust storms appear, winds and navigation problems are different. 'Although these problems could have been corrected with the assignment of air force pilots to the mission, Major General Vaught chose not to do this.

The helicopters would turn out to be the fatal link in the plan. The RH-53s were big, fragile, maintenance-intensive mine counter-measures aircraft and not well-suited for extended range special operations in a hostile environment. There were a myriad of technical problems that could ground them or render them unsafe. The engines had to be hydraulically cranked to start them. On-board power was frequently insufficient to accomplish this, so the aircraft were usually rigged to an auxiliary power unit (APU). In Iran, no such unit would be available, so compressed air cylinders would be used to crank the engine. If on-board power was insufficient, and the two cylinders were exhausted, the helicopter would become useless immediately.[7]

Unfortunately, they were the only aircraft even remotely suitable to the requirements of the mission and in position to support it. The technical problems would have to be dealt with as they arose. Compounding this problem, only eight of the helicopters could be deployed to the carrier without arousing suspicion from the Soviets and other foreign powers. As the only tactical insertion assets available, the planners were forced to accept the risk inherent in the use of these helicopters.

Since Vaught declined to direct an overall training plan, Kyle formulated the plan for the air force assets in close coordination with Colonel Beckwith, who formulated the ground plan. Training was conducted in the US and Japan, with MC-130s training in Okinawa, Florida, Arizona, North Carolina and Georgia.

Much of the training centered around the desert refueling operation. Originally, Kyle planned to airdrop large, 500-gallon fuel bladders onto the site from aircraft. However, problems arose with moving the bladders when they were on the ground. Eventually, the planners decided to use EC-130 transports, with palletized 3,000-gallon bladders inside them, to provide the fuel in the desert.

As the task force began testing the procedures they would use in the various portions of the operation, problems with the helicopters continued to arise. On

4 December, Kyle and Vaught took off from Yuma, Arizona, in one of the helicopters and were engulfed in a cloud of dust. Vertigo set in and the entire incident caused the two seasoned special operations veterans concern.

By February, with several rehearsals under their belts and a more complete intelligence picture, the planners made changes. The ground assault force would fly into Iran aboard MC-130s and C-130s, then transfer to the helicopters at the refueling site. The site chosen for refueling, called Desert One, was a remote spot in the Dasht E' Kavir desert. Its only drawback was an unimproved dirt road that ran through it.

The helicopters continued to present problems; an inspection of the aircraft aboard the USS *Nimitz* revealed that, due to a shortage of spare parts, two of the aircraft had been cannibalized for spare parts. Vaught told the Navy leadership in the Pentagon of this and the Navy reinvigorated the maintenance effort on all the RH-53s earmarked for the mission.

One final modification to the plan occurred in March, when the Pentagon significantly shortened the distance the rescue force would have to fly on the first night and eliminated the requirement for a mid-air refuelling.

Then, on 31 March, the Pentagon dispatched a team into Iran to reconnoiter and prepare Desert One. Retired Colonel (then Major) John Carney described his mission as follows:

I was the leader of a combat control team in support of the Desert One mission. As a member of the Joint Task Force, my initial mission on 1 April 1980 was to covertly insert to a site in the Dasht E' Kavir desert located some 300 miles southeast of the US Embassy in Tehran. I reconnoitered this area in order to mark out a landing zone for the future insertion of US forces. In a relatively short period of time I was able to gather soil samples, install a covert landing system, and assess over a mile-long desert strip for any hazards to C-130 landings. This site became known as Desert One. Twenty-four days later, I returned to Desert One on the lead aircraft, with a seven man combat control team ...[8]

By 7 April, the overall plan had been finalized as follows:

On night one, three MC-130s would depart carrying the ground assault force and the team of combat controllers. The first MC-130 would depart at dusk, followed an hour later by the remaining two. The lead MC-130 would act as pathfinder and its passengers would secure Desert One. The three EC-130s carrying the fuel would follow. Simultaneously, the helicopters would depart the USS *Nimitz*, en route to Desert One.

On the ground at Desert One, the lead aircraft would disembark the security and combat control teams, who would prepare the site. An hour later, the remaining two MC-130s would land, with two EC-130 refuellers three to five minutes behind them. With the first EC-130s on the ground, the first two MC-

130s would take off and head back to eliminate congestion at the site. The last EC-130 would then land. The EC-130s would line up abreast one another for the refuelling operation.

Fifteen minutes after the last EC-130 lands, the helicopters arrive and marshall behind the EC-130s to refuel. Once refueled, the helicopters depart for Desert 2, the hide site for the ground assault force. The MC-130 and three EC-130s depart Desert One conducting mid-air refuelling after they exit Iranian airspace.

Once they drop off the ground assault force, the helicopters proceed to their hide site about fifty miles away, where they land, establish defensive positions, and camouflage.

On night two, provided the Iranians have not detected the insertion, the Rangers take off at dusk, aboard four MC-130s, en route to Manzariyeh Airfield, near Tehran. They are followed by four AC-130 Spectre gunships; one provides fighter suppression at Mehrabad Airport on the outskirts of Tehran, one covers the embassy, one covers the airfield at Manzariyeh, and one is a backup. All refuel from KC-135 tanker aircraft over Saudi Arabia.

Two C-141 Starlifters depart Dhahran, Saudi Arabia, timed to arrive at Manzariyeh ten minutes after the airfield is secure. One is in an air ambulance configuration, the other in passenger configuration.

The ground assault phase takes place. As the hostages and troops arrive at Manzariyeh, they are sorted and placed on the two Starlifters in consonance with their medical condition. When all are loaded, the C-141s depart. After the C-141s depart, the Rangers fly out aboard the MC-130s, followed by the Spectres.[9]

President Carter approved this plan on 11 April 1980.[10]

On 24 April 1980, the mission began precisely according to plan. At 1750 hours, the lead Combat Talon had all four engines running and was loaded and ready for takeoff. At 1805 hours, the aircraft was airborne. Exactly one hour later, the second and third aircraft took off. The entire assault force was in the air. All the fixed wing aircraft would remain on schedule until they arrived at Desert One.

At 1830 hours, the helicopters started their engines. Lifting off on schedule at 1905 hours, the big helicopters headed for Desert One. Although it was a bit hazy, visibility improved once they crossed the Iranian coast.

At 2030 hours, the lead MC-130 entered a haze bank, but cleared it quickly. This was a *haboob*, a weather condition in which thick dust becomes suspended in the atmosphere, like a cloud. At the 1,000 feet altitude at which the Combat Talon was travelling, the visibility was relatively good. The aircraft hit another *haboob* at 2100 hours. This one limited visibility to about a mile. Unfortunately, conditions were much worse near the surface of the desert, where the helicopters would soon be travelling.

As the lead Talon was entering the second *haboob*, one of the helicopters damaged one of its rotor blades. Apprised of the condition by a warning light on the instrument panel, the pilot landed the aircraft and the crew chief confirmed the condition. One of the other helicopters then landed, rescued the crew, and continued on. There were now seven helicopters and they were running about fifteen minutes late.

At 2200 hours, the helicopters saw the formation of four C-130s pass parallel to them at about 2,000 feet altitude, just before they passed through the first haboob and entered the second. Visibility immediately dropped to between half and one-quarter of a mile. Two of the aircraft were forced to turn around and exit the cloud when they lost sight of the ground and the other helicopters. The two choppers landed. The other aircraft continued to press onward through the cloud.

As the helicopters were entering the cloud, the lead Combat Talon landed at Desert One. The landing system installed by Major Carney worked perfectly. The security force would soon be dealing with a busload of Iranians and an Iranian fuel truck.

At 2245 hours, the pilots of the two helicopters attempted to make another run through the *haboob*. As they re-entered the cloud, one of the helicopters lost its second-stage hydraulic system, a most dangerous condition, but continued on. The other helicopter pilot experienced failure of his compass and his pitch-and-roll indicator, both of which are essential for flight in limited visibility conditions. Further, his inertial navigation system appeared to be malfunctioning. The pilot aborted and headed back to the *Nimitz*.

Now there were six helicopters.

By 2320 hours, all the EC-130 refueling aircraft were staged to refuel the helicopters and the first two MC-130s were airborne again and headed back to the staging area. The helicopters were running ninety minutes behind schedule.

At 0025 hours the first two helicopters approached Desert One. Kicking up a dangerous amount of dust as they landed, the helicopters taxied in behind two of the EC-130s and began taking on fuel. The remaining helicopters straggled in until the last one closed at 0050 hours, close to two hours behind schedule, and began taking on fuel.[11]

Just after 0100 hours, 25 April, it all started to unravel. Helicopter number two, which had experienced the hydraulic failure, shut down, grounded by the senior marine helicopter pilot. Neither Kyle nor Beckwith could persuade the pilot to risk continuing the mission. The pilot further confirmed that he could not load the entire ground assault force on the remaining five helicopters due to weight constraints. Either the assault force would have to leave behind some twenty personnel, or the mission would have to be aborted. Beckwith, after conferring via satellite communications with Vaught, ordered an abort. The ground assault force began re-boarding the remaining fixed-wing aircraft.[12]

At 0225 local time, one of the helicopters lifted off to make room for another helicopter to refuel behind one of the EC-130s. The helicopter was immediately engulfed in dust, slewed sideways, and slammed into the cockpit of the EC-130. Kyle described the scene as follows:

> ... I heard a loud *whack*, then a booming explosion. As I turned, I saw a raging inferno engulfing the left side of Hal Lewis's tanker. The scene was erupting into a bizarre kaleidoscope of fire, dust, and smoke enveloping the aircraft ... At first, I thought the bladder system aboard the C-130 had exploded. Then through the leaping flames I saw the unearthly silouhette of the helicopter's blades slowly windmilling above the C-130's cockpit. The helicopter had drifted sideways almost 90 degrees to the right and slammed down onto the topside of the tanker's left inner wing section, coming to rest on top of the cockpit. The rear of the RH-53D was in the fire on the left side of the tanker, with only the twisted shell of the helo cockpit clear of the murderous flames.[13]

Shortly afterward ammunition began exploding, showering three of the helicopters with shrapnel. The helicopter crews abandoned their aircraft and began boarding the C-130s. At 0235 hours, the C-130s lifted off from Desert One and headed back to their staging area, where the joint task force would tend to its wounded and ponder its failure.

Consolidation of Air Force Special Operations, 1983

On 1 March 1983 all US Air Force (USAF) special operations units were consolidated, in response to the findings of the Holloway Commission Report. The Commander of 23d Air Force assumed overall administrative control of all the special operations units, which had been consolidated into the 1st Special Operations Wing (SOW) at Hurlburt Field, Florida. 1st SOW coordinated and directed the activities of all reserve and active component special operations squadrons (SOS). Its active component consisted of the 8th, 16th, and 20th SOS with the 8th SOS operating MC-130 Combat Talons and HC-130 Hercules Tankers, the 16th SOS operating the AC-130 Spectre gunships, and 20th SOS operating long range helicopters – the MH-53 Pave Lows and the HH-53 Jolly Green Giants. Additionally, there were four active SOSs located outside the United States. Providing the air force Combat Control Teams was the 1720th Special Tactics Group, also based out of Hurlburt.

A significant number of USAF special operations forces (SOF) were in the reserve components, including the 919th Special Operations Group (SOG) (AC-130A gunships), the 302d SOG (EC-130E command and control aircraft) and the Pennsylvania Air National Guard (EC-130E Volant Solo Psychological Operations aircraft).

The Drug War, 1983–5

One of President Reagan's major initiatives was to try to interdict the flow of illegal drugs into the United States. Beginning in April 1983, 1st SOW was the vanguard of this battle. Operation BAHAMAS AND TURKS (BAT) was an air force initiative to curb the heavy flow of illegal drugs through the Bahamas and Turk islands into the United States.[14]

The concept of the operation was that the 1st SOW would transport Drug Enforcement Agency (DEA) agents into areas where drugs were being trafficked. The DEA would make arrests. 1st SOW commenced the operation on 3 May and by the end of the month had logged quite a take. On the first day, aircrews in UH-1N helicopters assisted in the capture of a Cessna 210 aircraft with twenty-six duffle bags full of cocaine. The next day, they helped in the seizure of a twenty-foot boat with forty bails of marijuana aboard. On 4 July, American Independence Day, Operation BAT celebrated by capturing a Cessna carrying 863 lb of cocaine and a seventy-foot 'mother ship' carrying thirty tons of marijuana. By 4 August, Operation BAT had resulted in the confiscation of 1,243 lb of cocaine and 83,460 lb of marijuana. In addition to this, one hundred bales of marijuana and twenty-six packages of cocaine had been jettisoned at sea. 9,000 lb of marijuana had burned up in two aircraft crashes.[15]

Although originally envisioned as a short-term operation, BAT proved tremendously effective and continued on for two-and-a-half years. The cost of drug trafficking had gone up.[16]

Grenada, 1983

1st SOW would have two responsibilities during the Grenada intervention: delivering the Rangers to Point Salines and providing air-to-ground fire support to all the special operations forces fighting in the south. Combat Talons would deliver the Rangers to Point Salines. Spectres would provide the fire support.

At 0330 hours, Major Michael Couvillon piloted his Spectre into a firing orbit, 6,600 feet above Point Salines Airfield. His altitude was just outside the range of the ZU-23 20mm anti-aircraft cannons that intelligence reported the Grenadan forces might be armed with. Using all the sensors aboard, the sensor operators began identifying potential threats to the inbound MC-130s that were carrying the Ranger assault force. What they saw on the ground was a runway blocked with heavy equipment, concrete posts and other obstructions. On the ridge north of the runway, the sensor operators found four enemy air defense sites that appeared to be equipped with the ZU-23s.

This intelligence proved invaluable to the inbound Rangers. The Cubans knew from their intelligence sources that Rangers normally jumped from 1,000 feet altitude, so no doubt their guns were calibrated and crews trained to engage aircraft at that height. The Rangers decided to jump from 500 feet instead.[17]

This last minute change was right on target. As the lead Combat Talon approached the runway, most of the small arms, machinegun fire, and flak was above it. But one of the ZU-23s was putting effective fire in the flight path of the second Combat Talon forcing it and the remaining C-130s to peel off. Major Couvillon was given the word to deal with the problem.

Having identified and programed all the potential targets in the vicinity of the airfield over the past two hours, Couvillon's FCO selected the 40mm Bofors to take out the troublesome anti-aircraft emplacement. Although the fire control computer was intermittently malfunctioning, it provided the firing solution. Two shots destroyed the position. Then, for good measure, the Spectre took out the remaining three positions on the ridgeline.

The Rangers then called for some help with a machinegun that had two of their number pinned down behind a Cuban construction vehicle. Unfortunately, the computer malfunctioned and could not provide a firing solution and the Rangers were in dangerously close proximity to the target. The two Rangers had little choice, so they accepted the risk. With the computer malfunctioning, the navigator, Captain Bryan A. Lasyone, aimed the guns by carefully orienting the position of the entire gunship. Dozens of 40mm rounds and hundreds of 20mm rounds suppressed the fire, within fifty feet of the Ranger positions.[18]

Throughout the next two days, Spectre gunships were employed in a more conventional fire support role, in concert with artillery, helicopter gunships and fast-moving close-air-support aircraft. They suffered no casualties.

Conclusions

The air force had finally taken positive action to rebuild a robust special operations capability and the payoff began to show in Grenada. The special operations in Grenada had a few rough edges that were a consequence of incomplete planning, but that was overcome by the superb quality of the men and machines that executed the missions.

The actions at Grenada paved the way for effective air force special operations support in the latter part of the 1980s, particularly the Panama intervention. More importantly, Grenada served as a springboard for effective coordination between the air force and the other services, for the synchronization of special operations.

NOTES

1. Bill Sweetman, 'Forces of Darkness,' *International Defense Review*, June 1988, p. 676.
2. Daniel P. Bolger, *Americans at War 1975–1986; an Era of Violent Peace* (Novato, California, Presidio, 1988), pp. 31–84.
3. Colonel James H. Kyle, USAF (Ret.), with John Robert Eidson, *The Guts to Try* (New York, Orion, 1990), pp. 11–23.
4. Ibid, pp. 46–61.
5. Jeffrey P. Rhodes, 'The Machines of Special Ops,' *Air Force Magazine*, August 1988, p. 66.
6. Kyle, *The Guts to Try*, p. 211.

7. Ibid, p. 214.
8. US Special Operations Command Presentation, Association of the United States Army (AUSA) Convention, Washington, DC, 13 October 1992.
9. Kyle, *The Guts to Try*, pp. 178–84.
10. Bolger, *Americans at War 1975–1986*, p. 138.
11. Kyle, *The Guts to Try*, pp. 236 82.
12. Ibid, pp. 288–9.
13. Ibid, p. 295.
14. Herbert H. Kissling, *An Air Commando and Special Operations Chronology 1961–1991* (Hurlburt Field, Florida, First Special Operations Wing, Air Force Special Operations Command, United States Air Force), pp. 190–2.
15. Ibid, pp. 190–2.
16. Ibid, pp. 190–2.
17. Bolger, *Americans at War 1975–1986*, p. 305.
18. Ibid, p. 310.

PART IV

Honing the Edge 1987–92

CHAPTER 10

The New Order
Special Operations in a
Multi-Polar World 1986–92

The world changed radically as the 1990s began. Fortunately, US policy and military planners anticipated many of these changes correctly and launched visionary initiatives in both military and foreign policies.

As he began his term as President, on 20 January 1989, George Bush brought with him ample foreign policy and military experience. Bush, his advisors, and his cabinet were satisfied with the Reagan foreign policy legacy that was beginning to nibble away at the Soviet monolith and planned to continue that strategy for the next four years.

They were all in for a shock.

It is now known that since at least 1983 the Soviet economy had been careening uncontrollably down-hill like a juggernaut. Mikhail Gorbachev's desire to develop a market economy would have been exactly the right initiative twenty years before, but when the crunch came in the late 1980s the decline had taken on the momentum of a tidal wave. The best Gorbachev could do was try to ride the crest of that wave and pray he didn't hit a reef. In addition to economic decline, glasnost was spotlighting the myriad failures and tragedies brought on by seventy years of communist rule.

When Bush took office as President, relationships with some countries were being revised and, in a geopolitical game of mirrors, a number of America's erstwhile friends had become her enemies, and her enemies, friends. By the third anniversary of his inauguration, Bush had directed the military might of the United States against both Manuel Noriega of Panama, and Saddam Hussein of Iraq, who had both been clients of the United States in the early 1980s. Absolute power had absolutely corrupted the Panamanian strongman and the 'Butcher of Baghdad.'

In international relations many a nation has had to ally itself with evils in order to achieve its foreign policy aims. History is replete with such national experiences; Chamberlain appeased Hitler, the allies supported Stalin against the axis and so on. The ultimate outcome of such alliances is that eventually one has to defeat the devil decisively or pay him his due.

Panama, 1989–90

The history of Panama was stormy and turbulent until 1914, when the United States completed, opened and controlled the new canal between the Atlantic and the Pacific. To protect this new strategic asset, America firmly established and has since maintained a military presence there. From that point until 1968, Panama maintained a series of democratic and constitutional governments.[1]

This stability ended in 1968 as a military junta led by Major Boris Martinez of Panama's Army, the Guardia Nacional, overthrew the democratically elected government of President Arnulfo Arias. Shortly thereafter, Martinez was ousted by Colonel Omar Torrijos who had been aided by a young intelligence officer – Captain Manuel Noriega. Captain Noriega progressed as governments came and went, and he successively became Lieutenant Colonel, Chief of Intelligence and ultimately Commander of the Guardia, when he promoted himself to Brigadier General. He then renamed the Guardia, calling it the Panama Defense Forces or PDF. He had his own man, Nicolas Ardito Barletta, installed as President after rigging the 1984 presidential election between Barletta and Arias. This obvious fraud caused many Panamanians to take to the streets, but to no avail: Noriega had consolidated his power.

Since the Martinez/Torrijos coup, Noriega had been a strong personal ally of the United States, having attended several schools operated by the US Army. During his tenure as Chief of Intelligence under Torrijos he provided funds and airfields in support of US efforts to arm the Nicaraguan Contra rebels, stem the narcotics trade, and conduct special operations in El Salvador. Until 1984, the US administration had been willing to overlook his heavy-handed methods of expanding his power base and neutralizing political opposition. To the United States, Noriega represented a solid bastion against the spread of communism.

A bad situation got progressively worse. In 1987 Noriega decided to consolidate his hold over the Panama Defense Forces further and remove its Chief of Staff, his old friend Lieutenant Colonel Roberto Diaz-Herrera. However, Diaz-Herrera got wind of the move and publicly denounced Noriega for rigging the 1984 elections, murdering a popular idealist, Dr Hugo Spadafora, and assassinating Torrijos (evidence connecting Noriega to Torrijos' death is inconclusive, but such an act was certainly consistent with Noriega's *modus operandi*). This created an unprecedented public outcry which Noriega brutally suppressed with his riot squads, a group of thugs known as the 'Dobermans.' He also directed President Eric Arturo Delvalle, whom he had installed after removing Barletta, to declare a state of emergency and suspend the constitution. This prompted the US Senate to pass a resolution calling for the restoration of constitutional rights in Panama.

Throughout 1987, Noriega openly flouted all local and US efforts to curb his conduct. Upon his assumption of command at United States Southern Command (USSOUTHCOM), General Frederick F. Woerner publicly questioned the legitimacy of Noriega's government. This came right on the heels of the resolution by the US Senate. Noriega decided it was time to show the US that in Panama, *he* was the sole authority and could act with complete impunity.

In a carefully choreographed demonstration, Panamanian protesters rioted outside the United States embassy in Panama City as Panama Defense Forces and police stood by. On 'Black Friday,' 10 July, he ruthlessly suppressed popular demonstrations against his own regime as the Panama Defense Forces shot many and arrested thousands of protestors. By October, the Panama Defense Forces began a deliberate campaign to harass US service members and dependents. The situation was critical: President Reagan directed that all ties with Noriega be severed; General Woerner began preparing war plans designed to, at a minimum, curb Noriega's repression of Americans and Panamanians alike or, if necessary, remove him and his power base, the Panama Defense Forces, from the Panamanian scene.

Official Panamanian government harassment of US personnel became more intense and vicious as the US presidential election of 1988 approached. In January a US Navy lieutenant was arrested by the Panama Defense Forces and accused of spying. He was released nine hours later after being beaten and strip-searched. A Panama Defense Forces shotgun blast wounded the wife of a US Marine at her home in March. In June a Panama Defense Forces officer assaulted a US soldier and his wife at gunpoint, forced the soldier into the trunk of their car, and beat and raped his wife. The most heinous incident occurred when Panama Defense Forces troops stopped and searched two American school buses loaded with children. Brandishing AK-47s, they held the buses for several hours. Bomb threats at US facilities and gunpoint detentions became the order of the day for Americans in Panama.

As President Bush assumed office in January, the situation in Panama was critical, but his administration optimistically and unrealistically looked to the 1989 elections to depose Noriega. On the US domestic scene, irrespective of administration policy objectives, federal grand juries in Tampa and Miami, Florida handed down indictments against Noriega on 4 February for drug trafficking and dealings with South American drug cartels.

Another Panamanian election took place, with fraud and beatings in full public view. Noriega had now organized 'Dignity Battalions,' groups of armed thugs similar to Hitler's 'Brown Shirts,' who regularly rousted both Panamanians and Americans and strengthened Noriega's machines of control and repression. In the Panamanian national election Guillermo Endara and his vice-presidential candidates Ricardo Arias Calderon and Guillermo 'Billy' Ford decisively defeated Noriega's candidate Manuel Solis Palma, a situation Noriega reacted to with his most radical action yet. Panama Defense Forces soldiers boldly marched into the polls and confiscated accurate voting records and replaced them with fraudulent ones in front of US election observers led by former President Jimmy Carter. Two days after the elections, on 10 May, Endara, Calderon, and Ford were viciously assaulted by Panama Defense Forces riot police, the 'Doberman' gangs, while en route to a rally by their opposition party. The Dobermans shot and killed Ford's bodyguard. A photographer from the international weekly *Newsweek* photographed the bodyguard vomiting blood on Ford before he died.

US military personnel and their dependents continued to be harassed by the Panama Defense Forces. All other actions having no effect, Bush reacted with military movements, ordering Operation NIMROD DANCER, the deployment of almost 2,000 soldiers and Marines from the US to bases in Panama. Simultaneously he directed that 6,000 service personnel and dependents in Panama be evacuated from their local lodgings onto the bases.

At the end of September, General Maxwell Thurman, a legendary firebrand, was asked to postpone his retirement and take over USSOUTHCOM. Unlike the stereotypical General Officer, Max Thurman made his reputation in staff assignments rather than command, as a cold, calculating, and brilliant planner.

Coincidentally, a new Chairman of the Joint Chiefs of Staff was sworn in on 1 October. Army General Colin Powell, former National Security Advisor to Ronald Reagan and Commander of United States Forces Command, succeeded Admiral William Crowe.

Noriega's actions, which had elicited international censure, made it apparent even within the Panama Defense Forces that the situation could not persist. On the evening of 2 October, Major Moises Giroldi, Chief of Security for the Panama Defense Forces, staged a coup against Noriega but, when presented with the opportunity, Giroldi could not bring himself to kill Noriega, as called for. By the evening of 3 October, the coup attempt was history and Giroldi dead.

On 15 December, Noriega deposed his most recent Presidential lacky, Francisco Rodriquez, proclaimed himself 'Maximum Leader' and declared a 'state of war' with the United States.

On 16 December, he stepped into the abyss. That night, Marine First Lieutenant Robert Paz and three of his friends were driving through Panama City when they were stopped at a Panama Defense Forces checkpoint. The streets of the city were crowded and the people quite agitated over the present state of affairs within Panama and the tension between their country and the United States. Seeing the Michigan license plates on the American car, a crowd of about forty Panamanians rushed it. The Panama Defense Forces soldiers at the checkpoint allowed other cars ahead of Paz to pass, but insisted that the Americans halt. The Panama Defense Forces soldiers, waving their AK-47s, tried to pull the Americans from the car; the driver floored the accelerator and sped away. The Panama Defense Forces opened fire. One round entered the car through the trunk and struck Paz in the back, mortally wounding him. Paz died shortly afterward at Gorgas Army Hospital.

As Paz and his compatriots were speeding away from the checkpoint, a US Navy lieutenant and his wife arrived in time to observe the shooting. A Panama Defense Forces officer arrested the two Americans, took them into an office, blindfolded them with tape, and transported them to La Commandancia, Noriega's headquarters for the Panama Defense Forces. There, the lieutenant was beaten and kicked repeatedly in the groin as his wife looked on. Panama Defense Forces troopers threatened her sexually, physically assaulting, taunting and fondling her, and telling her that her husband would be unable to perform sexually after the repeated kicks to the groin.[2]

Thurman was notified of both incidents that evening and immediately phoned General Powell in Washington. After consultation with the Chiefs of Staff of the Uniformed Services and the Secretary of Defense, Powell and Lieutenant General Thomas Kelly, Chief of Operations (J3) for the Joint Staff, briefed the President. They discussed a full range of options available, but recommended one: Operation BLUE SPOON (later to be changed to JUST CAUSE),[3] a full-scale invasion of Panama. Secretary of State James A. Baker agreed. 'Okay, let's go' said Bush.

Within two days, Airborne Rangers from the 75th Ranger Regiment would chase a drunken Manuel Noriega out of the bed of his favorite prostitute and out of his position as 'Maximum Leader' of Panama.

There were two plans for US operations against Noriega. The first, designed to give ample time for him to understand the full political implications, allowed five days for the mobilisation. Prior to assuming his new duties, General Thurman spent time researching and familiarizing himself with the developing situation in Panama, reviewing the BLUE SPOON plan, and consulting with Powell. By the time he took over, both he and Powell were of the opinion that Noriega would only use warning time to prepare his defenses, ultimately resulting in an increased loss of American lives once hostilities commenced. Thurman turned this around.

The day he assumed command of USSOUTHCOM, he grabbed Lieutenant General Carl W. Stiner, Commander of XVIII Airborne Corps, gave him full responsibility for planning BLUE SPOON and appointed him Task Force South commander, with command of all forces involved in an invasion of Panama, should it come to pass. He told Stiner: 'Carlos, I've talked to the chief and I've talked to the chairman and you are my man for everything that has to be done there.'[4]

Stiner and his staff prepared a plan for a lightning attack that would require only forty-eight hours preparation. If they were going, no time would be given for Noriega to prepare his defenses.

Special Operations Forces Organization, 1987–93

JUST CAUSE was a complete integration of both conventional and special operations forces. Stiner had created a fully integrated plan using conventional forces against targets that were strongly defended and special operations forces against critical, high-profile, high-visibility targets. This integration proved highly effective and lethal. In February after indictments were returned on Noriega, General James Lindsay, who commanded United States Special Operations Command (USSOCOM), activated a small planning cell called the Joint Special Operations Task Force (JSOTF) to organize special operations in Panama and support USSOUTHCOM war planning. Lindsay's action ensured complete unity of effort and synchronization of special operations in both USSOUTHCOM and XVIII Airborne Corps war plans.

On 12 May, in conjunction with Operation NIMROD DANCER, Secretary of Defense Cheney ordered deployment of Army Special Forces and SEAL Units to Panama. In light of the belligerent and unpredictable nature of Panama Defense Forces activity, the Washington leadership considered it possible that Americans in Panama could be held hostage or become imprisoned as a bargaining chip for Noriega.

When Bush finally ordered the execution of JUST CAUSE, the efforts of USSOCOM and the JSOTF ensured that Army, Navy, and Air Force special operations forces were fully synchronized and complemented Stiner's XVIII Airborne Corps plan. Joint special operations had come a long way since the Iranian hostage rescue mission and the Grenada intervention. USSOCOM organization and leadership had finally solved most of the problems endemic to joint special operations.

The spectacular success that SOF experienced during JUST CAUSE was largely due to the leadership and organization of USSOCOM; but also the unified command plan of the United States Department of Defense (DoD) in general. Against various exigencies, DoD had established five permanent unified combatant commands (joint Army, Navy, Air Force, and Marine commands) with geographic areas of responsibility (AOR). Each of these commands was headed by a commander-in-chief (CINC) who was a four-star general or admiral. The CINC exercised authority over all combat forces in the AOR and was responsible for all contingency planning. They also coordinated their actions with other US agencies in the AOR: primarily the Department of State, but also such agencies as Treasury, Commerce, Transportation, Environmental Protection (EPA), and Justice. These regional unified commands were:

○ United States Atlantic Command (USLANTCOM at the time but changed to USACOM on 1 October 1993). USACOM operates primarily in the Atlantic and Caribbean basins.
○ United States Central Command (USCENTCOM). USCENTCOM operates in the Southwest Asia AOR which includes the Middle East, Sub-Saharan Africa, and South Asia.

○ United States European Command (USEUCOM). USEUCOM has responsibility for US military activities in Europe, to the Ural Mountains, the Mediterranean basin, and North Africa.
○ United States Pacific Command (USPACOM). USPACOM has responsibility for all US military activities in the Pacific basin, including northeast and southeast Asia.
○ United States Southern Command (USSOUTHCOM). USSOUTHCOM has responsibility for military operations in Latin America and is the headquarters that coordinated JUST CAUSE.

In addition to the regional commands, there were four other unified commands with global responsibility. Normally, the CINCs of these forces supported regional commands with various resources. These were functional, specialized commands that included:

○ United States Space Command (USSPACECOM). USSPACECOM is responsible for all military activities relating to the United States space program.
○ United States Transportation Command (USTRANSCOM). USTRANSCOM controls all strategic transportation activities and requirements world-wide. This command involves three of the four services (it has no Marine component) equally.
○ United States Special Operations Command (USSOCOM). USSOCOM has responsibility for all SOF based in the continental United States, but also trains and resources all SOF units world-wide.
○ United States Strategic Command (USSTRATCOM). USSTRATCOM has responsibility for all nuclear forces in the US Navy and Air Force.[5]

In the case of JUST CAUSE, General Lindsay, the CINCSOC, acted in a support role providing the Joint Special Operations Task Force (JSOTF) to General Thurman, the CINCSOUTH.

CINCSOC is primarily a resource manager. Through his staff he develops SOF strategy, doctrine and tactics, trains and educates his force, establishes SOF requirements and ensures that his units maintain a constant state of readiness. He also procures special operations peculiar supplies and equipment and ensures the interoperability of the component SOF units.

When USSOCOM was activated on 1 June 1987, the first CINCSOC was General James J. Lindsay. Born in Portage, Wisconsin, Lindsay boasted extensive and laudatory experience in special operations. His first special operations assignment was in Vietnam as commander of an 'A Team.' From then on he rotated between special operations and conventional assignments culminating in his command of USSOCOM. A Distinguished Service Cross, a

US Special Operations Command Organization

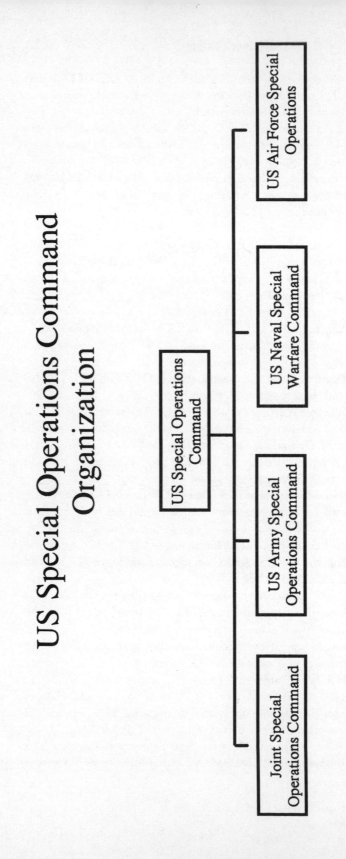

Figure 2

Distinguished Service Medal, four Silver Star and four Bronze Stars for Valor served as testimony to his gallantry in action and bravery under fire.

Each of the regional CINCs had a special operations staff element assigned to plan all special operations in the region and coordinate requirements both in-theater and with USSOCOM. In addition to these staff elements, some theaters have a separate special operations command (SOC).[6] Commanders of any JSOTF operating in the theater are normally subordinate to a conventional joint task force (JTF) commander or the theater CINC. The theater special operations commands are:

○ Special Operations Command – Atlantic (SOCLANT)
○ Special Operations Command – Pacific (SOCPAC)
○ Special Operations Command – Europe (SOCEUR)
○ Special Operations Command – South (SOCSOUTH)
○ Special Operations Command – Central (SOCCENT)

In addition to the theater special operations commands, the Commander, United States Forces – Korea has a special operations command (SOC-K) that plans special and unconventional warfare operations on and around the Korean peninsula.

This command structure ensures that all special operations are coordinated between the services, with conventional force commanders, and with other agencies working within the theater. It worked in Panama as follows.

As BLUE SPOON and other contingency plans were being developed, SOCSOUTH developed complementary special operations plans in coordination with USSOCOM. USSOCOM was included because it had to recruit, equip, train, and deploy the forces necessary to satisfy USSOUTHCOM operational requirements. When the President gave the order to go to war, the Joint Task Force (formed around the XVIII Airborne Corps) and the JSOTF assumed command of the forces they were allocated under the JUST CAUSE operations order. The Joint Task Force took command of all Army, Navy, Air Force, and Marine conventional forces involved in the operation. The JSOTF commanded all SOF involved except select Air Force special operations aircraft. These forces had been recruited, trained, equipped, and deployed by CINC-SOC. The missions that SOF components planned and executed in support of JUST CAUSE are discussed in detail in the three subsequent chapters.

The Gulf War, 1990–1

Once the Panama crisis was diffused, it looked like the American leadership could get back to the business at hand: declawing the Soviets. But, unknown to the American leadership, there was another problem yet to deal with. That problem was Saddam Hussein, and he had over a million men under arms, battle seasoned from their war against Iran. His ruthlessness and cruelty made Manuel Noriega look like a rank amateur.

Ever since the overthrow of Shah Reza Pahlavi, the American administration had considered Iran to be the major threat to its strategic interests in the Middle East. In 1979, Ayatollah Khomeini had successfully overthrown the Shah and established a theocracy in an Islamic fundamentalist revolution. Khomeini then installed a government, with immense popular support, that demanded strict adherence to the tenets of Shi'ite fundamentalism; in fact he ruled on the basis of this strict interpretation of the Koran. This placed the Iranian government and its people diametrically opposed to the Sunni Moslem monarchies (Saudi Arabia, Kuwait, and Jordan) and secular governments (Syria, Iraq, Israel, and the Soviet Union) in the region. Further, Ayatollah Khomeini had expressly stated that he wanted to export the revolution he had fostered in Iran to other Islamic states.

It was precisely this missionary zeal that prompted Saddam Hussein to go to war against Iran in 1980. Ostensibly with the goal of securing the Shatt-al-Arab waterway, his outlet to the Persian Gulf, Hussein attacked Iran in order to destabilize the Islamic Republic and depose its leadership. Unfortunately for him, the Iranians recovered from the onslaught, organized, and declared a jihad, or holy war, against him. They counter-attacked with a vengeance. Thrown back, the Iraqis found themselves on the defensive for six years, fighting for their very existence. In the intervening years, Hussein reformed his Army, and established and trained a formidable eight-division formation called the Republican Guards. He accomplished all this with considerable Soviet, European, American, Saudi and Kuwaiti assistance. Hussein was the West's bulwark against fanatical Islamic expansionism. He became 'our man' in the Middle East. By 1987, with new equipment and western training, his forces began a campaign which would eject Iran from his territory and secure the Shatt-al-Arab. By 1988, the war was over – in a stalemate, but Hussein had amassed a massive war debt and the fourth largest standing Army in the world: a most dangerous combination.

The price of oil was inextricably linked to Iraq's ability to repay its war debt. If the price of oil dropped below thirty-eight dollars a barrel, Iraq could not service that debt and its economy would become bankrupt. Therefore, dissent within the Organization of Petroleum Exporting Countries (OPEC) over the price of oil could severely damage the Iraqi economy. The Kuwaiti royalty, the Sabah family, advocated dropping the price of oil and on several occasions had sold their oil below set OPEC prices. This had resulted in heated exchanges between the oil ministers of all the OPEC countries at OPEC meetings. More to the point Iraq had told Kuwait that its practice of undercutting oil prices threatened the very existence of Iraq and was therefore tantamount to an act of war and Iraq would respond accordingly.

Iraq attacked and occupied Kuwait at 0200 hours local time on 2 August 1990. On the pretext of resolving a border dispute over ownership of the Rumaylah oil fields in northern Kuwait, Saddam Hussein embarked on a punitive expedition that would accomplish four objectives: punish the Kuwaitis for their perceived duplicity; depose the Sabah family; secure access to the sea, Kuwaiti water tables and oil fields; and establish a base for onward movement into Saudi Arabia.

Led by Saddam's Republican Guards, the Iraqi attack was vicious and as the hold on Kuwait was consolidated, Hussein declared it Iraq's nineteenth province and so looted the nation. The Iraqi military machine became one gigantic looting apparatus. They absconded with cars, grain, medical equipment and supplies, trucks, oil; anything that had any value.

Meanwhile, the Republican Guards were staged along Kuwait's southern border for an attack into Saudi Arabia. Their armor battalions were in attack formations. They had refueled, resupplied and moved their military stocks of food, fuel and ammunition to forward sites in Kuwait. Clearly, Saddam's war machine was ready to continue into Saudi Arabia.

As the Iraqi assault took place, President Bush was in a summit with Prime Minister Margaret Thatcher of the United Kingdom. Encouraged by the British Prime Minister, who provided a sound international perspective, Bush began to build an international coalition.[7] Not only was this a most barbaric and heinous aggression, but Hussein threatened the flow of oil. This was a significant problem to the United States, but it could rely on its own reserves if necessary. However, it was a major problem to the industrialized nations of Europe and Asia, who were almost entirely dependent on oil from the Persian Gulf. The United Nations began to enact a series of resolutions that censured Iraq for its aggression, established an economic embargo and authorized the use of force to expel Iraq from Kuwait.

American response was swift. Bush, Powell and Cheney conferred with King Fahd, the monarch in Saudi Arabia. To prove to Fahd that nothing short of Saudi Arabia's national survival was at stake, they showed him positive intelligence on Iraq's offensive capability and possible intentions. Fahd was alarmed, conferred with his Arab neighbors, and by 7 August the ready brigade of the United States 82d Airborne Division was winging its way to Saudi Arabia, arriving on the 8th.[8]

The 82d was an almost pitifully light force in view of the powerful Iraqi armored threat. They called themselves 'speed bumps in the desert,' likening themselves to the asphalt bumps that are placed in trafficways to slow traffic. But if Hussein had real offensive intentions, the sight of those stalwart airborne soldiers with the might of the United States following behind them made him blink. The Iraqi Army began to dig in and fortify Kuwait. They withdrew their supply stocks and replaced their elite armor formations with regular infantry troops. They prepared to defend the nineteenth province.

Efforts to build a coalition paid off and by February 1991, units from the United Kingdom, France, Italy, Canada, Australia, Belgium, Netherlands, Spain, Norway, Denmark, Portugal, Greece, Argentina, South Korea, Bangladesh, Morocco, Egypt, Senegal, Niger, Pakistan, Oman, the United Arab Emirates, Saudi Arabia and Free Kuwait Forces, were deployed against the Iraqi invaders. This was clearly a coalition of the new world order: Czechoslovakia and Poland sent support units and even Mujahedeen tribesmen of Afghanistan, fresh from expelling the Soviet aggressors, deployed to Saudi Arabia to help expel the Iraqis.[9] This coalition should have sent a clear message to Saddam that, as President Bush put it, 'this aggression shall not stand.'

The command in the United States responsible for planning and conducting military operations in southwest Asia was United States Central Command (USCENTCOM), located at MacDill Air Force Base, Florida and commanded by General Norman H. Schwarzkopf.[10] The USCENTCOM organization and functions paralleled USSOUTHCOM. Within a period of seven months, USCENTCOM had deployed to Riyadh, Saudi Arabia, and expanded not only to a wartime joint headquarters for US forces, but also the administrative and operational headquarters of all coalition forces. An allied effort, USCENTCOM became Joint Forces Central Command and took on the character of Supreme Headquarters Allied Expeditionary Force (SHAEF), the command that led to allied victory in Europe fifty years earlier.

The executive agent in USCENTCOM for special operations was Special Operations Command USCENTCOM or SOCCENT. Here the tables were turned from World War II. Whereas the British Special Operations Executive (SOE) had called the shots for allied special operations in Nazi-occupied Europe, it was now time for their proteges, the Americans, to orchestrate the effort.

General Carl W. Stiner had replaced Lindsay as CINCSOC following the latter's retirement after JUST CAUSE. Stiner had gained extensive experience with effective SOF integration as Commander of JTF South in JUST CAUSE. But this merely served as the capstone to an extensive career in special operations. A tough airborne officer from LaFollette, Tennessee, Stiner served his first tour with SOF in the 3d Special Forces Group at Fort Bragg, from 1964–6. Like his predecessor, General Lindsay, he then rotated between conventional and special operations assignments through the remainder of his career. A Defense Distinguished Service Medal and two Army Distinguished Service Medals were tribute to an exemplary career.

This became a campaign radically different from JUST CAUSE. Not only was this a joint effort but also an allied one. The Iraqi threat could not be neutralized with a lightning strike into Kuwait or Iraq; the threat was over one million strong with thousands of tanks, armored personnel carriers, artillery and an apparently respectable air force. The campaign was therefore planned and executed differently.

Even after intercession by General Powell and General Stiner, the new CINCSOC, General Schwarzkopf was extremely reluctant to use SOF behind Iraqi lines for fear that their deployment could telegraph his strategy. An orthodox, conventional warrior, Schwarzkopf was suspicious of these unconventional and unorthodox operators who sometimes required conventional units to 'pull their fat from the fire' when their plans went awry. It was only after the commander of the British forces, Lieutenant General Peter de la Billiere (an old SAS hand), convincingly argued the point that Schwarzkopf permitted them to be used in a clandestine role, in enemy territory.[11] However, Schwarzkopf supported the extensive use of Air Force SOF during the air campaign. On the friendly side of the line, Schwarzkopf maximized the capabilities of SOF to advise and train allied Arab formations in US combat procedures and small unit tactics.

Psychological Operations (Psyops), a recent addition to the SOF arsenal, were instrumental in the conduct of Operation DESERT STORM. Their effective planning and execution significantly reduced the loss of life on both sides and was a major contributing factor to the rapid coalition victory.

Civil affairs and psychological operations units were particularly valuable picking up the pieces and getting order restored in Kuwait following the cessation of offensive operations. Civil Affairs units, composed primarily of reserves called up for the war, were instrumental in reestablishing and restoring public services to operation after the coalition victory. US Civil Affairs units supervised the repair of water and sewage systems, rebuilding of roads, clearing of battle damage, restoration of electrical power and the reestablishment of municipal government.

Kurdish Relief, 1991–3

President Bush called for the Iraqi people to overthrow Saddam Hussein on several occasions during the Gulf War crisis. In addresses directed at the Iraqi people he told them that the only lasting way for them to end the tyranny that was bringing so much pain was to oust Saddam. Taking this as a cue, Shi'ite Iraqis in southern Iraq and Kurdish tribes in the north attempted armed revolutions. They believed that once they began the revolution, President Bush would provide them with military assistance; but this was not Bush's intent at all. They began their revolutionary activity and pleaded for American and coalition assistance, but the pleas fell on deaf ears. Consequently, the Shi'ite rebellion in southern Iraq was immediately and ruthlessly suppressed by the Republican Guards who had managed to escape the Kuwaiti theater as Bush ended the war.

Kurdish leaders also tried to exploit Iraq's weakened condition by conducting operations against Iraqi forces in the North, and with the Shi'ite rebellion suppressed, Saddam began a campaign of repression against the

Kurds, who fled into the mountains of northern Iraq and into refugee camps in southern Turkey.

Still recovering from the combat against Iraq, SOF were called to protect and assist Kurdish refugees in southern Turkey and northern Iraq, who were being systematically harassed by the Iraqi Army. In Operation PROVIDE COMFORT, US SOF moved into northern Iraq and established safe havens for these refugees; providing protection from the Iraqi military, medical attention, food and shelter.

During the Gulf crisis, Special Operations Command, Europe (SOCEUR) had deployed to Incirlik Air Base in Turkey to orchestrate special operations against northern Iraq. During the war they assisted in rescuing downed pilots and searching for Scud missiles. After the war, they planned and organized Operation PROVIDE COMFORT. The 39th Special Operations Wing (later redesignated the 352d Special Operations Group), 10th Special Forces Group (Airborne), United States Civil Affairs and Psychological Operations Command (USACAPOC), engineers, US, Dutch and British Marines conducted the operation and succeeded not only in providing humanitarian aid, but also in returning the Kurdish refugees to their homes.

Meanwhile, around the world, SOF continued to provide assistance to developing nations by fostering democratic ideals, depoliticizing and professionally developing military forces, and building educational and logistics infrastructures. In addition to existing US initiatives in Latin America and Asia, US SOF began security assistance programs in Sub-Saharan Africa.[12]

Conclusions

Coinciding with the establishment of USSOCOM, a fundamental change took place in the character of special operations. In contrast to special operations of the past, the operations conducted in the late 1980s and early 1990s emphasized minimizing casualties on both sides. In both Panama and the Persian Gulf, SOF personnel repeatedly exhibited compassion not only for the civilian populations affected by the wars, but also their vanquished enemies. In particular, SOF actions clearly demonstrated that the US action was not against civilians, but against military aggression and political corruption.

NOTES

1. Thomas Donnelly, Margaret Roth, and Caleb Baker, *Operation Just Cause; the Storming of Panama* (New York, Lexington Books, 1991), p. 2.
2. Bob Woodward, *The Commanders* (New York, Simon & Schuster, 1991), p. 133.
3. According to Bob Woodward, in his book *The Commanders*, Lieutenant General Kelly changed the name BLUE SPOON to JUST CAUSE after a telephone call from General James W. Lindsay, Commander of the US Special Operations Command. 'Do you want your grandchildren to say you were in Blue Spoon'? asked Lindsay. Kelly saw the point.

4. Donnelly, Roth, and Baker, *Operation Just Cause*, p. 55.

5. In 1991, President Bush announced a unilateral nuclear arms reduction initiative that included the consolidation of all nuclear forces under a newly formed USSTRATCOM. Under the terms of that initiative, the US Army gave up its entire nuclear capability. This action completely eradicated the United States tactical (battlefield) nuclear capability.

6. US Special Operations Command Public Affairs Office Memorandum to the author, with enclosures, Subject: Security Review of Manuscript, dated 9 September 1993.

7. Bruce W. Watson, et. al., *Military Lessons of the Gulf War* (London, Greenhill, 1991) pp. 19–20.

8. Woodward, *The Commanders*, pp. 245–56.

9. Watson, *Military Lessons of the Gulf War*, p. 135.

10. Ibid, p. 135.

11. General Sir Peter de la Billiere, *Storm Command; A Personal Account of the Gulf War* (London, HarperCollins, 1992) pp. 191–2.

12. Richard H.P. Sia, 'U.S. Increasing Its Special Forces Activity in Africa' (*Baltimore Sun*, 15 March 1992), p. 1.

CHAPTER 11

Swords to Plowshares
Army Special Operations in
the New Order 1986–92

As the 1980s drew to a close, Army special operations forces (SOF) continued to be used in support of conventional operations and took on extensive nation-building and foreign internal defense (FID) missions. Conflicts in Panama and the Persian Gulf clearly pointed out a new direction of evolution in army special operations. In comparison with earlier, bygone days, nation-building and foreign internal defense operations took on a significantly greater importance in American policy. In two major American conflicts that took place in the last decade of the twentieth century Army SOF exhibited timely initiative and flexibility when, as a result of unforeseen consequences, it came to the aid of oppressed peoples in Latin America, the Middle East, and Africa.

Since the Korean war, successive presidents and secretaries of defense had designated the Army as the principal service in providing foreign military training assistance and fighting low-intensity conflicts (LIC). The John F. Kennedy Special Warfare Center and School was established to accomplish the former mission and develop the operational doctrine to accomplish the latter. However, the Carter administration eliminated this Army mission.

The succeeding Reagan administration reinstated the mission in the early 1980s in response to the findings of the Holloway Commission Report on the Iran rescue mission and several other independent and government studies and panel discussions. These studies also resulted in the creation of the position of Assistant Secretary of Defense for Special Operations and LIC (ASD SO/LIC). Although Special Forces and Rangers trained extensively for LIC missions, few such missions were executed.

The exception to this was hostage rescue, usually undertaken as a result of a terrorist act, which falls into the category of low-intensity conflict (LIC). Secretary of Defense Caspar Weinberger and Admiral William Crowe had acted with alacrity on the findings of the Holloway Commission and, by the end of the Reagan administration, the United States had developed a highly effective hostage rescue capability in the Special Forces.

Even so, the one documented Special Forces hostage rescue mission was executed during Operation JUST CAUSE, the US intervention in Panama: a conventional warfare setting. Since this rescue was executed solely by the Army, with no Navy or Air Force involvement, the 'jury remains out' on America's joint service hostage rescue capability. Since there has been no recent crisis requiring a joint service hostage rescue operation, it remains to be seen if such a capability is a reality.

Special Forces also provided training and advice to the El Salvador military on how to reduce the Communist insurgency. In 1989 this assistance enabled government forces to break the stalemate with the insurgents on the field of battle. Furthermore, the loss of aid from Nicaragua caused by the fall of the Sandinista regime and the elimination of Soviet aid severely crippled the rebels, forcing them to the conference table where they struck an agreement to cease hostilities and disarm in return for a greater say in the government.

Although doctrine from the late 1980s and early 1990s envisioned that Army SOF would principally operate in the low-intensity conflict (LIC) environment, the facts are that most special operations from 1987 onward were conducted in the context of mid-intensity conflicts.

In spite of their specialized LIC capabilities, Army SOF were used primarily for 'economy of force' missions in conventional conflicts. These are missions in which a small force performs a task that normally would require a much larger force. Commanders assign economy of force missions to subordinate units in situations where they are prepared to risk failure of low priority missions so that they may concentrate forces elsewhere against a higher priority one.

Panama, 1989–90

Operation JUST CAUSE was the largest deployment of Army special operations forces (ARSOF) since the Vietnam war. Every branch of ARSOF was represented and they executed the full gamut of SOF missions. This time, in contrast to Grenada, they were assigned only those missions that best suited their unique capabilities.

In Grenada, planners assigned ARSOF missions as an afterthought, perhaps as a means to ensure that SOF was not left out of the operation and to maintain visibility. No doubt, SOF planners felt they needed a role to vindicate themselves after the tragedy in Iran four years before. Further, unless they could prove their worth, they would have trouble justifying their expense to the US Congress. Unfortunately, the lackluster SOF performance was a direct consequence of haphazard employment.

This was not the case in JUST CAUSE. This time, the plans were in place and the Joint Force Special Operations Component Commander (JFSOCC) assigned the Army missions based on unique Army SOF capabilities. Nowhere was this more evident than in hostage rescue. In the early hours of JUST CAUSE, the Special Forces and Rangers each conducted hostage rescue operations characterized by cunning, surprise, daring and superb training. These operations

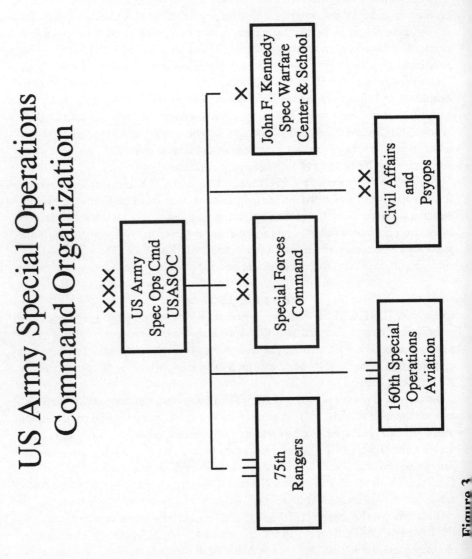

Figure 3

vindicated ARSOF from the failure at Desert One and established them as one of the world's premiere hostage rescue teams.

DIRECT ACTION

After Vietnam, the Airborne Rangers made a radical transition from their traditional role as a small-unit, deep reconnaissance and raiding force. With the consolidation of Ranger units into the 75th Ranger Regiment, the Rangers took on the role of an elite infantry shock force in contrast to their former emphasis on small unit operations in support of conventional forces. US planners first employed the Rangers in this role during the operation to take Point Salines Airfield during URGENT FURY, the US intervention in Grenada, but that operation had been fraught with numerous difficulties. During the intervening years, between Grenada and Panama, the Rangers took stock of their performance and rigorously trained to improve on it. It was this demanding training that enabled them not only to excel at these 'shock' missions, but also gave them the flexibility to deal with an unexpected hostage crisis.

When the US intervened in Panama, three key airfields had to be seized rapidly and simultaneously: Tocumen Military Airfield, Omar Torrijos International Airport, and Rio Hato Military Airfield. Noriega could escape by air using any one of these airfields, which necessitated their rapid seizure. Lieutenant General Carl Stiner, Commanding General of XVIII Airborne Corps and the Joint Task Force, assigned these as H-Hour objectives to the 75th Ranger Regiment. Colonel Buck Kernan, the Commander of the Rangers, assigned the Tocumen/Torrijos airfield complex as the H-Hour objective for 1st Battalion, 75th Ranger Regiment, with C Company of his 3d Battalion attached. The remainder of the Regiment seized Rio Hato.

At 0103 hours, following preparation by the ubiquitous AC-130 Spectre gunship and AH-6 Little Bird helicopters, the four C-130 Hercules and seven C-141 Starlifters carrying the Rangers throttled back for the jump. Charlie Company of the 3d Battalion, jumping from the four Hercules aircraft, would assault and secure Torrijos International main terminal while 1st Battalion would assault the military side at Tocumen.

The timing of the assault at 0103 hours should have put Charlie Company at the terminal during the late evening and early morning lull in passenger traffic. This was not the case, however. A Brazilian airliner that was scheduled in at 2245 hours had arrived late and disembarked its passengers. Consequently, as the Ranger assault began, there were almost 400 civilians in the terminal.

After landing in elephant grass across the runway from the terminal the commander of Charlie Company and his fire support officer slogged to the airfield. As they did so, the commander monitored, on the radio, the progress of his platoons as they moved in and seized their initial objectives. 1st Platoon was to establish a blocking position at the airport entrance. 3d Platoon was to seize and secure a fire station north of the terminal. 2d Platoon took up an attack position at the Eastern Airlines baggage area for its assault on the terminal.

As 2d Platoon approached the terminal, the platoon leader saw a Panamanian looking at them from around the corner. It was obvious to them that this was no soldier. As the Lieutenant raised his rifle, the civilian disappeared. One of the Rangers immediately charged and shot out the lights as his fellows assaulted the building to find, around a corner, four Panamanians squatting with their hands in the air. After taking them into custody, the platoon took up an attack position facing the terminal.

1st Platoon, after securing the Airport entrance, cut through a chain link fence and moved toward a restaurant. The first squad sent an interpreter into the restaurant to ask the occupants to surrender, which they did. The platoon then established a security perimeter around the restaurant.

3d Platoon was about to find itself locked in mortal combat. As it approached the fire station, a fire truck raced out of the garage. One of the Rangers leveled his M-16 rifle and fired three tracer rounds in front of the windshield, which caused the driver to stop and then turn back. Arriving back at the fire station, the driver bailed out of the truck and ran into the back of the fire station before the platoon could stop him. As the advance squad approached, they were confronted by fifteen Panamanian civilians shouting obscenities at them. After rejecting the idea of throwing a grenade into the fire station as a 'convincing device,'[1] an interpreter warned the Panamanians that they had better surrender. They did.

3d Platoon then began its approach to the terminal proper. Suddenly one of the terminal windows shattered as they were taken under fire by two PDF soldiers firing through the glass. Laying down a base of fire, the platoon hastily entered the terminal as the two soldiers fled into a men's toilet.[2] Sergeant Reeves and Private First Class (PFC) Forbes charged through the door of the toilet and Reeves entered the first stall. No soldier. As Reeves began to enter the next stall, he was shot in the shoulder by one of the PDF soldiers who had waited inside a stall to ambush the Rangers. Reeves was hit twice more before going down. Forbes tried to shoot the soldier but his weapon malfunctioned, so he left the bathroom and reported to Specialist Eubanks, who together with Sergeant Thorland and PFC Kelly, was securing the area outside the door. Breathlessly, Forbes told his fellow squad members of the action in the bathroom and that Ranger Reeves was down and wounded.

Thorland, Eubanks and Kelly then charged back into the bathroom to get Reeves. As Thorland recovered the wounded Ranger, Kelly and Eubanks covered their exit, ensuring that if the PDF reappeared from a stall, they would be met by a hail of bullets. Sergeant Reeves then provided the trio with a detailed report of the situation inside the bathroom as Kelly tended to his wounds.

Throwing a grenade through the door to try to eliminate the PDF quickly, Specialist Eubanks and PFC Kelly again assaulted the bathroom but Eubanks' Squad Automatic Weapon (SAW) malfunctioned. The grenade had been ineffective as it became lodged between stalls, which mitigated the blast. The Rangers did, however, retrieve Sergeant Reeves' weapon.

Doggedly, Kelly and Eubanks rushed the door one last time, with Eubanks breaking right and Kelly breaking left as they entered. The two then crouched on either side of the room and waited. One PDF soldier peeked around a corner shouting obscenities. Eubanks shot him in the neck and the soldier went down, babbling incoherently. The second soldier lunged out of a stall and grabbed Eubanks' weapon. With a shot to the head, Kelly killed him instantly. Then without warning, the first soldier rolled over and tried to draw his pistol. Kelly kicked him through a window and out onto the tarmac twenty-five feet below. To the Rangers amazement, the PDF soldier got to his feet and attempted to draw his pistol again when PFC McKinney, an M60 machinegunner securing the terminal, cut him down.

Now it was 2d Platoon's turn.

As 3d Platoon finished its encounter 2d Platoon entered the terminal. The platoon leader, deployed one squad to each floor. 3d Squad moved up the escalator to the third floor[3] and was immediately attacked by a group of Panamanian security agents barricaded in the airport security office. The agents started burning papers which the Rangers believed might be of interest to US authorities. After describing the situation to his platoon leader, the Ranger squad leader, in Spanish, ordered the group to surrender. The agents responded with more gunfire.

Throwing a grenade through the door to stun or kill the PDF, the squad assaulted the room. The grenade was overly effective: it had not only killed the five agents in the room, but also fanned the fire and activated the sprinkler system, which proved ineffective in combating the blaze. The company commander ordered the squad to evacuate the room as the heat grew intense.

As they followed 3d Squad up the escalator to the third floor, 1st squad heard women sobbing. Moving across the terminal, it sounded like there were dozens of civilians, their shouts and screams echoing through the terminal. Suddenly they heard a heavily accented voice shout: 'Don't shoot! We're civilians.'[4] Looking down to the main floor of the terminal the Rangers saw literally hundreds of civilians. Simultaneously, the company commander began getting reports at his command post of civilians in other parts of the terminal. The passengers from the Brazilian flight were everywhere. It was a tight situation, but so far no civilians had been hurt. 3d Squad redeployed to the main terminal, with the 2d Squad, and began evacuating civilians. One Panamanian told the 2d Squad leader, Sergeant Anderson, that he had seen a woman and a baby go into the baggage claim area on the first floor.

A team of two Rangers entered the baggage claim area, which was dark. Through their night-vision goggles, the team saw a group of nine armed PDF soldiers holding a woman and her baby hostage. The baby was crying. The Panamanian who had reported to the squad leader had neglected to tell him about these soldiers. On orders from the squad leader, the Rangers, using one of the civilians as an interpreter, ordered the PDF to surrender. The response: no dice. They had hostages and they were staying right where they were. The woman, who by her accent was identified as an American, yelled for the Rangers to leave as the PDF had threatened to kill her and her baby.

But the Rangers were not going anywhere. The platoon leader redeployed his squads to isolate the area and located the airport security manager, who offered to act as a go-between with the PDF soldiers holding the hostages. The lieutenant had his own Spanish-speaking Rangers monitor the negotiations to keep the security manager honest. As the discussions went on, one Ranger broke into a room adjacent to the baggage area to establish a sniper position. After more than two hours of negotiations the PDF soldiers remained intransigent and finally opened fire on the Rangers.

This was the last straw for the Ranger commander; he had enough. When the PDF fire ceased, he shouted to the PDF that if they did not surrender in five minutes, he would simply kill them all. The PDF dropped their weapons and lay down on the floor. After the woman and her baby emerged from the room, and were safeguarded, the PDF came out, their hands over their heads, and were taken into custody.

When they were relieved by elements of the 82d Airborne Division at 0700 hours the next morning, Charlie Company, 3-75th Rangers handed twenty-one prisoners and 398 civilian detainees over. One woman suffering from smoke inhalation had been treated by a platoon medic. The prisoners had been handcuffed while the civilians were asked to sit quietly and remain calm. One of the platoon leaders bought some food from a vendor for about ten children, who had become quite hungry after all the excitement.

None of the Rangers was killed in the assault, although Sergeant Reeves was seriously wounded. Seven Panamanian military had been killed but, with the exception of one case of smoke inhalation, not a single civilian was harmed.

AVIATION MISSIONS

Army special operations helicopters supported both conventional and special operations throughout the campaign in Panama. Like their Air Force counterparts, one of their primary functions was to provide heavy, precise firepower in congested areas where collateral damage was to be avoided. One of the helicopters specially designed for this mission was the AH-6 Little Bird. Mounting either rockets or mini-guns, the Little Birds are perfectly suited to the close-in combat that characterizes urban warfare. It is not surprising that

AH-6s were selected to suppress sniper fire in the vicinity of the PDF head-quarters, La Commandancia, in Panama City when conventional units assaulted it on 20 December 1989.

But the airframe is really only a small part of the capability. Skilled and experienced pilots are the key to reaching the full potential of the entire weapons system. It may be one of the best helicopters in the world, but it is useless if its crew is incompetent. The 160th Aviation Regiment, at Fort Campbell, Kentucky, takes only experienced volunteers. Once assigned to the Regiment, the aviators rigorously train in all types of special aviation missions in all conceivable circumstances. This process may very well produce the best helicopter pilots in the world and was demonstrated by the actions of Chief Warrant Officer (CWO) Fred Horsley and Captain (CPT) George Kunkel at La Commandancia.

On 20 December, Horsley and Kunkel were flight lead for a group of Little Birds whose mission it was to support the ground assault on La Commandancia. Flying low-level, nap-of-the-earth with night-vision goggles, they encountered heavy ground fire just as they crested a hill en route to La Commandancia. Flying through the ground fire, the two pilots began their mission of suppressing sniper and heavy weapons fire emanating from a sixteen-storey high-rise apartment building overlooking the headquarters. Unknown to either pilot, however, the initial ground fire they encountered coming over the hill had mortally wounded their Little Bird.

They initiated their first attack run, mini-guns blazing, against some snipers on the rooftop of the apartment building. As they completed the run, Horsley saw that Kunkel was fighting the controls to get the helicopter to respond so Horsley grabbed his controls to assist. The aircraft continued towards the ground. With extremely limited response from the controls, the two pilots tried to aim for an open area on their right. They managed to level the aircraft before it crashed into the ground, skidding across a courtyard and crashing into a concrete post. As the aircraft caught fire, Horsley bailed out immediately, but Kunkel's flight vest became entangled in his harness and debris forcing him to have to struggle to free himself. Since Kunkel's side of the aircraft was blocked by a wall, he crawled out on Horsley's side and joined him forward of the burning aircraft. They were inside La Commandancia.

The scene looked like Armageddon. The Little Bird was blazing and the two pilots were taken under enemy fire from several locations. Compounding this problem was the AC-130 Spectre gunship that was laying down preparatory fires for the ground assault. These fires thwarted several escape attempts by the two aviators.

Suddenly the volume of fire inside the compound subsided as the volume outside increased to a deafening roar. Task Force Gator, of the US 5th Infantry Division, had begun its assault. Taking advantage of the lull, the aviators darted between two buildings to the outer wall, which was topped by barbed wire. Suddenly, Horsley heard a rustling in nearby bushes, drew his pistol and turned, poised to shoot. He was confronted by a PDF soldier with his hands raised, who hurriedly explained that everyone who was not dead had run away, and that he wanted to surrender.

The two aviators decided that Kunkel should go over the wall and make contact with Task Force Gator, since his night-vision goggles were still partially operational. Throwing his vest over the barbed wire and vaulting the wall, Kunkel darted down the street, shouting 'Bulldog,' the running password for US Forces. Making contact with elements of Task Force Gator, Kunkel then returned to the wall for Horsley and the Panamanian prisoner. As Horsley was boosting the Panamanian over the wall, the AC-130 opened fire again. Startled, Horsley vaulted over the Panamanian, who was atop the wall, to the street outside. When the firing stopped, the two pilots pulled the Panamanian to safety. They then linked up with Task Force Gator and were evacuated to a high school, where they contacted their unit.

ECONOMY OF FORCE

Economy of Force missions are not the optimum use of Special Forces personnel so the Army leadership is reluctant to use them in this role, because they are a scarce, precious resource that is difficult and expensive to replace. Fortunately, few Special Forces personnel are lost in these operations simply because they are so resourceful and tenacious. They simply refuse to be overcome by the enemy. So it was at the Pacora River Bridge, in Panama.

The capture of Manuel Noriega was top priority for US forces during the intervention. For Operation JUST CAUSE, the 3d Battalion, 7th Special Forces Group, designated as Task Force (TF) Black, was assigned the mission of tracking him. Additionally, the Task Force was to interdict lines of communication between the PDF general staff and its garrisons, in order to decapitate the PDF command and control structure.

To accomplish this second mission, Colonel Jake Jacobelly, the 7th Group Commander, assigned three targets for surveillance and four targets for seizure. The targets to be seized were: the Pacora River Bridge, Tinajitas, Fort Cimmaron, and a television tower that would be used by American Psychological Operations (Psyops) personnel.

Tinajitas was the garrison of a PDF company that could shell the US Army headquarters at Fort Clayton with mortars. The company could also deploy to assist the garrison at La Commandancia, the PDF headquarters, when it came under attack.

Fort Cimmaron was the garrison of Battalion 2000, the elite unit that had come to Noriega's rescue during the Giroldi coup, earlier in the year. Jacobelly planned a direct assault on Cimmaron to either destroy the unit or force it to surrender.

The Pacora River Bridge presented a choke point on the route from Fort Cimmaron to Torrijos Airport, a Ranger objective, so Colonel Jacobelly assigned A Company, 3d Battalion, 7th Special Forces Group, under the command of Major Kevin Higgins, the mission to establish a blocking position on the bridge at H-hour.

Higgins was originally scheduled to lift off from Albrook Air Station at 0010 hours, so that the company would be in its blocking position by the 0100 hours, or H-hour. As Higgins' troops were preparing to embark, at 0005 hours, they began taking fire from Dignity battalion troops outside the fence.

As if this unexpected attack was not bad enough, the battalion operations officer came running out to the flight line and told Higgins that H-hour had been moved forward to 0045 hours. Furthermore, intelligence reported a convoy moving toward the bridge. Higgins got his company loaded immediately, the helicopters lifted off amid the gunfire, and screamed for the bridge. What follows is a first-hand account of the action.

On December 20th, 1989, my Special Forces unit was to secure the Pacora River bridge and deny enemy access to it. The mission was to prevent the Battalion 2000 from sending troops, ammunition, and weapons to reinforcing Panama Defense Forces at Torrijos International Airport where the Rangers and 82d Airborne had mounted an effective assault. Prior to departure from Albrook we received fire from Panama Defense Forces. We were on our way in three MH-60 helicopters with our 24-man element. Within fifteen minutes we were over the objective. The enemy convoy was below us now. We arrived at the bridge at the exact moment the lead vehicle of the enemy convoy began to cross. We then dismounted the helicopters and onto the road. Within seconds, four men jumped out into the road, and in succession, fired light anti-tank weapons at the lead vehicles of the enemy convoy. The convoy kept coming. We then launched the mother of all anti-tank weapons, the AT-4. This did in fact stop the enemy convoy. We then called on our Air Force Combat Controller to service the enemy convoy with an AC-130 gunship. This was very effective. After the AC-130 gunship stopped firing, the enemy dismounted their vehicles leaving the engines running, lights on and doors open. We then called for another hit from the Spectre gunship to take out the lead vehicle's engine. The first 105 Howitzer round that was fired did in fact take out the lead vehicle's engine. After Spectre stopped firing once again, my medic and I approached the bridge to emplace claymore mines. As I was emplacing my claymore mine I saw three enemy soldiers approaching my position. I then rolled out into the road, shooting at point blank range killing one and wounding two. We continued to hold our position. At 0600 hours our quick reaction forces arrived. No Americans were harmed.[5]

Had it not been for the flexibility and superior training of the troops involved in this operation, it might very well have failed. With the adjustment in H-hour and the information on the convoy, the helicopter pilots had to adjust their routes to shorten flight time: no easy task given the congested air space over Panama that night. Moreover, because of the firing at Albrook, the aircraft had taken numerous hits, making their airworthiness questionable.

Once A Company arrived and secured the bridge, they found their enemy to be particularly tenacious. They would attempt counter-attacks, in small groups, during any lull in the Spectre firing. At one point, an undetermined number of Panamanians got under the bridge, but a medic threw several grenades under the bridge, stopping the movement.

Upon arrival of the Quick Reaction Force, at 0600 hours, Higgins had the entire force sweep the area. Several enemy soldiers were found cowering in houses. The enemy wounded were treated by Special Forces Medics. Following the sweep, A Company established checkpoints on the bridge. Finally, at 1430 hours that afternoon, the Special Forces were relieved by the 82d Airborne Division, whereupon they returned, with their prisoners, to Albrook.

OPERATION MA BELL

Innovation is a key characteristic of Army special operations. It is innovation that frequently enables SOF to undertake some tasks more efficiently and safely than conventional forces. Operation MA BELL[6] clearly illustrated the tremendous influence small SOF units can generate through the innovative use of combat power.

The Special Forces company that relieved Major Higgins at Pacora River was subsequently relieved by troops of the 82d Airborne Division and commenced a mission to neutralize enemy independent forces located in four western provinces of Panama. The objective of this operation was not to destroy these units, but to force their surrender with minimum casualties.

AC-130 Spectre gunships, army helicopters and conventional troops from the 7th Infantry Division provided support to the Special Forces for this operation. A key component of the plan was the use of the local telephone system, which caused the soldiers to dub it Operation MA BELL. Here is the company commander's account of how this operation proceeded:

A Special Forces A Team would be flown by helicopter to a landing zone near the Panamanian garrison. As we off-loaded the aircraft, the AC-130 would orbit around the Panamanian garrison. Speaking Spanish, I would use the phone, located sometimes in a farmer's home, and call the Panamanian commander. I would then tell him to look up in the sky at the AC-130 and then threatened death, unless he surrendered. The AC-130 proved to be a powerful threat and a great motivator. All missions were accomplished, no shots were fired, no civilians killed, and no civilian property damaged. In one garrison, we raised the Panamanian flag ... symbolizing that our goal was not to defeat Panama, but to liberate the Panamanian people from years of corruption and tyranny. This operation, in my eyes, embodies the value of Special Forces training in unique, special skills. It also embodies the Special Forces motto: De Oppresso Libre – To Liberate the Oppressed!'[7]

CIVIL AFFAIRS

President Bush was adamant that the US objective was to free Panama from the clutches of a renegade dictator and eliminate the instruments of repression that kept him in power. With that objective achieved, the United States had to help the Panamanians restore order before it disengaged. Bush wanted that done rapidly so the Panamanian people could get on with their lives.

Panama had a freely elected president before the US intervention. Guillermo Endara had been elected in May but Noriega stole the election from him. Therefore, the US policy was quickly to install Endara and his administration to their rightful positions, to fill the vacuum left by the removal of the Noriega regime.

This objective became the mission of a relatively new tool in the arsenal of US Army Special Operations Command: the newly formed US Army Reserve Special Operations Command (USARSOC). The majority of USARSOC units were in the reserves, although they did have one active duty unit, the 96th Civil Affairs (CA) Battalion, located at Fort Bragg, North Carolina. Consequently, the 96th CA Battalion deployed with the Rangers to Panama in the early morning hours on 20 December.[8]

As the Rangers were clearing and securing Tocumen Airfield, Torrijos International Airport, and Rio Hato Airfield, soldiers of the 96th ran collection points for prisoners, wounded and civilians. They later assisted units of the 82d Airborne Division when they linked up with and relieved the Rangers.

Our mission was to help the Panamanians get their country running again. To do that, we had to be on the ground during the initial invasion to coordinate with the military intelligence, military police and ground-forces commanders. We continued activities during ongoing operations to render humanitarian assistance.

Major Harold E. Williams
Commander, A Company
96th CA Battalion

After parachuting into to the Tocumen/Torrijos complex, the soldiers of the 96th split up, accompanying the assault forces going into both airports. At the PDF barracks at Tocumen, Corporal Ricardo Barrios performed the first civil affairs action of the intervention: he processed detainees by sorting out which were bona fide prisoners-of-war and which were civilians. At the Torrijos Airport Terminal, 96th CA soldiers conducted field interrogations and searches for information of immediate tactical value to the Rangers. During this procedure, Sergeant Miguel Barbosa-Figueroa discovered there were eight Department of National Investigations (DENI) agents still hiding in their office. He and another soldier then went and found the agents, forcing them to surrender.

Once the initial assaults were over, the 96th immediately found that they needed a lot of help in their mission to get Panama back on its feet. Unfortunately the only potential reinforcement for the 96th was in the reserves, and President Bush had decided against a reserve mobilization. Consequently, USARSOC put out a call for volunteers within twenty-four hours of the invasion. Initially 600 reservists answered that call to participate in Operation PROMOTE LIBERTY and the number grew to several thousand before the operation was over.

The reserve civil affairs soldiers were organized into the Civil Military Operations Task Force, or CMOTF, under the command of Colonel William H. Stone, Commander of the 361st Civil Affairs Brigade in Panama. President Endara requested American assistance to advise his government ministries as they organized. Colonel Stone then organized CA teams to advise the finance, public works, health and justice ministries, as well as the Office of the President. Brigadier General Bernard Gann, the director of plans and policy for USSOUTHCOM, operationally controlled these teams.

Under this program, US civil affairs soldiers helped to provide humanitarian aid to civilians displaced by the fighting, to restore the public health system, and to get the local and national law enforcement agencies reformed and running again. Unfortunately, almost everyone in Panama with law enforcement experience had been in the PDF. Rather than leave these people out 'in the cold,' President Endara decided to co-opt them by retraining them and incorporating them into the new law enforcement system. US personnel helped to inculcate responsiveness to law and civilian rule into these reformed policemen.

Although severely hindered by the lack of a reserve mobilization, the civil affairs activities undertaken in support of Operation JUST CAUSE were crucial to getting order restored in Panama. They assisted in the re-establishment of strong democratic institutions that serve as a bulwark against tyranny. The US Army Civil Affairs effort resulted in a rapid restoration of democratic freedoms, essential services, and the speedy disengagement of US combat forces.

The Gulf War, 1990–1

No sooner had the bulk of Army SOF redeployed from Panama, than they were confronted with another mission. On 2 August 1992, Iraqi forces invaded

Kuwait. Since the US had no immediate capability to respond to the aggression, the prime concern was to deter further Iraqi aggression against Saudi Arabia. Within days the 82d Airborne Division was holding the line.

Following UN resolutions, General Norman Schwarzkopf, Commander-in-Chief, Joint Forces Central Command, was faced with building a coalition force from scratch. Although British and French forces had their NATO experience to guide them in coalition warfighting procedures, the Arab forces had not actively participated in any sort of collective security relationship. This presented myriad problems. To start with, the Egyptian, Syrian, Saudi Arabian and other Arab units had to learn how to participate in an allied formation. All the allies had to learn each other's procedural, organizational and cultural idiosyncrasies. As with Iraq, much of the Arab allied equipment was of Soviet make, making enemy vehicle recognition a major problem. Getting this coalition force to fight as a team, in short order, would be a monumental undertaking.

Faced with this task, Schwarzkopf called in the 5th Special Forces Group, from Fort Campbell, Kentucky, to help.

COALITION WARFARE

During a command post exercise a month before the invasion, Colonel Jesse Johnson, the Commander of Special Operations Command USCENTCOM (SOCCENT), and Lieutenant General John Yeosock, Commander, 3d US Army, had discussed the role of Special Forces in coalition warfare. The fundamental issue was how to integrate disparate allied forces together for a coordinated attack.

Then came the invasion of Kuwait, which led to the real need for an international military coalition.

Initially, on 13 August 1990, Navy SEAL platoons deployed into Saudi Arabia to advise and assist Saudi National Guard units on the frontier in controlling close air support, should have been needed. SEALs were initially selected for this mission because General Schwarzkopf had delayed deployment of the 5th Special Forces Group in order to free up available airlift and sealift assets to get his conventional firepower into theater as quickly as possible. SEAL advisory operations were highly successful, but had to be terminated when the 5th Special Forces Group arrived to relieve them on 5 September, so that the SEALs could get on with vital maritime missions.

5th Group was to provide liaison and conduct foreign internal defense (FID) operations with the Royal Saudi Land Forces (RSLF) and, as they arrived in theater, with the Pan-Arab forces. General Schwarzkopf assigned a second mission to conduct special reconnaissance and early warning along the Saudi–Kuwaiti frontier, since he lacked timely, precise, tactical intelligence about what was happening there. By November, six A Detachments, in concert with

Saudi paratroopers, were manning nine border outposts. During the day they conducted combined mounted patrols throughout their sectors, trained with their Saudi counterparts, maintained liaison with flank units, and visually reconnoitered from border forts. At night the Saudis conducted mounted patrols at high speed with headlights blazing – much to the dismay of the Special Forces soldiers – to find line-crossers and refugees, as well as to look for any indications of attack.

As the conventional forces arrived in theater, General Schwarzkopf directed the 5th Group to assist with the reconstitution of the Kuwaiti Army. Only one Kuwaiti army unit escaped Kuwait with any of its equipment. It was reconstituted as an armor brigade, with brand new Yugoslavian T-84 tanks, purchased from Yugoslavia complete with the technical manuals. Over time, USCENTCOM constituted an additional five Kuwaiti light infantry brigades from Kuwaiti refugees, expatriates, and students who had returned from abroad to help free their homeland. The Special Forces trained each of these units and assisted in equipping them. They paid particular attention to making sure the recruits were trained in basic human rights, the Geneva Conventions and basic civil affairs.

The Kuwaiti Army in training was considerably different from the US Army. There was no professional non-commissioned officer (NCO) corps, and consequently, officers were responsible for everything. Generally, these officers were arrogant and not particularly well schooled in military art and as a result the Kuwaiti units became highly dependent on their Special Forces advisors for direction and leadership.[9]

Concurrently, other Special Forces soldiers were formed into four-man advisor teams and deployed in all the Pan-Arab units down to battalion level. They brought their own communications gear and interpreters to make sure that their units could maintain communications with their coalition partners and to iron out any confusion that arose once the battle was joined. These teams provided General Schwarzkopf with 'ground truth' information on their unit's locations, status, capabilities and intent. They were also prepared to jump in and exercise leadership, if necessary.

When the ground war started there were 106 of these teams deployed throughout the coalition. In the Egyptian and Saudi sectors, Special Forces troops led the way through the obstacle belts and were the first troops up on their first day's objectives. In the Saudi zone, Special Forces troops provided flank security and unilaterally engaged in close combat to clear a number of enemy units hindering the Saudi advance. They suffered no losses.

The result of the Special Forces effort was that the theory of coalition warfare became a reality. Two heavy, allied corps of Pan-Arab forces became effective, contributing members of the coalition team, and ultimately liberated Kuwait City. As the free Kuwaiti forces made their victorious entrance, they were accompanied by their partners: the 5th Special Forces Group (Airborne).

The 5th Group also performed several special reconnaissance missions in support of the 3d US Army. These teams were inserted up to 165 miles inside Iraq to provide early warning of enemy counter-attacks. Teams were deployed to observe the Iraqi theater reserve, the Republican Guards, as well as the roads between central Iraq and Kuwait. Should they spot any troop movements, into or out of the theater, they were to report. These teams were placed under the operational control of the XVIII Airborne Corps, in the far west, and the VII Corps to their immediate east, which was the main effort.

On 23 February 1991, Special Reconnaissance missions (SR) 008B and 005[10] were inserted deep into Iraq and had quite similar experiences. SR 008B was a three-man team commanded by a Master Sergeant that infiltrated to the Euphrates river valley, deep in Iraq, the night before the coalition ground attack. Under the operational control of XVIII Airborne Corps, the team was to report on any Iraqi forces or military vehicles moving into or out of the Corps sector.

As their helicopter landed and the team disembarked, they aroused, one member said, '250 dogs' that immediately began barking. No doubt the team was inserted near a camp of wandering Bedouins, who were always accompanied by large numbers of dogs. Alarmed, the team ran four kilometers to their hide site and dug in. The site was located in a mound of dirt in a cultivated field, near the intersection of two drainage ditches. By daylight they were well hidden and reporting on the highway traffic and railroad running through their area.

As the sun rose, the fields began to fill up as shepherds and their families tended their grazing goats, sheep and camels. With all this traffic, it was only a matter of time before the team was discovered. Then at midday it happened: a little girl and her father peered into the rear exit hole of the site and saw the team. Two members of the team charged out to capture the pair, only to discover twenty more Bedouins watching. Releasing the man and the girl, the team packed a rucksack with their essential gear and had moved down the drainage ditch approximately 100 meters when the Bedouins opened fire on them. The Iraqi government had put a price on the head of downed pilots, and the Bedouins had apparently mistaken these soldiers for pilots. The team ran another 100 meters down the ditch.

As the first shots were fired, the team radio operator called for immediate close air support and an emergency exfiltration. As the team worked its way up the ditch, they saw the Bedouin man who had originally discovered them stopping buses loaded with enemy soldiers. Team members began to selectively engage Iraqis who were firing from rooftops across the highway. As some of the enemy soldiers tried to flank the team, they took them under fire.

An hour-and-a-half after the battle began, an F-16 fighter rolled in responding to the call for air support. Unable to identify the team's location on the ground, the fighter dropped a 1,000lb bomb, allowing the team to adjust subsequent bombing runs from its crater. The Iraqi attack stalled as the pilot continued his attack with cluster bombs, killing some fifty enemy soldiers. But between runs, the enemy relentlessly pressed the attack, attempting to encircle the team.

In the mid-afternoon, the team leader heard the approach of their exfiltration helicopter – an MH-60 Black Hawk from the 160th Special Operations Aviation Regiment (SOAR) flown by Chief Warrant Officer James (Monk) Chrisafulli. According to the team leader, the Blackhawk 'was screaming down the road, going around 140 knots, on one side of a 20-foot power line, six feet off the deck.' The team popped a white pen flare to mark the location and the pilot jumped the helicopter over the power line, 'put the nose straight at us, swung it all the way around straight up, and then he slammed it right in.' Another team member later recounted: 'It was some flying. Matter of fact, my mouth kind of dropped. I just never saw flying like that.' The team at first feared that the helicopter had been shot down, but later realized that 'no, it was controlled . . . like a ballet with that aircraft.' As the team charged out of the ditch for the helicopter, the door gunners laid withering fire on the Iraqis with their mini-guns. As the soldiers mounted up, the pilot lifted off and, at an altitude of perhaps ten or twenty feet, roared back to friendly lines. The aircraft had been so heavily damaged by enemy fire that it was grounded for the remainder of the war.

Chief Warrant Officer Chrisafulli and his copilot, Chief Warrant Officer Randy Stephens, were awarded the Distinguished Flying Cross. The team leader was awarded the Silver Star for Gallantry. The remainder of the soldiers involved in this action were each presented with the Bronze Star for Valor.

CIVIL AFFAIRS AND PSYCHOLOGICAL OPERATIONS

CEASE RESISTANCE –
BE SAFE

To seek refuge safely, the bearer must strictly adhere to the following procedures.

1. Remove the magazine from your weapon.
2. Sling your weapon over your left shoulder, muzzle down.
3. Have both arms raised above your head.

4. Approach the Multi-National Forces' positions slowly, with the lead soldier holding this document above his head.
5. If you do this, you will not die.

Coalition Psyops Leaflet
(English Translation from Arabic)

When President Bush called a halt to offensive operations on 28 February, it
caused a problem for the Commander of the 3d Brigade, 82d Airborne Division. Forward of his brigade's positions was Tallil Air Base, the largest Iraqi Air
Force base in southern Iraq, and he was under orders to seize it. Just as he was
getting ready to take this objective, the President called 'quits.' Fortunately, the
450th Civil Affairs (CA) Company, a reserve unit from Riverdale Maryland, was
attached to his brigade and their commander had a plan.

Under the command of the 450th CA Company Commander, a Lieutenant
Colonel, the Brigade Commander established Task Force (TF) Psyops consisting of the 450th, some military police, and utility helicopters. Tanks and
attack helicopters would be on call if the unit got into trouble. Their mission
was to talk the Iraqi troops at Tallil into either fleeing or surrendering.

The operation began as a helicopter flew over the air base and, via loudspeaker, broadcast a message to the Iraqis to surrender. Immediately following
the broadcast, the Task Force infiltrated the air base and seized the control
tower. Again the 450th broadcast a surrender message, this time from the
control tower. Several Iraqis opened fire, but as they realized their situation
appeared hopeless, some fifty of them surrendered. About 100 Iraqis took off
running to the north and fled the base.

The booty: twenty top-of-the-line Iraqi jets, five Soviet-made helicopters,
and tons of supplies. The base had been taken without US forces firing a shot
and hence was not part of the offensive operation.

On 1 March, Task Force Psyops turned over the base to the 1st Battalion,
505th Parachute Infantry Regiment, and was disbanded. The 450th returned
to its normal mission of controlling civilians, refugees and prisoners-of-war. The
unit ended the war by establishing Camp Mercy, in southern Iraq, to provide
aid and comfort to Shi'ite Iraqis that fled Iraqi governmental persecution.

As a result of a request to the US Department of Defense by the Emir of
Kuwait, the Joint Staff, through USSOCOM, directed the United States Civil
Affairs and Psychological Operations Command (USACAPOC) (pronounced
ew sah kay' pok) to organize civil affairs specialists into the Kuwaiti Task Force
(KTF). The Civil–Military Operations Task Force used in Panama served as a
model for the KTF which assisted the various ministries in the Kuwaiti government in preparing for the reestablishment of basic governmental infrastructure.

Simultaneously, a Combined Civil Affairs Task Force (CCATF) undertook emergency restoration of essential services. This group concentrated on the immediate provision of food, water, medical support, electrical power, sanitation, telecommunications and transportation. The objective was to relieve the immediate suffering of the Kuwaitis, until government and business began functioning again.

The Kurdish Uprising, 1991–3

As the Gulf War concluded, Special Operations Command, Europe (SOCEUR) planned the conduct of Operation PROVIDE COMFORT to provide humanitarian aid to Kurdish tribesmen who had rebelled against the Iraqi government. The 1st Battalion, 10th Special Forces Group (Airborne), from Bad Tolz, Germany, units of the US Army Civil Affairs and Psychological Operations Command (USACAPOC), along with Air Force, Marine, and coalition units conducted the operation to provide food, shelter, and supplies to the Kurds, and ultimately return them to their homes in northern Iraq.

The mission of the 10th Special Forces Group (Airborne) and USACAPOC units was to coordinate the administration of refugee camps established in southern Turkey. 10th Group teams deployed into Kurdish mountain camps and coordinated aerial resupply operations with MC-130 Combat Talon Hercules and, later, MH-53 Pave Low, CH-47 Chinook, and RH-53 Sea Stallion helicopters. 1st Battalion, 10th Group began moving into the camps on 16 April 1991. A Company deployed to a camp at Isikveren, Turkey with an estimated 80,000 Kurds. B Company deployed a few days later to care for the 70,000 people at Yekmal. C Company was split up to cover smaller camps. When the 2d Battalion, 10th Special Forces Group (Airborne) arrived from Fort Devens, Massachusetts, it deployed to camps at Pirinceken, Uzumlu, and Cucurka, near the Iranian border, containing a total of over 180,000 Kurds.

The Special Forces soldiers worked not only with their civil affairs partners, but with several non-governmental organizations as well. *Medecins sans Frontiers* (Doctors Without Borders), a French organization, the international Red Cross, and the Red Crescent were already working in some of the camps. In those camps where effective medical organizations were already functioning, the SF allowed them to continue. Where there was no medical organization, the Special Forces established one.

On 20 April, the coalition established a safe haven for the Kurds, in northern Iraq. As conventional coalition forces from the Netherlands, United Kingdom, and the United States cleared Iraqi military units from the territory in northern Iraq, Special Forces, Civil Affairs, and Psychological Operations soldiers coordinated the movement of Kurdish refugees back into their homes. The major challenge was to convince the Kurds that they would be safe in their homes in Iraq. Working with Kurdish and Iraqi leadership, the US leadership negotiated on behalf of the Kurds for their safety. Once the Kurdish leadership was convinced that their people would be secure, they encouraged their return to their homes.

As of this writing, a small coalition force remains in southern Turkey at Silopi to intervene should Iraqi persecution of the Kurds resume. Responsibility for the security of Iraqi Kurds has been handed over to the United Nations. The coalition legacy was best summed up by a senior American officer, who said: 'The Iraqis would like to view our involvement here as just another tile on the mosaic. For us, it must be more than that. The picture isn't clear until the last tile is in place. The question to our leadership is: who places the last tile on the mosaic?'

Conclusions

The most recent stage in the development of Army SOF has clearly shown that they are not only superb warfighters, but have become particularly effective in crisis intervention: operations short of war. Special Forces, Rangers, and Special Operations Aviation regained the standards of excellence they had demonstrated in the latter stages of Vietnam. Skilled integration of psychological operations personnel and equipment with both special and conventional forces effectively saved lives and articulated to enemies and allies alike US foreign policy concerns. Finally, the civil affairs units for the first time were able to prove their worth, as they moved in and assisted devastated nations and governments in repairing the damage of war.

Operation PROVIDE COMFORT was a relatively new concept that had to be undertaken because of a tremendous foreign policy gaffe: the US should not have advocated rebellion against Saddam Hussein unless it was prepared to assist. So dictates the law of unintended consequences. Iraqi Shi'ites paid for this error with their blood. Many Kurds lost their lives and property when they rebelled with the expectation of American assistance. Although late in coming, US Army SOF saved many Kurdish lives when it intervened in Turkey and northern Iraq to mitigate Kurdish suffering and return survivors to their homes. Unfortunately, until Saddam Hussein and the present Iraqi political system are gone, the Kurds and Shi'ites will remain in jeopardy because of their ill-fated, US-instigated, rebellion. This is one of the most important lessons of the Gulf War, but it should have been learned thirty years before, at the Bay of Pigs, in Cuba.

NOTES

1. Thomas Donnelly, Margaret Roth, and Caleb Baker, *Operation Just Cause; the Storming of Panama* (New York, Lexington Books, 1991), p. 206.
2. Office of the Historian, US Army Special Operations Command, papers, untitled and undated, describing various special operations during Operation JUST CAUSE (unclassified), Tab H, Ranger Hostage Rescue.

3. Specialist Eubanks' account of this operation states that this action took place on the third floor of the terminal. Donnelly, Roth and Baker, in their book, indicate it took place on the second floor. In this case the author went with the eyewitness account.

4. Donnelly, Roth and Baker, *Operation Just Cause*, p. 210.

5. US Special Operations Command Presentation, Association of the United States Army (AUSA) Convention, Washington, DC, 13 October 1992.

6. 'Ma Bell' was the popular nickname for the American Bell Telephone company.

7. US Special Operations Command Presentation, Association of the United States Army Convention, Washington, DC, 13 October 1992.

8. *Special Warfare* (Spring, 1990). This account comes from an untitled compilation of work from several authors including Lieutenant Colonel Jeffery Greenhut and Captain Gerry Gray of the 354 CA Brigade, Captain Cynthia Crosson of the 353 CA Command, Captain Robert N. Gable of the 486th CA Company, Lieutenant Colonel Susan Schenk of the 364th CA Brigade, Captain Terry Henry of the 96th CA Battalion, and Staff Sergeant Kirk Wyckoff of the JFK Special Warfare Center and School.

9. Greg Walker, 'From Refugees to Liberators' *Soldier of Fortune* magazine, June 1992, p. 64.

10. A superb account of SR 005, commanded by Chief Warrant Officer Richard 'Bulldog' Balwanz, is contained in the May 1992 issue of *Soldier of Fortune* magazine.

CHAPTER 12

Naval Special Warfare in the New Order 1986–92

The men of Naval Special Warfare (NSW) conducted a wide variety of missions during the late eighties and early nineties, although their operations received little media reporting. In addition to their contributions to the actions in Panama and the Persian Gulf, Navy special operations forces conducted several behind-the-scenes operations in Latin America and the Philippines in support of Presidential initiatives. Political high visibility, original and unconventional plans, and sudden, violent action characterized the missions planned and executed by modern maritime special operators.

Persian Gulf Operations, 1987–90

In 1987, the decade-old conflict between Iran and Iraq began to interfere with commerce and freedom of the seas in the Persian Gulf, just as USSOCOM and its NSW component, Naval Special Warfare Command (NSWC) were being established. The Commander of the Middle East Force (CMEF), a standing Naval headquarters presence in the Persian Gulf since 1948, transitioned virtually overnight into Commander, Joint Task Force Middle East (CJTFME). Part of the force structure identified to support this organization and its expanded mission was a relatively heavy SOF contingent under the leadership of NSW officers.

In August 1987, Naval Special Warfare Groups (NSWG) One and Two were alerted to deploy forces to the Persian Gulf to support military operations collectively referred to as Operation EARNEST WILL. EARNEST WILL was put into motion to provide protection for US and allied flagged bulk petroleum carriers and other ships crossing the Persian Gulf. The operation evolved into a military presence that deterred offshore hostile activities by both Iraqi and (principally) Iranian forces, strengthened ties with the Gulf nations and set the stage for the tight coalition effort needed in 1991 during Operations DESERT SHIELD and DESERT STORM.

The NSW assets which deployed for four-month periods were organized as a NSW Task Group (NSWTG) comprised of two NSW Task Units (NSWTU). Combatant craft and certain Army helicopters were to form the core of the force package for the next twenty-four months, conducting around-the-clock

Naval Special Warfare
Command Organization

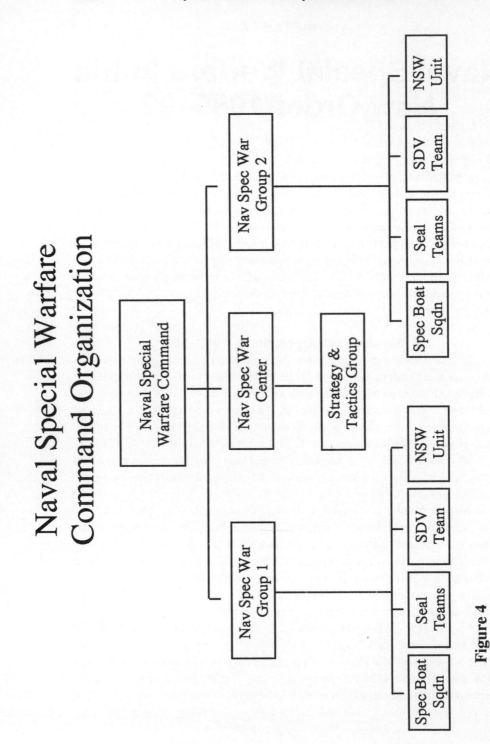

Figure 4

operations to protect the natural sea lines of communications and US interests in and around Bahrain from hostile action by Iranian forces.

The initial NSWTG Commander, co-located with CJTFME on his flagship, conceived the concept of Mobile Support Bases (MSBs) which would function as afloat staging areas for the NSW forces and other attached offensive, defensive and support assets.[1] Two MSBs were established, each supporting a NSWTU. The MSBs were, in fact, leased offshore oil field support barges that were turned into floating fortresses. They were normally positioned in the natural choke point between the Iranian island of Farsi in the central Persian Gulf, and the shallows in Saudi Arabian territory to the west. In these international waters the NSW mission was to sustain day and night patrols with patrol craft and helicopters to deter Iranian activity and watch for floating mines that could endanger commerce or other maritime activity.

The MSB concept, which was a revisit to a concept born during Vietnam, proved to be an unqualified success. These were true joint military endeavors. In addition to the assigned NSW contingent, normally a SEAL platoon, two MK III Patrol boat (PB) detachments of four boats and a headquarters element, there was a reinforced US Marine platoon assigned to provide barge security, a Vulcan anti-aircraft detachment from the 82nd Airborne Division with two weapons (20mm gatling guns) for air and surface defense, two rotary wing detachments comprised of four to six observation and Combat Search and Rescue (CSAR) aircraft, as well as headquarters augmentees from all services supporting intelligence, communications, medical, and maintenance requirements.

Almost immediately after being established in 1987, the collective efforts of this task force resulted in the capture of an Iranian craft (the Iran Ajr) confirmed to be engaged in mine-laying activities. Other Iranian small craft attempting hostile mischief were engaged and dispatched (blown out of the water, sunk, or simply chased away) by attached helicopters. Combatant craft and assigned SEAL platoons continually rehearsed and trained for various offensive missions to counter increasing Iranian boldness.

In late 1987 armed army helicopters engaged an Iranian speedboat in the central Persian Gulf. The craft, a 43-foot Swedish-built Boghammer, was sunk by the effects of a 2.75-inch rocket. For intelligence exploitation purposes, it was raised from its resting place at a depth of over 100 feet and initially found a home on one of the MSBs. It was returned to a naval engineering activity, rebuilt and used for radar measurement studies. It was subsequently transferred to Special Boat Squadron One where it was used as an aggressor craft during fleet pre-deployment training. It served, along with a 31-foot Iranian Guards gunboat that was found adrift after a minor surface engagement in the Gulf and returned to the US, as a realistic and effective training aid for numerous west coast-based ships heading for potential confrontations with similar craft during and after Operation EARNEST WILL.

Four-month deployments (six for the Marines) were routinely without benefit of liberty ashore. Personnel would arrive in Bahrain, transfer to a (leased and unarmed) support vessel, cross to their assigned MSB, and remain there almost totally out of sight of land for the duration of their deployment. The harshness of the environment – over 100 degrees Fahrenheit air temperatures, 100 percent humidity, ninety-five degree water temperature and high winds/ frequent dust storms (at sea!) – presented challenges to men and equipment. Combatant craft required constant maintenance and the harshness of the sea conditions took their toll on the aluminum MK III PBs, requiring several to be completely rebuilt after withdrawal and all to require continuous repair. Weapons, even if not fired, had to be cleaned daily, and electronic equipment continually failed. The primary key to the successes of this military endeavor revolved around the young sailors as well as the soldiers, airmen, Marines and some Coast Guardsmen, led by their senior petty officer/chief petty officer supervisors, and their unfailing efforts to sustain operational capabilities. This 24-month operation was accomplished without any personnel or material casualties.[2]

Also in support of CJTFME was a four-boat harbor/anchorage security detachment based in Bahrain. This detachment, resourced from Special Boat Unit Eleven (a Naval Reserve Force command) operated MK II PBRs (Patrol Boats, Riverine), Vietnam vintage craft designed for use on inland waterways. This detachment, in theatre from day one of the operation, conducted patrols of the inner harbor of Bahrain and the offshore anchorage (called Sitrah) nearly twenty-four hours each day for two years. Many of the men who served their four-month tour, working out of wooden sheds at the end of Mina Sulman pier, were reservists who volunteered for this duty. They performed professionally and effectively, although almost totally outside the operational environment for which they normally trained.

Toward the end of the joint commitment to EARNEST WILL, the assigned SEAL platoon began to cross-train with Bahraini and Saudi Arabian special forces, establishing relationships that would prove invaluable during the early stages of coalition operations in the Gulf War of 1990-1.

It is not too bold to say that without the original ingenuity that established the MSB concept and the follow-on support efforts of NSW, and augmenting conventional and special operations force assets, this military endeavor might not have been the success that it was.

Panama, 1989

As USSOCOM was going through adolescence in its maturation process as a command, another major military confrontation involving numerous SOF assets occurred in Central America. On the night of 20 December 1989, a series of well-planned and rehearsed military actions commenced within the confines of the Panama, under the operational name of JUST CAUSE.[3] NSW forces were to see intense and varied involvement, conducting a variety of high-visibility missions supporting both unconventional and conventional strategies.

A critical operation involved sinking a 65-foot Panamanian patrol boat at Balboa Naval Station, just south of Miaflores locks. This craft could have either sortied and complicated gaining quick control of the Pacific entrance to the canal or been used by Noriega to make good his escape.

Four combat swimmers from SEAL Team Two clandestinely placed explosives that sent the craft quickly to the bottom. However, the operation began to deviate from the original plan almost as soon as it began. One member of the team described provided this account of the action:

On the night of December 19, 1989, I was one of four divers from a SEAL Team who was inserted into the waters of the Panama Canal. Our mission was to attach huge sacks of plastic explosives to the hull of . . . an armed 65-foot coastal patrol boat that belonged to the Panamanian Navy, and was to be used as a means of escape for General Noriega. We used an oxygen re-breather which allowed us to remain submerged for over three hours without making any bubbles. We successfully completed infiltration to the target and secured our charges to the hull and continued on to the extraction location. At exactly 0100 hours on December 20th, at a time preset by us before entering the water, the charges detonated, and the vessel sank beneath the waters of Balboa harbor. Throughout the mission, we had to react to numerous situations which forced us to use all the tricks of the trade from years of combat-proven training. During emplacement of the charges, several fire fights on shore broke out, resulting in a series of underwater explosions in close proximity to us. While there is nothing a diver can do about underwater explosions, except try to avoid them, our level of training allowed us to continue the mission, uninterrupted. Next, while en route to the extraction location, a freighter making its way up the canal, forced us to dive to a depth of over fifty feet in order to avoid being run over. That exposed us to a different type of threat since pure oxygen can be toxic at depths greater than twenty feet. It was instantly apparent that our emphasis on the highest possible physical fitness standards was about to pay off. Our mission lasted about four hours and was the exact type of mission SEALs train for every day.[4]

NSW personnel conducted several other missions, which included positioning a SEAL force to engage PDF (Panamanian Defense Forces) units bottled up on Flamenco Island. These PDF forces were never a threat to the operation.

To seal off one escape route for the PDF and Noriega, a small flotilla of special boats, augmented by a small SEAL contingent, detached from Rodman Naval Station to control the Caribbean entrance to the canal at Colon. The MK II PBRs prevented attempts by PDF to flee by sea, captured numerous and surrendering PDF troops and hundreds of weapons.

One particularly unique action had a three-man team of SEALs and 'boat people' (slang for sailors specializing in special boat operations) in an indigenous canoe called a *cayuga* positioning themselves offshore east of Panama City to observe the approaches from Torrijos Airport down Avenida Balboa. They provided real-time reporting on PDF movements that could have disrupted friendly operations.

Unfortunately, of the several NSW missions which complemented the overall battle plan, the one involving the largest number of personnel was to have disastrous results.

As the capture of Noriega was a primary objective of Operation JUST CAUSE, Paitilla Airfield had to be secured to prevent Noriega from using its aircraft to make good his escape. This objective was five miles northeast of the entrance to the Panama Canal and a known location of one of Noriega's aircraft. The mission given to a SEAL contingent from NSW Group (NSWG) Two was to deny Noriega the use of this airfield and specifically his Lear Jet. The following synopsis focuses on the vulnerabilities of the plan and the people who executed it.

The mission itself was relatively simple. A force of SEALs would land from sea during hours of darkness and proceed to the aircraft, disable it, foul the runway with obstacles and establish a security position in case Noriega or his henchmen showed up at the airfield. With a MK III PB[5] served as an escort and command and control platform for the mission, over eighty SEALS and Air Force Combat Control Team (AFCCT) personnel crossed the five miles to Paitilla in F-470 Zodiac inflatable boats. While en route to the beach landing site Joint Task Force commander advanced the timetable for the mission, causing the mission commander to rally his forces afloat for an orders update. Once seaward of the airfield, swimmer scouts proceeded ashore to observe and report any activity.

Paitilla is essentially in downtown Panama City, being bounded on the north and west by residential high rise buildings and to the east by an area of slum dwellings. The airfield is 5,000 feet long running north and south. Along its western boundary is a series of hangars; a lesser number are along the eastern boundary, with the terminal being on the northeast corner of the complex.

The swimmer scouts determined that there was no observable enemy activity and gave the signal to land. The boats proceeded to shore and the operators moved tactically inland and assumed positions ready to advance on their objective. At this time, a radio message again changed their timetable, due apparently to a report that Noriega was inbound on board a helicopter from Colon.

The force package, organized into three platoons and a headquarters/support element, was complemented by an AC-130 gunship overhead. The SEAL platoons began a hasty patrol, at a run, toward the hangar and encountered several civilians. These were told to stay away from the runway.

For inexplicable reasons, the AFCCT could not establish contact with the AC-130; a critical failure as the AC-130 had sensors that could detect and classify activity on the ground. It also had devastating firepower that would attack any activity it observed with pin-point accuracy. When the lead element of the assault team passed the target hangar en route to a security position, they were ambushed by a PDF security unit and took several casualties. The SEALs returned a high volume of effective fire on the hangar suppressing the hostile fire. A second burst of gunfire resulted in a casualty in the reserve platoon that was now hustling across the runway to give support. The SEALs again responded with effective suppressive fire, established a security perimeter, and tended to their wounded. Three SEALs were now dead with a fourth to die later while en route to a hospital in the US. Seven men were wounded, five seriously. The SEALs called for a medical evacuation helicopter, which arrived over an hour later to evacuate the casualties. Reinforcements also arrived. A firm security position was established in the terminal building where the total force remained for the next thirty hours, after which they were relieved by elements of the 82d Airborne Division.

The action at Paitilla is still an excellent case study on whether or not a given mission is appropriate for a special operations unit. While unit-level tactics and techniques are essentially the same, or at least variations on a theme for all military units required to engage in ground maneuver, certain principles of warfare must be observed during the decision process leading to mission allocation and during detailed mission planning for a special operation. A brief analysis of Paitilla as it related to these primary axioms may provide insight on the basic question – whose mission should this have been and how should it have been executed?

Several factors should have been considered by the Joint Task Force planners when they determined which force was best suited for this mission. A key factor in determining that a special operations unit is suited for an operation is the necessity for economy of effort. Any military endeavor should plan on a primary assault force, a command and control element and a reserve. Even in a small squad or fire-team sized action this provision should not be overlooked. A force of eighty-four SEALs and AFCCT operators was an excessively large force for this or any other special operation meant to remain low key. Mission planners considered the large number of personnel necessary to ensure the ability to maintain security and command and control while simultaneously performing certain tasks requiring strength and separation of elements.

The plan to foul the airstrip by pushing aircraft and rolling stock on to the tarmac may have justified, to some, the need for more personnel. But the nature of a large force maneuvering in a relatively confined area made it impossible to conceal the intentions, let alone the actual presence of a nearly company-size force. There is solid evidence that during the beach landing some Panamanians, who may have been off-duty PDF personnel, noticed the movement of the bulk of the force (but not the swimmer scouts). Seeing several dozen obviously armed men land on sovereign Panamanian territory naturally prompted at least one individual to report this activity to the security force, estimated to be approximately sixteen PDF personnel. This early detection, coupled with the apparent need to accelerate the time frame for execution, caused the majority of the assault team to proceed down the length of the runway at a run, ignoring available cover and concealment, in order to get to a position to deny the use of the target aircraft. Early detection allowed the PDF security force, already on alert status, to ambush the lead SEALs in the open in a withering cross-fire.

As an alternative, a smaller number of Joint Task Force personnel could have been tasked to enter the facility and survey the primary target area, confirming the assumed situation. A smaller force could also have positioned itself to engage the security forces with standoff weapons and/or the AC-130, and could have satisfactorily fouled the runway with one or two well placed obstacles. This smaller force could have been supported by a larger reserve either afloat or at another location ready to helo-envelop the facility to provide an assault or capture force. A tactical command and control element could have been positioned afloat or in a nearby building, several of which were easily accessible prior to the operation. This type of technique would have preserved the benefits normally associated with a special operation and minimized the risk to those involved.

Two other key factors in determining the propriety of special operations are surprise and security. The large force size working in a confined, urban area, made surprise a difficult goal to achieve. The restrictive and accelerated time schedule precluded the cautious approach and movement around the target area normally required by SEAL doctrine. Such a cautious approach would have cleared the potential danger areas to the flanks of the runway and allowed time to recon the targeted hangar with all available means of observation equipment before boldly approaching it without benefit of cover and concealment. Several poor assumptions appear to have been made by the planners, not the least of which was the anticipated lack of hostile activity on the facility. These assumptions seemed to support the cancellation of any security precautions.

The apartments or 'high ground' immediately surrounding the airfield should have been considered (as later proved) to be hostile. A smaller overall force, or at least a smaller advance portion of the larger force could have been used to secure the flanks and 'high ground' along the route of approach, offering the ground force commander a more secure route to the primary target area, resulting in an enveloping maneuver that would have wrenched the tactical advantage from the opposition.

Yet another shortfall was provision for adequate command and control. In spite of the fact that this action occurred only five miles from the NSWTG headquarters, communications failed at crucial times. These failures delayed the arrival of medical evacuation (which was not and should have been on-call to begin with), and delayed communications with the overhead support gunship. A dedicated command and control element for this mission was appropriate, but may have been better served if alternate reliable means of communication had been planned and available. Millions of dollars' worth of equipment in the hands of highly trained (and irreplaceable) operators means nothing 'if the call doesn't get through.' Visual signals, laser spots or other non-RF (radio frequency) means to communicate in an emergency should have been available. These means could have included strobe light signals, chemical light signals, laser emissions (from a laser designator) or even a cellular telephone.

The need for superior firepower, particularly with regard to SEAL employment, is usually another factor in determining whether to use a conventional or special operations unit.[6] No one who observed the Lear Jet hangar after the engagement could doubt that significant firepower had been brought to bear on that target during the exchange between the PDF security force and the SEALs. But again, the restrictive rules of engagement (ROE) that required that the aircraft not be destroyed, but damaged, appeared to give more importance to a replaceable piece of hardware than to the personnel who were intended to inflict 'minor damage,' cutting the brake lines, to it.

An underestimation of the enemy's knowledge of the terrain, their resolve to do their duty and their ability and willingness to fight contributed to the unfortunate outcome of this operation. Although there is some disagreement, reliable sources have indicated that an elderly security watchman was the only Panamanian killed and that the other PDF troops on the facility made good their extraction with only minor wounds after initial contact.

Superior firepower is only effective when brought to bear in a such a manner that it defeats the enemy's goals and contributes to mission success. The point could be made that the mission was a success since Noriega did not use Paitilla as a means of escaping from Panama, but conversely, that a successful escape from this particular airfield was even remotely possible is questionable. The available firepower, from the AC-130, the ground force themselves, or from the MK III PB offshore (equipped with an 81 mm mortar and within range of the hangar area) was more than adequate to deal with any realistic defensive or counter-attack threat. In the case of Paitilla, the restrictive ROE prohibited preemptive use of any of these fire support assets until an engagement was initiated by the defending force, the very engagement that cost the lives of four men.

Debate over this action will and should continue to be studied during the future training of NSW and other SOF planners. Of note: afterwards, NSWC decided to increase the number of SEALs that had to attend the Army's Ranger School to better prepare them for multi-platoon ground operations. The bravery and dedication of those young men on the ground at Paitilla on 20 December 1989 cannot be questioned. The suitability of the mission as it was planned for a SOF unit should be objectively addressed or future generations of SEALs may look back, draw the wrong conclusions, and model their operations inappropriately.

Philippine Insurrection, 1990

Shortly after Operation JUST CAUSE, in the summer of 1990, another real-world situation required the involvement of NSW assets.

The Special Boat Detachment assigned to NSWU One in Subic Bay, Republic of the Philippines routinely trained with Philippine Navy counterparts in simple boat handling and tactical interplay. Two of the detachment's MK III Patrol Boats and crews were scheduled to train with the Philippine Navy Assault Boat Unit based at Cavite Naval Station in Manila Bay. This unit was also equipped with MK IIIs, although the Philippine version was less well armed. The craft were secured at the naval station and the American crewmen, with the exception of an on-board watch section, had spent the night in a local hotel.

Upon returning to the station the next morning, the crews had to negotiate crowds of military and civilians milling around the main gate. The Philippine officer assigned as their liaison spotted the Americans and ushered them into the compound. The American lieutenant in charge of the detachment noticed that the Filipinos were not displaying their normal insignia and unit designators. He also noticed that everyone was armed and their weapons all had magazines inserted – not a normal situation. His discussions with the liaison officer determined that a coup was in progress and that most of the Philippine Naval personnel were no longer in support of the government led by President Corizon Aquino. This explained the uniform modifications.

The liaison officer indicated that this was a Philippine problem of no concern to the Americans and told them to return to their base in Subic Bay. The crewmen proceeded to their craft and readied them for sea. The young lieutenant, accompanied by the liaison officer, went back to the hotel to gather as many of his sailors' belongings as possible. Upon his return, following a confrontation with a group of armed men who apparently disliked Americans at that particular time, the patrol boats got underway.

Without warning, Cavite was suddenly attacked by a flight of Philippine Air Force F-5 fighter-bombers. Possibly mistaking the American craft for 'rebel' patrol boats, two aircraft diverted toward the American craft dropping several 500lb bombs in close proximity and making strafing runs. The craft were now taking evasive action and the crew feverishly loading the single .50 caliber machinegun for which they had ammunition when the aircraft disengaged before causing any damage, either because they were out of ammunition or because they noticed the American flag and identification roundel on the top of the wheelhouse. For whatever reason, the crews were thankful and, at flank (maximum) speed, made their way to Subic Bay.

The MK III crews were ordered to mount all weapons, take on combat loads of ammunition, and put to sea. For the next seven days the two 65-foot craft patrolled the mouth of Manila Bay, in company with a frigate, awaiting possible orders to support an evacuation of Americans from the US embassy, a mission that had been rehearsed many times prior to and during each detachment's deployment for several years. Although this mission was not required, it and several others were planned in detail.

One was a bold plan to rescue President Corizon Aquino from Malacanan Palace in downtown Manila.

The president's palace is located on the Pasig River, several miles east of the mouth of the river, where it flows into Manila Bay. Anti-government factions had threatened to capture the president and her supporters, thus putting the United States in an awkward position since its ambassador had committed to showing firm, albeit passive support to the elected government. When Aquino's personal safety appeared in jeopardy, plans were prepared to extract her from the palace. This presented an ideal opportunity to employ Special Operations Forces, primarily the NSW assets based in Subic Bay. Several personnel assigned to that unit had extensive knowledge of the area of Manila around the palace. Also, the geography of the area supported a clandestine approach by way of the Pasig River to a point immediately behind the palace grounds.

Several options were open to the on-scene planners, including use of indigenous craft, that would permit an unobtrusive approach to the compound, or Special Boat Detachment assets, which would signal an obvious, well armed American involvement. Also available were Special Operations helicopters that could have delivered a rescue team vertically. But these last two options would also be overt gestures which could have had unpredictable or undesirable effects on the civil conflict. The plan decided upon, but never executed, involved a combination of clandestine and overt phases that offered the best chance of success without endangering US forces, Philippine forces or densely populated downtown Manila. Once again, the Special Operations option offered conventional military leaders an economical means of achieving objectives with a minimal chance of a potentially dangerous escalation.[7]

The NSWU One staff, assigned SEAL platoons, and the Special Boat Detachment stood down as the coup attempt was quelled without significant overt US involvement.

The Gulf War, 1990–1

On 7 August 1990 the alert order reached NSWG-1 to begin planning to move forces to Saudi Arabia in support of Commander in Chief, Central

Command (CINCCENT). Personnel on local exercises in Southern California were recalled, SEAL platoons preparing for deployments were realigned and detailed logistics planning began. Immediately, CNSWG-1 sent a trusted and experienced officer, who was then serving as Commanding Officer, Special Boat Unit Thirteen, to MacDill Air Force Base, Florida as liaison with CINCCENT planners, a position this officer filled for the next seven months on the staff of Commander, Special Operations Command Central Command (COMSOCCENT).

Within seven days, initial logistics plans were finalized and equipment staged for onload aboard the first C-5 and C-141 aircraft that were to transport forward a NSWTG. Ammunition, food, combatant craft (and their spare parts), personal equipment, communications vans and Nuclear, Biological and Chemical equipment were loaded and sent winging east. After numerous mechanical problems at various locations worldwide, all aircraft arrived at Dhahran, Saudi Arabia and were off-loaded. Within three weeks the initial personnel, who were the first SOF and among the first US forces in theater, were expanded to an ashore NSW force structure that reached over 200 personnel.

The advance party in Saudi Arabia faced the challenge of arriving without a definite base identified for their use. A location called Half Moon Bay was selected as the initial site for the NSWTG headquarters. This location was normally a beach recreation area for local ARAMCO (Arab America Oil Company) employees. The NSWTG fortified it and established communications and training sites soon after their arrival.

In addition to establishing the command and control, site surveys of other forward locations took place as did the immediate operational employment of the NSWTG's combatant craft detachments. These comprised four 'previously owned' 37-foot speedboats that had seen earlier duty in the US during fleet training, and were designated to protect Maritime Prepositioned Ships (essentially floating warehouses used for contingency storage) offloading along the Saudi coastline.

SEALs also linked with Saudi counterparts and began unit bonding and basic combined training in laser target designation (for 'smart' munitions employment) and aircraft beacon operations. They also honed their tactical and command and control skills.

When DESERT SHIELD began, the Saudi Navy had an organization they referred to as SEALs. Small numbers of these personnel trained with their American counterparts during Operation EARNEST WILL. The Saudi training unit for these personnel was co-located with the training unit for the Saudi Marines at Ras al Ghar, a vast facility just south of the large Saudi naval base at Jubail.

The Saudi basic SEAL training was modeled after late 1960s versions of

BUD/S training, and even used instructor guides from that period. Instructors were primarily American civilians on contract to the Saudi government who claimed to, but did not necessarily, possess special operations backgrounds. The national ethic in the devout Muslim nation of Saudi Arabia made their version of a SEAL turn out very differently than the US Navy counterpart. Once 'qualified,' Saudi SEALS were assigned to high-level security duties rather than remaining together in a single special operations command.

Only two SEAL platoon equivalents were actually in existence. A key fear in a monarchy such as Saudi Arabia seemed to be that a highly trained, motivated and well-equipped SOF-type force could present a credible threat to the crown, possibly not unfounded. Consequently, Saudi SEAL platoons did not play a key role in coalition special operations.

Within weeks an NSWTU was established at Ras al Ghar to be followed by others at Ras al Mishab and afloat on a Kuwaiti powered barge set adrift by the Iraqis and captured by the Saudis. NSW personnel also supported liaison tasks with the two remaining Kuwaiti patrol boats, a German-built Lurssen 45-meter and a 57-meter Patrol Guided Missile Gunboat. Combined training with Saudi counterparts and Combat Search and Rescue (CSAR) detachment training with offshore Naval ships complemented surveillance duties along the Saudi–Kuwaiti border near the coast.

The harshness of the environment, remembered by many Operation EARNEST WILL veterans, was hard on man and machine. All NSW operators followed the 'one is none, two is one' axiom when planning and executing missions. Murphy's Law[8] was inevitable in this theater, not just a possibility. Excellent logistics support, from both in-theater and US sources ensured sustainment of primary war fighting abilities.

When DESERT SHIELD began to evolve into DESERT STORM, the men of the NSWTG were acclimatized and ready for action, be that action an operational engagement or the order to return home. The former began to take place on 30 January 1991 when an Iraqi armored column attacked the Saudi Arabian town of Khafji. En route to Khafji, certain Iraqi elements took the coastal route that was under surveillance from a border observation post manned by men from a SEAL Team One platoon. This platoon had called in air strikes and provided information on enemy troop movements to their immediate north, prior to being forced hastily to withdraw south as the Iraqis continued their advance. The most disconcerting outcome of this engagement, from the standpoint of the men at the NSWTU at Ras al Mishab, was the wanton destruction by the Iraqis of the telephone exchange in Khafji used by the Americans to make personal phone calls to the US.

When offensive operations began on 17 January 1991, they were complemented by an almost flawlessly executed series of over 200 NSW missions. One of the early missions was the recapture of the Kuwaiti island of Qaruh by

SEALs staging from the USS *Nichols*. SEALs staging from surface ships engaged and recaptured several oil platforms in Kuwaiti waters and recovered a downed F-16 pilot from the Gulf. One of the aforementioned 'previously owned' high-speed boats was originally tasked with the latter mission when the airman bailed out close to the coast, but rough seas caused structural damage requiring it to abort and return to base. The young crewmen did a superb job of damage control, it transpired, since once back in port it became obvious that the craft was badly damaged and sinking.

SEALS conducted several successful clandestine beach reconnaissance missions along the Kuwaiti coastline and successfully reconned over twenty square miles of the Gulf by SEAL Delivery Vehicle (SDV) in search of mines that could endanger an amphibious assault.

One coalition special operation involved a Kuwaiti resistance element attempt to infiltrate over the beach into Kuwait City. This attempt was made from a small number of high-speed boats at night, but the Kuwaitis requested immediate withdrawal when they encountered virtually impenetrable beach defenses. This mission, albeit ultimately aborted, was accomplished without compromise or even detection by the enemy.

One of the final coastal operations of the war was credited with diverting the attention of two Iraqi divisions that would have otherwise been in position to block the US Marine thrust, or 'end run,' into Kuwait City. A detachment of four, 40-foot high-speed boats proceeded north toward Kuwait City from Ras al Mishab. This first-hand account was provided by the young commander of that platoon:

I was commander of a Navy SEAL platoon whose mission was to conduct a deception operation on the Kuwaiti coast, south of Kuwait City. Our task was to convince the Iraqis that the amphibious invasion that they had been expecting was in fact taking place on the east coast of Kuwait. Departing our base from Ras Al Mishab in four high-speed boats we transitted to a point seven miles off of Mina Saud. I led my platoon of fifteen SEALs, in three rubber boats, to a position five hundred meters off the Kuwaiti coast. Then six of us swam to the beach, each carrying haversacks of twenty pounds of C-4 plastic explosives. We laid the charges on the beach and set the charges to detonate at 0100 hours, exactly three hours prior to the commencement of the ground war. We swam back to our rubber boats and rendezvoused with two of our high-speed boats. At 1230, the other two boats opened fire on the beach from three hundred meters off the shore. Their sustained fire was followed by floating charges, which exploded off the shore over the next fifteen minutes. Five minutes later, our haversacks lit up the beach. In reaction to our deception, Central Command intelligence indicated that elements of two separate Iraqi armored divisions remained in-place, on the coastline, thereby posing no threat to approaching coalition ground forces.[9]

Among the first allies in Kuwait City were personnel from the FAV (Fast Attack Vehicle) Detachment manned by SEALs (and one Special Forces 'exchange' officer). The primary mission of this small element was CSAR and headquarters security.

Almost immediately upon consolidation of the allied position in Kuwait and Iraq, plans formed to redeploy forces to CONUS. Having served the longest in theatre, the NSW contingent was among the first to redeploy home.

Although the NSWTG ashore saw the majority of action during the conflict, NSWTUs were afloat with the Amphibious Task Forces resourced from both the Pacific and Atlantic fleets. Their activities were mostly limited to underway missions, since CINCCENT decided against conducting an opposed amphibious landing. In support of the coalition embargo against Iraq, several hundred Visit, Board, Search and Seizure (VBSS) missions were accomplished onboard commercial ships in the Persian Gulf, Arabian Sea and Red Sea. These missions were extremely hazardous because of the vertical assault and underway boarding tactics necessary to get the VBSS teams quickly aboard suspect vessels and because of the total lack of reliable intelligence on potential opposition to the search. No US casualties were incurred during any of these missions, which continued well after the armistice.

Conclusions

DESERT STORM demonstrated the benefit of using SEALs as they were intended to be used. As much of a success as was DESERT STORM, it was doubly so for the NSW contingent. Using obsolete equipment such as aging high-speed boats, staging from platforms that needed to be rebuilt before they could be useful, and being restricted (again) by ROE that limited the degree of aggressiveness that could used, were problems that were all overcome by exceptional leadership, courage down to the junior petty officer level, planning and innovation.

Since World War II, naval special warfare forces – SEALs, and their UDT forefathers, Special Boat Unit personnel, and their small combatant craft forefathers, and the myriad unsung support personnel who receive no glory but are irreplaceable in the operational equation – have been continually involved in the American government's military responses to the needs of its allies and own national interests. They have endured difficult training regimes because they are expected to accept difficult missions. They are not supermen who are immune to injury or death. They have time and again proven their worth and will continue to do so into the unknown, but no less dangerous future confronting the world community.

NOTES

1. Personal knowledge of the author.
2. Personal knowledge of the author.
3. Malcolm McConnell, *Just Cause* (New York, St. Martins, 1991).
4. US Special Operations Command Presentation, Association of the United States Army (AUSA) Convention, Washington, DC, 13 October 1992.
5. In M. McConnell's book *Just Cause*, the MK III PB is described as being a fiberglass-hulled craft. It is actually constructed of aluminum. MK II PBRs (Patrol Boats Riverine), which were also heavily involved in this operation, have fiberglass hulls.
6. From an interview with a NSW officer assigned to NSWU Eight during JUST CAUSE.
7. From an interview with the Special Boat Detachment lieutenant who was present in Cavite at the start of the coup.
8. 'Murphy's Law' is an axiom that states: if anything can possibly go wrong, it will, and at the worst possible time. The origin of this axiom is unknown.
9. US Special Operations Command Presentation, Association of the United States Army (AUSA) Convention, Washington, DC, 13 October 1992.

CHAPTER 13

Air Force Special Operations in the New Order 1986–92

Air Force special operations forces rarely took the lead in any special operation, unlike their Navy and Army counterparts. They had two roles: one being that since the days of the old AC-47 gunships, they had provided special, precision, fire support to units on the ground. Their other role was transportation: the clandestine infiltration and extraction of cargo and personnel in denied or hostile areas. Prior to the aborted Iranian hostage rescue mission, conventional air force helicopter and fixed-wing transport aircraft conducted most of these missions. Among the many lessons learned from the failure of the aborted mission into Iran was that effective SOF insertion and extraction required unique, specialized equipment operated by specially trained pilots and crews.

Devastating, heavy machinegun and cannon fire delivered from an aircraft in a pylon turn remained the most effective method of providing precision fire support in a benign air defense environment. For this purpose, the air force continued to rely on the AC-130 Spectres, originally fielded in Vietnam. Of course they had been upgraded with more advanced sensors, navigational gear, more and better armaments, but the airframe and the tactics remained essentially the same.

A new AC-130U model Spectre will begin to be fielded in the late 1994 timeframe. Twelve AC-130H gunships will be upgraded to the new model. In the H model, two M-61s will be replaced with a GAU-12/U 25mm gatling gun. This new gun is hydraulically powered and fires the same ammunition as the 25mm Bushmaster that was found on the American Bradley infantry fighting vehicle. This provides the capability of firing armor-piercing kinetic energy, high-explosive, and standard ammunition. All guns and sensors are controlled by a new battle management center that provides firing solutions enabling the guns to lock on and track targets. A Global Positioning System (GPS) and suite of navigation systems similar to that in the MC-130 provides this aircraft with an all-weather capability. Further, the addition of a radar ground mapping system provides an all-weather target acquisition and tracking capability. The aircraft has an upgraded electronic counter-measures system with improved chaff and flare dispensing systems.

The men of the 1720th Special Tactics Group, consisting of four squadrons,[1] were essential to special operations as they had the mission of coordinating air force special operations support with ground forces. The Group provided Special Operations Weather Teams (SOWT) and Combat Controllers to ground SOF to synchronize air and ground operations.

Combat controllers were infiltrated into an area by a variety of means set up and operate either a drop or landing zone. These airmen also served as pathfinders, emplacing navigational aids and target designation gear.

The four man SOWTs conducted clandestine infiltration of target areas to collect meteorological data for air operations. They were highly trained paratroopers with small arms, mountain and SCUBA training. They carried a Belt Weather Kit (BWK) that contained a complete, miniaturized set of weather observation equipment.[2]

Relying on NVGs and thermal imagers, these soldiers sped through the night on motorcycles, all-terrain vehicles and trucks. Chief Master Sergeant (CMSgt) Robert Boyle aptly described the activities of these soldiers:

> Any air traffic controller can land aircraft and any medic can treat wounded people. It takes a whole different kind of guy to jump out of an airplane at 800 feet while bullets are coming up at you. You hit the ground in the dead of night, run around with 500 Army Rangers. You have to create order out of chaos, then start landing airplanes. You've got to keep artillery over you, direct gunship and helicopter fire, and clear people and planes on and off the airstrip. They've got to have the presence of mind to direct things when things go wrong. It's not the life for everyone; only the special ones.

Panama, 1989

Operation JUST CAUSE, the US invasion of Panama, saw extensive use of Spectres with very little use of the Combat Talon special operations transportation aircraft. Because of their precision firing capability, Spectres were the ideal fire support system for the urban warfare that characterized the US intervention. Artillery is simply too indiscriminate and inaccurate to provide extensive fire support in cities and developed areas and is almost impossible to deploy clandestinely. So, like their predecessors in Vietnam, the Spectres were called upon to provide fire support in almost every battle occurring on the first night. The 16th SOS, the Spectre Squadron from Hurlburt known as the 'Ghostriders,' was fully engaged.

The Spectres were made to order for these fire missions.

Pacora River Bridge

A Spectre gunship, call sign Air Papa 05,[3] began its turn over the Pacora River Bridge at 0045 hours, or H-hour on 20 December 1989. Air Papa 05 was to provide fire support to A Company, 3d Battalion, 7th Special Forces (SF) Group (Airborne) as they secured the bridge. One of Noriega's elite units, the Battalion 2000, would have to transit that bridge in order to intervene in the Ranger assault at Tocumen/Torrijos Airfield complex. A Company, commanded by Major Kevin Higgins, comprised only sixteen lightly armed personnel. They would be reliant on Air Papa 05 to provide the precise, measured firepower that would enable them to stop a battalion of well-trained troops.

Air Papa 05's sensor operator was observing events on the ground and discussing them with his Fire Control Officer (FCO). Both had noted that 400 meters north of the bridge a convoy of trucks was approaching and as yet the SF unit was nowhere to be seen. Suddenly, from the south, three MH-60 Black Hawk helicopters banked over the convoy and landed adjacent the bridge. Both the sensor operator and FCO were concerned because the convoy was bearing down rapidly on the bridge and they could not fire until they established contact with Tech Sergeant John Ecklof, a one-man air force Combat Control Team, accompanying the Special Forces. They watched as the helicopters landed, disembarked their passengers and departed the area.

Immediately, a soldier ran out into the middle of the road on the south side of the bridge and fired a missile at the lead truck. It had no effect. Three more soldiers fired at the vehicle with no effect. Finally, a team of soldiers ran out in the road and fired a missile, which stopped the lead truck. Simultaneously, the FCO heard Tech Sergeant Ecklof on the radio; he needed immediate fire on the convoy as it was attempting to bypass the lead vehicle. The FCO readied the 20mm gatling guns as the sensor operator illuminated the lead vehicle with the covert illuminator.[4] The FCO obtained the firing solution from the computer and engaged the guns. Sounding like a chain saw cutting sheet metal, the M-61s fired. On target, the second vehicle started burning and the remainder of the convoy stopped. Enemy troops could be seen jumping out of trucks, running for cover. The sensor operator then flipped on the infrared searchlight to aid the friendly forces on the ground. As enemy soldiers attempted to assemble into groups, Air Papa dispersed them with gatling guns.

Ecklof then asked Air Papa 05 to disable the lead vehicle with its 105mm howitzer. The FCO acknowledged the request and the sensor operator illuminated the hood of the vehicle with his laser. The gun fired, causing the tail of the aircraft to jerk. A couple of seconds later, the shell blasted through the hood and engine of the truck.

Rio Hato Airfield

Seventeen minutes after the Spectre attack began at Pacora River, Air Papa 03 began its pylon turn over the Rio Hato runway in Panama. In precisely one minute, a flight of twenty C-130s would arrive and airdrop a battalion from the 75th Ranger Regiment onto the runway. Air Papa 03 was working this mission with two Army Apache helicopter gunships. Glint tape, which is highly visible with Low-light level television (LLLTV) systems, marked the tops of the two helicopters as they engaged anti-aircraft guns and enemy soldiers on the runway. Sitting behind the gun positions in a dark cubicle on Air Papa 03 were the sensor operators, observing the Apaches as they serviced the airfield. One operated the infrared sensor, the other the LLLTV and laser designator/rangefinder (LDTR). In concert with the Fire Control Officer (FCO) they identified potential targets. They had one.

'We've got a live one on that first ZPU skipper,' the FCO said to the pilot to let him know that he was planning to engage. There were two ZPU-4 anti-aircraft guns in position to protect the airfield; one was unattended. A Panamanian Defense Forces soldier had just dashed from cover to mount the firing saddle of the second gun as the Apache gunships left the area. He could probably hear the drone of the Spectre and the approaching C-130 Hercules carrying the Rangers. The FCO had the range to use any one of his weapons, the gatling guns, the Bofors, or the howitzer cannon. After consulting the pilot, he selected the howitzer. The sensor operator illuminated the ZPU with his laser designator by flipping switches on the control console. The FCO confirmed the sighting, checked the fire control solution, and received confirmation of the solution from the computer. 'Okay' he said as he released the safety switch on his console and the pilot and sensor operator depressed their buttons, firing the cannon. The aircraft rocked slightly as the cannon erupted; two seconds later the sandbagged ZPU position disappeared in a flash, followed by smoke and dust. As the dust cleared, the FCO and sensor operators saw that there remained only a smoking crater where the sandbagged gun position had been.[5]

As Air Papa 03 resumed her patrol, the C-130s had throttled back and were disgorging Rangers over the airfield. They could descend without fear of effective anti-aircraft fire. Air Papa 03 would not resume firing until all the Rangers were on the ground and she had contact with the air force Combat Control Teams.

LA COMMANDANCIA

La Commandancia, in Panama City, was Noriega's headquarters for the PDF. Its rapid neutralization was essential if US forces were quickly to subdue the PDF and minimize losses on both sides. The capitulation or destruction of La Commandancia was essential to the success of the US mission. The installation was located in the urban center of Panama City, completely surrounded by tall buildings and apartment complexes. On the ground, Task Force Gator would conduct the assault on the headquarters. Task Force Gator consisted of mechanized infantry companies from the 5th Infantry Division (Mechanized), an Airborne Infantry company with light tanks from the 82d Airborne Division and light armored vehicles from the 2d Light Armored Vehicle Battalion from the US Marines. The 5th Battalion, 1st Field Artillery provided some of the fire support.

But on this constricted battlefield, hemmed in by civilian homes and office buildings, cannon artillery was of limited value. Consequently, the Joint Special Operations Task Force Commander assigned two Spectres to provide the precision fire support necessary to cover Task Force Gator effectively and minimize collateral damage.

Gunships were already raining fire on La Commandancia when the soldiers of C Company, 1st Battalion, 508th Infantry (Airborne) began their assault. Since 2245 hours (H-hour) the gunships had been conducting a vicious bombardment of the facility, so that by the time Task Force Gator arrived, it was a mighty conflagration. One gunship pilot described the mission as follows:

> I was the aircraft commander of Papa 06, one of two AC-130H Spectre Gunships that orbited La Commandancia during Operation JUST CAUSE. The Commandancia was the headquarters of the Panamanian Defense Forces and was situated in downtown Panama City within a walled compound amongst a group of barracks ... These barracks were preplanned targets. Our mission was to participate with the ground forces in the decapitation of the PDF and the destruction of their command and control facilities. Specifically, our job was to use our 105mm howitzer to knock down three of the barracks adjacent the compound. In the opening minutes of the conflict, we put three rounds of 105 into each of these barracks and that was sufficient; they began to burn almost immediately. After that, we received an urgent call from some friendly forces that were receiving fire from the Commandancia, itself. So, we disengaged from the barracks and I flew the aircraft into a firing orbit over the Commandancia and we proceeded to put approximately 53 rounds of 40mm through the roof, to suppress the enemy fire. The remainder of our mission was spent over the US Embassy in Panama City, protecting it ...[6]

But on this mission confusion reigned. Smoke, flame and dust may have been obscuring the sensors aboard the gunships, making targeting difficult. Additionally, PDF mortars may have been firing, although US mortar locating radars never found them. Several soldiers in Delta Company, 4/6 Infantry (Mechanized) were convinced that the Spectres were engaging them since there was never any sign of PDF mortars. As one infantry crew dismounted its armored personnel carrier (APC), artillery rounds impacted on the dismount point as the crew ran for cover. Then the APC was hit and caught fire. As the crew began moving, fire from the sky exploded directly in front of them. They changed direction and another round cut them off. In all, a total of twenty-six members of the second platoon of Delta Company were hit by the fire: over half of the platoon.[7]

But as the assault developed, the Spectre fire became more focused, so that it completely devastated La Commandancia. Ultimately it proved highly effective, but its contribution was marred by the suspicion that these Americans may have fired on their compatriots on the ground.

In all, the air force deployed a total of 9 AC-130A and H series Spectres to Panama for the intervention. Their integration into the campaign was a credit to the USSOCOM and Air Force Special Operations Command (AFSOC) planners who effectively integrated the use of the Spectres with the units they supported. Although the USSOCOM planners deserve credit for integrating the Spectres into the campaign plan, the air force Combat Control Teams deserve the credit for making sure that the Spectres were effectively employed and synchronized with ground operations. In close combat, the potential for fratricide by supporting fires is a real hazard, and the AFCCTs performed a tremendous service by making sure that the devastating fire was placed on the enemy and not on the friendlies.

Air Force Special Operations Command (AFSOC), 1990

Following Operation JUST CAUSE, the air force Chief of Staff established the Air Force Special Operations Command (AFSOC) at Hurlburt Field in May 1990 as the air force component of United States Special Operations Command. Its mission was to organize, train, equip and educate air force special operations forces for worldwide deployment and assignment to regional unified commands to conduct a variety of missions: unconventional warfare, direct action, special reconnaissance, counter-terrorism, foreign internal defense, humanitarian assistance, psychological operations, personnel recovery and counter-narcotics operations. AFSOC also took over supervision of the US air force Special Operations School and Special Missions Operational Test & Evaluation Center.

Simultaneously, with the consolidation of AFSOC, the Pacific and European special operations squadrons were consolidated under the newly activated 39th and 353d Special Operations Wings, respectively. These new Wings reported directly to their theater unified commanders, via the Joint Force Special Operations Component Commander (JFSOCC). This enabled the unified commanders in the Pacific and in Europe to fully integrate air force SOF into their planning.

Three unified commands had no permanently stationed AFSOF assets: US Atlantic Command (USACOM), US Southern Command (USSOUTHCOM), and US Central Command (USCENTCOM). For operations in their areas of responsibility (AOR), USSOCOM and its components plan for and deploy packages of SOF units from all over the world, as needed. Air force SOF involved in Panama came primarily from Hurlburt field. USCENTCOM's requirements in the Persian Gulf were filled from the resources of the 1st SOW at Hurlburt and the 39th SOW in Europe.

US Air Force Special Operations Command Organization

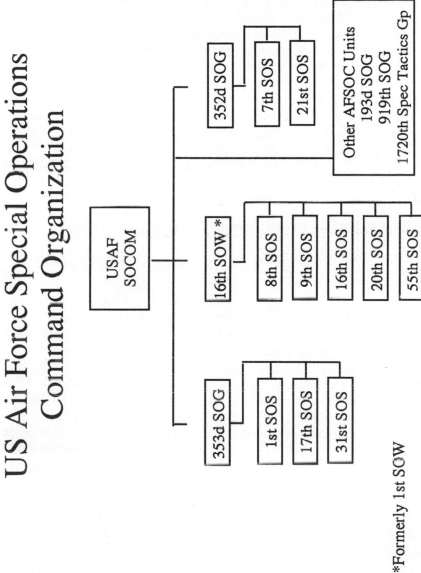

*Formerly 1st SOW

Figure 5

The Gulf War, 1990–1

Following their deployment to Panama, the men from Hurlburt redeployed, inspected, and repaired their aircraft. Since they are subject to deployment anywhere in the world, at any time, they worked around the clock after their return from Panama to make sure their aircraft were put back in top-notch condition. Once the post-operational maintenance was completed, they continued their training regimen to keep gunnery and flying skills sharp.

No sooner had they settled into their training and maintenance routine, than the 8th and 20th Special Operations Squadrons (MC-130 Combat Talon and MH-53 Pave Low helicopters, respectively), were alerted for deployment to Saudi Arabia following the Iraqi invasion of Kuwait. Almost simultaneously, the 21st Special Operations Squadron deployed to Turkey. In place by Christmas, AFSOC then alerted the 71st Special Operations Squadron (Air Force Reserve) (HH-3 helicopters), to deploy in January. As the air war kicked off on 17 January, AFSOC was there to support General Norman Schwarzkopf, the Commander-in-Chief, US Central Command, with a full arsenal of high-technology weaponry.

> We don't drop any better than any other crew in MAC (Military Airlift Command) can; we just go where the others can't.[8]
>
> *Lieutenant Colonel Donald James*
> *Navigator,*
> *8th Special Operations Squadron*

The new special operations transportation capabilities got a 'baptism of fire' during the Persian Gulf war. That conflict, more than any other, allowed the air force to demonstrate the advanced technology, skill, creativity and resourcefulness its special operators had acquired since the fiasco at Desert One, just ten years before. The stunning success of special operations transport and rescue missions is a tribute both to new flight technology and the skill of the crews that operate the aircraft.

Many of these missions harkened back to the days of the 1st Air Commando Group in Burma and the European 406th Squadron, nicknamed the 'Carpetbaggers.' The primary objective of these new 'Carpetbaggers' was to get into the target area and out, completely undetected; no easy task with aircraft the size of passenger buses flying in a highly lethal anti-aircraft environment. But to their credit they managed superbly, rescuing downed pilots, infiltrating and exfiltrating ground operators, and delivering missiles, bombs, and leaflets with no aircraft losses.

THE MC-130 COMBAT TALON

Most MC-130s belong to the 8th Special Operations Squadron (SOS), based at Hurlburt Field, Florida. The 8th, along with other AFSOC units, deployed to the Persian Gulf in 1990 in support of Operations DESERT SHIELD and DESERT STORM. Interestingly, the combination of precision navigation systems and HSLADDS on board the Talon suited it well as not only a transport, but also a bomber. On 6 February, 1992, MC-130H Combat Talons from the 8th dropped two 15,000lb BLU-82 Daisy Cutter bombs into Iraqi minefields and defensive berms (man-made walls of sand or dirt) to blast a corridor for US Marines to use during their ground attack.[9]

The problem was that the Iraqis had constructed a formidable barrier system composed of technologically advanced land mines, tank ditches, fire trenches filled with crude oil, and defensive berms that coalition forces would be required to breach in order to attack the Iraqi forces occupying Kuwait. Unfortunately, US mine clearing technology was not equal to the task and US leaders attempted a number of solutions. One unsuccessful solution, which was tested at Fort Irwin, California, involved bellying in B-52 Strato-Fortress aircraft at 3,000 feet and using a string of 500lb bombs to blast a corridor. Unfortunately, the Iraqi mines were designed to withstand overpressure detonation. Finally, on the recommendation of Lieutenant Colonel Thomas Beres, 8th SOS Commander, Colonel George Gray III, 1st Special Operations Wing (SOW) Commander and Army Colonel Jesse L. Johnson, the Joint Force Special Operations Command Commander (JFSOCC), Central Command ordered the 8th SOS to execute the BLU-82 mission to assist the breaching operation. Although the BLU-82s did not completely clear the minefields their use contributed significantly to a Marine advance so rapid that General Schwarzkopf advanced the time of his main attack by fourteen hours.

During the course of DESERT STORM, the 8th SOS dropped nine more Daisy Cutters, the entire theater stock, and was nicknamed the '8th Bomb Squadron.' The BLU-82s were dropped in pairs, from 17,000 feet, to stay out of range of the enemy anti-aircraft artillery. The average circular error from the aim-point was about fifty yards, the equivalent of a direct hit with the BLU-82's 12,600lb of explosive. The explosive effects of the bombs were so powerful that ground forces later entering the target area found that every enemy soldier within three miles was dead. The explosion resembles a nuclear detonation and is so striking that a British SAS team 110 miles from the target reported to its headquarters 'Sir, Sir, the blokes! They've just nuked Kuwait.'

One of the BLU-82s was dropped in a minefield inside a wadi in Kuwait, which protected a truck park that was part of a British objective. Unfortunately, USCENTCOM was not able to get any bomb damage assessment (BDA) on the mission before the ground attack commenced. When British soldiers hit the first line of defense, they found it abandoned. When they hit the second, they encountered numerous Iraqi defenders – all dead in their foxholes.

Yet another mission was conducted over Failakka Island, a potential objective of the US Marines. Three of the bombs were dropped just seconds apart. Instantly, every radar and anti- aircraft weapon on the island went out of commission.

To exploit the full effects of these bombing missions, they were followed up by leaflet drops telling the Iraqis that these were the first of many bombs to come and that they should surrender or die. After one such leaflet mission, an Iraqi battalion commander crossed over to the coalition side and provided detailed maps of all the minefields in his sector. The 8th dropped a total of 17 million leaflets, which were found in the hands of many of the tens of thousands of Iraqi soldiers who surrendered.

The 8th also refueled MH-53 Pave Lows and conducted several clandestine insertion and rescue operations. Its four Talon crews flew forty sorties for a total of 135 hours during the campaign.[10] None of the Combat Talons was lost.

THE AC-130 SPECTRE

Surprisingly, nine active and reserve component Spectre gunships deployed to the Persian Gulf and provided fire support for a number of operations. Surprising because the Spectres were ill-suited for missions in Kuwaiti Theater of Operations since the Iraqi Army had a formidable air defense capability; something the Panama Defense Forces lacked. However, their stellar performance in Panama was one factor contributing to the decision to deploy them.

The Spectres were controlled by the Central Command Air Force (CENTAF) Commander, Lieutenant General Charles Horner and his staff, an aberration from normal command and control procedure for these aircraft. By doctrine, the Joint Forces Special Operations Component Commander, and the commander of the Theater Air Force Special Operations Component plan for and task Spectre missions in support of the theater Commander-in-Chief's (CINC) operational requirements. This procedure ensures that the unique characteristics, capabilities, and limitations of the aircraft are considered during operational planning; a conventional air staff has significantly less special operations planning expertise to draw from.

This fluke caused several problems for the gunship crews: for example, although the aircraft are designed to operate only in a benign enemy air defense environment, they were assigned several missions over enemy territory. In another incident, a Spectre was misidentified by its controlling AWACS (Airborne Warning and Control System) aircraft as an A-10 Thunderbolt, a much smaller, more maneuverable, fighter-bomber. As a result of this mistake, the pilot commented that the conventional air staff seemed to have the mistaken impression that the Spectre was nothing more than a 'giant fighter-bomber, equipped with fourteen ejection seats for its crew.'

Tragically, this unusual command and control arrangement may have been a contributing factor in one Spectre mission that ended badly.

On the morning of 31 January, elements of the Saudi Army National Guard, the Qatari Battalion, and the 1st US Marine Division launched a successful counter-attack against the Iraqi 5th Regular Army Division that had begun its attack the day before. A Spectre gunship provided fire support.

At dawn, the Spectre, call-sign 'Spirit 03' flew an armed reconnaissance mission in support of the coalition forces engaged at Khafji. In addition to providing reconnaissance reports of Iraqi movements to the forces in contact, Spirit 03 had been specifically tasked to eliminate a Free-Rocket-Over-Ground (FROG) missile site. She was free to engage targets of opportunity provided she coordinated with forces on the ground. On arrival, Spirit 03 immediately identified the FROG unit and, as the rising sun turned the horizon to a fiery hue, hammered the unit with both its 105 and 40mm guns. She completely destroyed this potent and fearsome threat to her compatriots on the ground. Her mission a success, Spirit 03 and her crew flew out to sea, toward the emerging sun, to touch the hand of God.

What downed her is uncertain and the air force has not commented. Most likely she was hit by a shoulder fired surface-to-air missile (SAM). Her loss was a costly lesson and probably caused the air force leadership to discontinue the gunship missions in the Gulf.

THE MH-53 PAVE LOW

We don't like getting any higher than we would have to fall.[11]

Captain Dennis Jones
Pilot
20th Special Operations Squadron

The MH-53 Pave Low is one of the fastest helicopters in the US military inventory and was originally designed for search and rescue operations. The helicopter has 1,000 lb of armor plate and the pilots sit in titanium seats. Unlike the unarmed Combat Talons, Pave Lows are equipped with both 7.62mm mini-guns or .50 caliber machineguns that can be fired with one hand. In addition to armaments, the bird has chaff and flare dispensers and a sophisticated electronic counter-measures system on board.

The navigation package is similar in sophistication to the one on board the Combat Talon. These helicopters use a terrain following/terrain avoidance radar, combined with a FLIR system and NVGs to navigate. A recent improvement is a terrain-following capability from the Navstar Global Positioning System (GPS) satellites that is superimposed on the pilot's NVGs via fiber optics. The craft requires a crew of two pilots, two flight engineers, and two gunners. In addition to the crew, the Pave Low can carry up to thirty-seven troops, making it a superb platform for the insertion of raiding parties.

The helicopters have an automated hover feature that gives the pilots pinpoint accuracy in retrieving downed flyers or other personnel on the ground. The twin engines and titanium composite rotor blades allow for a rapid deceleration from cruising speed into a hover. With two lines running off the cargo ramp and one off the rescue hoist, a full load of troops can rappel out of the aircraft in twenty seconds.[12]

Experienced air force pilots consider the MH-53 one of the most fatiguing of all aircraft to fly in degraded visibility. Pilots fly for no more than thirty minutes at a time before turning over controls to the copilot. The pilot on the controls flies the aircraft on instruments while the other pilot monitors systems and visually checks through the windshield for obstacles.

Most of the air force's Pave Lows are in the 20th SOS, located at Hurlburt Field, and in the 21st SOS, based at RAF Alconbury in the United Kingdom. Both units deployed in support of Operations DESERT SHIELD and DESERT STORM, the 20th to Saudi Arabia and the 21st to Turkey. As it turns out, the MH-53s of the 20th SOS started the Gulf War.

Four MH-53J Pave Lows led the way for US Army Apache attack helicopters that blasted an air corridor through the Iraqi air defenses allowing the might of the coalition air forces to attack Baghdad undetected early on the morning of 17 January 1991.

Task Force Normandy, consisting of two hunter-killer teams, conducted the operation. Each team was composed of two Pave Lows, leading four Apache helicopter gunships from the 101st Aviation Brigade from Fort Campbell, Kentucky. Each was to attack a ground control intercept radar site in far western Iraq. Communications at the sites had to be knocked out within thirty seconds of each other, as they had overlapping coverage. If the sites were not attacked simultaneously, one would be able to alert Baghdad of the impending coalition attack, with potentially disastrous consequences for coalition flyers. This action would create a 'radar black' corridor for the allied air sorties to fly through. One site was fourteen miles inside Iraq, the other twenty-five miles.

This raid was absolutely essential to the opening of the air campaign and Colonel Gray assured Schwarzkopf of 100 percent success. When Schwarzkopf received this assurance, he told Gray: 'Okay, Colonel, you get to start the war.'[13]

The lead pilot of the mission was Major Bob Leonik. He is the epitome of what the air force looks for in a special operations pilot. He is no 'seat of the pants' pilot as is often depicted in popular movies. His missions are characterized by excruciatingly detailed planning. Routes and actions are wargamed to minimize the surprises. When he encounters the unexpected, Leonik deals with it with cold, objective, calculation; he reacts quickly and effectively.

Although he had considerable confidence in his aircraft, the environment had already pointed out some technological shortcomings. Visibility with NVGs was degraded because sand in the air made it difficult to discern ground from sky. Already four helicopters had burned into the Saudi sand dunes as testimony to this problem.

At precisely 0220 hours, 17 January 1991, Leonik's Pave Low crossed the Iraqi border. Leonik dodged around Bedouin camps to avoid being heard, ducked into dry wadis to get under radar and worked his way through an extensive system of observation posts. In pitch black conditions he was totally reliant on his instruments and sensors. He prayed that his instruments were giving him accurate information – a screw-up meant fiery death. He nearly had a heart-attack when his navigation console went blank – until he switched on the backup. At eight miles from the target, the pre-arranged stand-off attack position for the Apaches, he dropped chemical light sticks. An Iraqi sentry saw him jettison the chemlites and turned to run for the bunker. He never made it. As he opened the bunker door, a laser-guided Hellfire missile from one of the Apaches blasted the installation. Five seconds later, the other radar installation erupted in flame and noise and the lead pilot of the other team broadcast the code word for success: California. 'They did it!' Leonik yelled into the radio.

Back at USCENTCOM headquarters, Schwarzkopf monitored the Pave Low traffic and heard 'California.' 'Thank God', he muttered. Meanwhile, as Leonik worked his Pave Low back to friendly territory, he looked above him to see a sky that looked several hundred times more congested than the traffic pattern at Kennedy international Airport in New York. The air campaign was on. 'Go, go, go!' he yelled into the intercom.[14]

One of the auxiliary missions of both the 20th and 21st SOS was search and rescue. For inexplicable reasons, the air force decided not to deploy its newly re-created Air Rescue Service, with its new HH-60G Blackhawks, to the Gulf. Given the already saturated sea and airlift capabilities during the buildup, air force planners no doubt sacrificed the deployment of this unit and counted on the 20th and 21st SOS to handle any downed pilot.

Search and rescue (SAR) got off to a rocky start in the Gulf. One of the early missions was delayed seventy-two hours due to a highly complex set of bureaucratic circumstances. US Air Force Colonel David Eberly and his copilot, Lieutenant Colonel Thomas E. Griffith were searching for Scud missile launchers in their F-15 Eagle on 19 January 1991 when they were shot down in northwest Iraq. The first delay in a rescue attempt was probably the most galling: Special Operations Command, Europe (SOCEUR) had to wait for diplomatic clearance from Turkey to launch two of its MH-53s. Once Turkey provided the clearance, they had to await Syrian permission for their helicopters and an HC-130 refueler to cross Syrian airspace. Yet another problem was that the two downed pilots were some ten miles from where they had been reported shot down. Further complicating attempts to locate the flyers was the fact that the homing equipment in use was extremely imprecise, with an error potential of up to fifteen miles. Army Special Forces teams working the area were unable to locate them. In spite of the extensive search, the Pave Lows never actually found the downed pilots, and they were captured.

Navy Lieutenant Devon Jones was the first pilot successfully rescued by the 20th SOS. He and his navigator were shot down in their F-14 Tomcat. The Pave Lows barely got there in time. Two trucks full of Iraqi troops were closing on Jones' location when the SAR team arrived. Calling in A-10 Thunderbolts[15] to deal with the trucks, the Pave Lows rescued Jones, but were unable to get his navigator before he was captured. The Pave Low commander said of this mission:

> At 0730 local time, my crew and I were alerted that a Navy F-14 had been shot down in northern Iraq and that at least one crewman had punched out. After getting the pilot's location, which was just west of Baghdad, it became obvious that we were going to have to penetrate a serious anti-aircraft environment. However the Pave Low was designed with just that mission in mind. The fact that the mission would be conducted entirely during daylight hours was a concern, but we knew the Iraqis would be combing the desert in search of the Navy crew. When we received clearance to launch a rescue attempt, we headed north. Picking our way through the known enemy guided missile positions it took us an hour and a half to reach our search area – so long in fact that twenty minutes after arriving we were running low on fuel and had to return to base. We refueled at our forward base, located inside Saudi Arabia, and headed back north. In constant contact with AWACS we eventually established contact with two A-10s who had located the downed pilot and were providing cover. At approximately 1430, we established contact with Lieutenant Jones and headed in to pick him up. At the same time, the A-10s spotted an Iraqi vehicle moving at full speed toward his position. The A10s rolled in and as we landed, we could see the results of their work: the Iraqi truck exploded and was burning with a vengeance. We returned to base with Lieutenant Jones safely on board. It was over eight hours after our initial launch.
>
> *Captain Tom Trask*[16]

Pave Lows flew some sixty cross-border missions during the course of the conflict, with no combat losses.

THE MH-3 'PAVE PIG'

A defining characteristic of all SOF is their unique ability to improvise and jury-rig equipment to accomplish whatever the mission requires. A classic example of this is the MH-3 Pave Pig. The MH-3Es were 1967–9 vintage helicopters; veterans of the Vietnam war. Originally they were configured as Super CH-3C Jolly Green Giants that flew special operations missions in Vietnam. Activated in 1987 at Davis-Monthan Air Force Base in Tucson, Arizona, the 71st Special Operations Squadron, an Air Force Reserve unit, operated the Pave Pigs.

A significant amount of AFSOF is found in the reserves, and the 71st is an excellent example. The majority of its pilots and technicians are citizen-airmen, a modern version of the minutemen of the American Revolution. Lieutenant Colonel Lawrence Rolle, a vice-president of Marco Crane and Rigging Company of Phoenix, Arizona, commanded the unit in 1989. He, along with four fellow members of his unit, made the supreme sacrifice when they died that year in a crash during a training mission. Other members of the unit were teachers, tool and die makers, and software engineers.[17]

The aircraft they flew, the MH-3, had been considerably modified and upgunned since its Vietnam days. MH-3s are now equipped with FLIR and Trimble Global Positioning System receivers. Following the Gulf War they received flare and chaff dispensers and mini-guns. During the war, crew chiefs stood in the doors with flare pistols to ward off heat seeking surface-to-air (SAM) missiles. Despite the new electronics, the pilots remained highly reliant on NVGs as their prime navigational aid.

The Pave Pig is flown by a pilot, copilot, flight engineer and one or two crew members who watch for threats, take care of passengers, and man the machineguns. The flight engineer works the forward looking infrared and the copilot operates the satellite global positioning system.

Mobilized on 21 December 1990, the 71st SOS arrived aboard C-5 Galaxy transports at King Fahd Airport, Riyadh, Saudi Arabia less than a month later on 10 January. By 13 January, they had trained and become operational with the mission of providing over water search and rescue in the Persian Gulf, using a pier as a forward operating base. It was here that one crew learned that the MH-3 can be airborne from a dead stop in ninety seconds. This unusual statistic was discovered by a Pave Pig crew when the pier came under an Iraqi missile attack.

Although there was no need for them to recover any downed pilots, one of their MH-3s did locate the wreckage of Spirit 03, a Spectre Gunship from the 16th SOS shot down on 31 January 1991 near Khafji. When the ground campaign kicked off, the squadron was forward deployed to provide medical evacuation (MEDEVAC) and on 24 February MEDEVACed five critically wounded Saudi soldiers located between Iraqi anti-aircraft sites.

At the conclusion of the Gulf War, the 71st returned to Davis-Monthan, where it trained in rescue work and engaged in counter-narcotics operations. The unit was scheduled to become a conventional air national guard unit in late 1993 and early 1994.[18]

Conclusions

Overall, this most recent stage in the evolution of air force special operations can be considered a stunning success. Clearly the most significant achievement has been the development of a highly effective and reliable air transport capability for SOF. The spectacular missions flown during the Gulf War, in particular, testify to the manner in which air force SOF rose to the challenges posed by the failures of the 1970s and 1980s.

Improvements in the quality of air force combat control techniques were especially evident in Panama. Air force Combat Controllers parachuted with Rangers into airfields and immediately began controlling landing and fire support operations as the Rangers secured the facilities. These men were particularly important as they worked with ground units to provide timely and lethal fire support from the ubiquitous Spectres.

The establishment of the Air Force Special Operations Command (AFSOC) to resource special operations requirements was a positive step forward. Its creation ensured that the arcane, but nevertheless extremely important requirements of AFSOF are not ignored by the more conventionally oriented resource managers, force and doctrine developers in the Pentagon. Equally importantly, the AFSOC structure provides the previously unavailable opportunity for upward and lateral mobility to career-oriented officers and enlisted personnel who are proficient in special operations. AFSOC provides a vital link between force modernization, doctrine development, and personnel acquisition and training that guarantees SOF forces the correct mix of equipment and trained personnel to meet current and future challenges.

NOTES

1. US Special Operations Command Public Affairs Office Memorandum to the author, with enclosures, Subject: Security Review of Manuscript, dated 9 September 1993.
2. Jeffrey P. Rhodes, 'Any Time Any Place,' *Air Force Magazine*, June 1988, p. 74.
3. US Special Operations Command Public Affairs Office Memorandum, with enclosures, Subject: Security Review of Manuscript, dated 9 September 1993.
4. Ibid.
5. Malcolm McConnell, *Just Cause* (New York, St. Martins, 1991).
6. US Special Operations Command Presentation, Association of the United States Army (AUSA) Convention, Washington, DC, 13 October 1992.
7. Thomas Donnelly, Margaret Roth, and Caleb Baker, *Operation Just Cause; the Storming of Panama* (New York, Lexington Books), pp. 151–2.
8. Jeffrey P. Rhodes, 'The Machines of Special Ops,' *Air Force Magazine*, August 1988, p. 65.
9. Benjamin F. Schemmer, '8th Special Ops Squadron Nicknamed 8th Bomb Squadron After BLU-82 Missions,' *Armed Forces Journal International*, July 1991, p. 37.
10. Schemmer, p. 37.
11. Rhodes, p. 64.
12. Rhodes, p. 64.
13. Benjamin F. Schemmer, 'USAF MH-53J Pave Lows Led Army Apaches Knocking Out Iraqi Radars to Open Air War,' *Armed Forces Journal International*, July 1991, p. 34.
14. Douglas Waller, 'Secret Warriors,' *Newsweek*, June 17, 1991, pp. 22–3.
15. US Special Operations Command Public Affairs Office Memorandum, with enclosures, Subject: Security Review of Manuscript, dated 9 September 1993.
16. US Special Operations Command Presentation, Association of the United States Army (AUSA) Convention, Washington, DC, 13 October 1992.

17. Major Anthony J. Epifano, 'A Special Little Weapon to Throw at the Enemy,' *Citizen Airman*, July 1989, p. 4.
18. US Special Operations Command Public Affairs Office Memorandum to the author, with enclosures, Subject: Security Review of Manuscript, dated 9 September 1993.

PART V

Epilogue

CHAPTER 14

Special Operations in the Next Century

Special operations, and the forces that conduct them, have become steadily more prevalent since the Kennedy initiatives of 1961. The collapse of the Soviet Union as an imperial power has eliminated the need for a large American military capability to keep Soviet imperial designs in check. What have emerged, however, are regional threats to American vital interests. The military focus now is simultaneously to downsize force structure to realize fiscal savings, and maintain a capability to protect American vital interests effectively around the world.

More importantly, President Bush and, more recently, President Clinton have recognized that in the 'new world order' military confrontation has been and should continue to be replaced by peacetime competition. The primary threat to American interests is economic and the large American defense capability put a necessary but nevertheless unfortunate brake on economic growth. It is significant to note that for several years Japan has been out-producing the US in consumer goods, with virtually no defense establishment to speak of since the responsibility for her defense was assumed by the US since World War II.

In short, America's foreign policy aims have shifted from maintaining a sphere of influence to the protection of vital interests, allies, and human rights. President Clinton has espoused a foreign policy that American force will only be used to protect her vital interests; otherwise, she will only provide monetary and military hardware support to her allies and to United Nations in support of humanitarian relief and human rights protection operations.

Whether by design or by accident, these are the sort of missions at which, over the years, American special operations forces have come to excel. President Kennedy envisioned SOF as a tool to use in low-intensity-conflict operations, where military personnel had to possess not only heightened warrior skills, but, more importantly, the skills to build and foster relationships with allies. It was by building such interpersonal relationships that SOF were expected to forestall crises in the third world. If America's foreign aid programs could cement relations with nations whose welfare and friendship was vital to American interests, costly wars to protect those interests might be avoided.

Further, SOF employment doctrine for combat emphasizes minimizing

237

casualties to non-combatants and non-military facilities; in all the military services, SOF missions target a discrete, military objective. Although special operations have caused occasional civilian casualties and damage, this is rare. On the other hand, military and para-military forces threatening American interests are fair game, and SOF have traditionally caused significant damage to enemy military forces, their equipment and installations.

With the Panama intervention, even this has begun to change, as SOF attempted to encourage or coerce the surrender of Panamanian Defense Forces (PDF) without violence. This policy makes allowances for the fact that most military personnel, serving outlaw nations, are not responsible for the actions they are ordered to take but are doing so because of either intimidation, sense of national responsibility, or both. Recently, American SOF doctrine has recognized that SOF can frequently be more effective and productive by coopting military opposition. This is particularly important after the crisis, as these former 'enemies' can be helpful in rebuilding their nations following the downfall of a corrupt regime.

Recent Special Operations

Several recent special operations provide insight into the vast potential of SOF to support American foreign policy into the next century. Missions recently undertaken are characterized by innovation, initiative, courage and respect for human rights.

SOUTHWEST ASIA

Immediately after DESERT STORM Naval Special Warfare Task Units (NSWTU) assigned to the Amphibious Ready Groups (ARG) continued to engage in peacetime activities. Off the coast of Bangladesh combatant craft (24-foot rigid inflatable boats) were assigned to supported the relief efforts after devastating floods caused massive damage and loss of life in that country.

In 1991, when the American embassy in Mogadishu, Somalia was put at risk by bands of poorly disciplined, yet dangerous armed brigands, a combined force of marines and SEALs flew over several hundred miles in US Marine Corps CH-53 helicopters into the embassy grounds from ships of their parent Marine ARG (MARG). They provided security until the host ships closed the coast and dispatched more helicopters to evacuate the embassy staff. The force was under constant danger from a numerically superior group of hostiles and were subjected to ineffective sniper fire throughout their assignment. The mission was completed without casualties to either side.

In an effort to alleviate the massive famine brought on by the civil war in Somalia, the US conducted Operation RESTORE HOPE in the fall of 1992. Prior to the Marine landing on the beaches of Somalia at the start of the operation, SEALs embarked on ARG 1-93 conducted several clandestine beach surveys. Immediately prior to the Marine landings at daybreak, the media filmed uniformed personnel on the beach initially described as 'heavily camouflaged SEALs.' The personnel in the news clips were, in fact, not SEALs. This was confirmed very quickly by the SEAL ARG liaison officer calling his superior in California (on a cellular telephone from the deck of the flagship) and because some of the photographed personnel were wearing headbands instead of bush hats. The wearing of bush hats, not bandannas, is a tactical uniform requirement prescribed by Commander-in-Chief, Special Operations Command.

In June 1993, after US forces had turned over peacekeeping responsibilities in Somalia to the UN, Mohammed Aideed, a local warlord, launched a major campaign to strengthen his political and military position in the Somali capital of Mogadishu. Pakistani United Nations troops had been patrolling the streets around Aideed's Mogadishu neighborhood in order to deter his attempts to intimidate militarily the local population with his bands of armed thugs. Frustrated by the UN efforts to curb his conduct, Aideed's forces attacked the Pakistani troops on 12 June 1993, killing some twenty-four of them and wounding many more. The United States responded with a deployment of AC-130 gunships to the embattled region. For eighteen hours, the gunships, in concert with other aircraft, systematically destroyed Aideed's arms caches as well as his armed compound and residence, forcing Aideed into hiding. Four Somalis were documented killed in the US attacks although, in an attempt to propagandize the incident, Aideed's people claimed twenty were killed.

In August 1993, the Pentagon dispatched 400 Rangers in an effort to improve the deteriorating situation in Mogadishu. The Ranger deployment responded to increasing acts of violence against US military logistics personnel who were delivering humanitarian aid shipments to needy Somali civilians. Because the security situation in southern Mogadishu had deteriorated to the point that it was impeding the reestablishment of economic and political stability, a capable and rapidly deployable force was needed to deal with the bandits. The Rangers were ideal for the mission.[1]

THE FORMER SOVIET UNION

In early 1992, the US was in the process of restoring ties with Mongolia, the nation bordering both the People's Republic of China and Russia. Until 1991, Soviet troops had occupied Mongolia but had withdrawn as the Soviet empire collapsed. Having been dominated militarily by the Soviets since World War II, Mongolia began the process of developing its own defense establishment to protect her borders and requested assistance from the United States.

The language barrier was the first obstacle to effective communications between the US and Mongolia and it was vitally important that this barrier be broken if the US was to be able to provide military, or for that matter, any other assistance to Mongolia. Few in the United States spoke Mongolian, and almost no one in Mongolia spoke English, but most of the Mongolian military had spoken Russian to their former Soviet counterparts.

So, the vanguard of American involvement in Mongolia was a female Russian linguist; a non-commissioned officer from the 18th Airborne Corps deployed by United States Army Special Operations Command (USARSOC). Deployed on a six-month assignment to Ulan Bataar, Mongolia, the 18th Airborne Corps Sergeant First Class taught English to the Mongolian general staff as a precursor to future US/Mongolian military-to-military exchanges. Fascinated that the soldier was a female *and* a paratrooper, the Mongolians invited her to participate in an airborne jump with their own paratroopers. The sergeant was pleased to accept the invitation and, after jumping from a Soviet transport, became the first American soldier in history to be awarded and authorized to wear the Mongolian airborne qualification badge.

In the winter of 1991–2, many of the outlying areas of the former Soviet Union were under threat of famine, because of the extensive decay of their transportation system. The US undertook Operation PROVIDE HOPE, in an effort to alleviate food shortages in regions experiencing the most severe deprivation. PROVIDE HOPE was a food airlift that brought relief supplies into several of the former Soviet republics in central Asia.

Again, the language barrier was a serious hindrance to this mission; the C-141 Starlifter crews had to be able to communicate with Russian-speaking air traffic controllers and the food distribution had to be coordinated with Russian-speaking civil authorities on the ground. To facilitate communications, US Army Special Forces soldiers who spoke Russian flew in the cockpits of the Starlifters engaged in the operation.

In addition to assisting the pilots in communicating with air traffic control authorities, the soldiers coordinated the distribution of the food at their destinations. As ethnic fighting was manifest in several of the republics, in an unusual twist the soldiers coordinated with local *Spetsnaz* (former Soviet special operations forces) personnel for security of the American aircraft – the very forces they would have fought if the two world superpowers had ever been at war.

AFRICA

In March, 1992 the US activated the new 3d Special Forces Group (Airborne), whose orientation is sub-Saharan Africa and the Caribbean.[2] Special Forces soldiers from the 3d Group were immediately deployed in some eight African countries providing a wide variety of military support. In Cameroon, medical specialists from a reserve US Army Civil Affairs and Psychological Operations Command (USACAPOC) unit inoculated some 58,000 people against meningitis and treated another 1,700 for a variety of other ailments. SOF medical personnel were also providing medical and educational support to try to stem the spread of the Acquired Immune Deficiency Syndrome (AIDS) disease in Africa, which is close to achieving epidemic proportions in some parts of that continent.

FORMER YUGOSLAVIA

With the breakup of former Yugoslavia, ethnic Serbian forces in the region of Bosnia-Hercegovina began a systematic campaign of 'ethnic cleansing' in order to rid predominantly Serbian areas of Muslim families. In a campaign characterized by vicious atrocities and a cruelty unseen in Europe since the Nazi period in Germany, forces of the predominantly Serbian Yugoslav National Army surrounded and isolated predominantly Muslim cities, then subjected them to indiscriminate artillery shelling and small arms fire in order to kill off their inhabitants.

By February of 1993, the food situation in several besieged Muslim communities was desperate and, in response to a United Nations initiative, the US commenced participation in Operation RESTORE HOPE, an emergency airlift of supplies to some of desperate areas. Using a system honed and refined by the 352d Special Operations Group at RAF Alconbury in the United Kingdom, C-130 Hercules aircraft of the 435th Air Wing began dropping 1,500lb bundles of food and medical supplies by parachute to the starving populations of several Bosnian towns to augment overland delivery of relief supplies by the international community.

The Adverse Weather Airborne Delivery System (AWADS), has proven tremendously accurate. Resupply drops to the besieged town of Srebrenica in March 1993 had substantially reduced the hunger there and almost all supplies were landing in Muslim hands.

An excellent example of the accuracy of AWADS was demonstrated when the United Nations Commander in Bosnia, French Lieutenant General Philippe Morillon requested batteries to power his satellite telephone during a trip to Srebrenica in March. That night, Morillon's staff heard a crash of landing pallets outside their command post. Running outside to determine the source of the commotion, they found a bundle, specially marked with red chemical lights, containing the batteries.[3]

The Future of Special Operations

Humanitarian aid and nation assistance operations present the most promising arena in which SOF will be employed in the coming years. SOF already have a fine tradition of establishing new contacts in third-world countries and fledgling democracies, and America can take full advantage of this powerful capability. Below are some of the more critical issues that SOF should be used to address.

The spread of AIDS in Latin America and Africa is real cause for concern, with huge populations at risk because of ignorance and inadequate health facilities. The mass communications techniques perfected and employed by US Psychological Operations units could be put to effective use in educating third world populations in how to prevent or reduce the spread of this disease. Regional medical capabilities could be improved as civil engineers and medical units could build and staff hospital facilities, while indigenous personnel are brought to the US for training.

In nations recently liberated from the yoke of totalitarianism, Special Forces and SEALs could establish military-to-military contacts to be expanded by exchanges between conventional military personnel. These exchanges would have two objectives: (1) to provide local militaries with the training to deal with threats to their fledgling governments and (2) to discourage the military threat to the civilian government through an effective military professional development program.

The trouble in former Yugoslavia presents the most immediate quandary to President Clinton; the deployment of conventional forces would only serve to put them at risk and probably do little to stabilize the situation. The long term solutions are best left to those who are in a better position to influence in a practical manner the economic, political, and military situation in the Balkan region. However, America does have its robust special operations capability, which could be used to deter some of the more atrocious behavior on all sides. American SOF should continue to retain its precision direct action and intervention capabilities in order to lend credibility to American foreign policy objectives and strategies.

What distinguishes American special operations forces and special operators from their more conventional counterparts is a highly developed sense of imagination, extreme flexibility, and determination. The possibilities for their employment in pursuit of American initiatives, or the betterment of mankind's lot, are limited only by the imagination of the political and military authorities who employ them. With visionary leadership, these special men and women are a powerful instrument of national policy, whose skill as peacemakers will be far more critical to America in the twenty-first century than their combat potential.

NOTES

1. *The Stars and Stripes*, 'U.S. Sending 400 Rangers to Beef Up Somalia Force', Vol. 52, No. 129, pp. 1–2.
2. Richard H.P. Sia, *Baltimore Sun*, 'US Increasing its Special Forces Activity in Africa,' 15 March 1992.
3. John Lancaster, *The Washington Post*, 'U.S. Airdrops Said to Be on Mark,' 26 March 1993.

GLOSSARY

TERM	DEFINITION
A Team	Unit of twelve Special Forces soldiers
ABCCC	Airborne Command, Control, and Communications
AFCCT	Air Force Combat Control Team
AOR	Area of Responsibility
ARG	Amphibious Ready Group
ARSOF	US Army Special Operations Forces
ARVN	Army of the Republic of Vietnam
ATC	US Air Transport Command
AWACS	Airborne Warning And Control System
AWADS	Adverse Weather Airborne Delivery System
B Team	Headquarters team that exercises command over several A Teams
BDA	Bomb or Battle Damage Assessment
BLT	Battalion Landing Team
BUD/S	Basic Underwater Demolition/SEAL Training
C Team	Headquarters team that exercises command over several B Teams in a theater
CA	Civil Affairs
CBI	China–Burma–India Theater of Operation in World War II
CCATF	Combined Civil Affairs Task Force
CCRAK	Combined Command for Reconnaisance Activities in Korea
CCTS	Combat Crew Training Squadron
CIA	US Central Intelligence Agency
CIDG	Civilian Irregular Defense Group

CINCCENT	Commander-in-Chief, US Central Command
CINCEUR	Commander-in-Chief, US European Command
CINCLANT	Commander-in-Chief, US Atlantic Command
CINCLANTFLEET	Commander-in-Chief, US Atlantic Fleet
CINCPAC	Commander-in-Chief, US Pacific Command
CINCSOC	Commander-in-Chief, US Special Operations Command
CINCSOUTH	Commander-in-Chief, US Southern Command
CJTFME	Commander, Joint Task Force Middle East
CMOTF	Civil-Military Operations Task Force
CNSWG	Commander, Naval Special Warfare Group
CPX	Command Post Exercise
COMSIXTHFLT	Commander, US Sixth Fleet
Det WestPac	Detachment, Western Pacific
DOD	US Department of Defense
FAC	Forward Air Controller
FCO	Fire Control Officer
FLIR	Forward-Looking Infrared
FMLN	Farabundo Marti National Liberation Front (El Salvador)
FPL	Popular Forces of Liberation (Nicaragua)
FROG	Free Rocket Over Ground
GPS	Global Positioning System
H-hour	The exact time that a military operation begins
HALO	High-Altitude Low-Opening
HLZ	Helicopter Landing Zone
HSLLADS	High-Speed Low-Level Aerial Delivery System
IFF	Identification Friend or Foe
JACK	Joint Advisory Commission Korea
JCS	US Joint Chiefs of Staff

JFKSWCS	John F. Kennedy Special Warfare Center and School, Fort Bragg, North Carolina
JFSOCC	Joint Force Special Operations Component Commander
JSOC	Joint Special Operations Command
JSOTF	Joint Special Operations Task Force
JTF	Joint Task Force
JTX	Joint Training Exercise
KTF	Kuwaiti Task Force
LAW	Light Anti-tank Weapon
LCPL	Landing Craft, Personnel, Light
LDNN	South Vietnamese maritime special operations personnel
LIC	Low-intensity conflict
LLDB	South Vietnamese Airborne Special Forces
LLTV	Low-Level Television
LRP	Long-Range Patrol or Long-Range Patroller
LSSC	Light SEAL Support Craft
LVT	Landing Vehicle, Tracked
MAC(V)SOG	Military Advisory Command (Vietnam), Studies and Observation Group
MARG	Marine Amphibious Ready Group
MAU	Marine Amphibious Unit
MIKE Force	Mobile Strike Force
MSB	Mobile Support Base
MSSC	Medium SEAL Support Craft
MSSG	Marine Service Support Group
MTT	Mobile Training Team
NAVSPECWARCOM	US Naval Special Warfare Command
NJM	New Jewel Movement
NSW	Naval Special Warfare

NSWG	Naval Special Warfare Group
NSWTU	Naval Special Warfare Task Unit
NSWU	Naval Special Warfare Unit
NVA	North Vietnamese Army
NVG	Night-Vision Goggles
OECS	Organization of Eastern Carribean States
OG	Operational Group
Op-31	Naval component of MAC(V)SOG
Op-32	Air Force component of MAC(V)SOG
Op-33	Psyops component of MAC(V)SOG
Op-34	Component of MAC(V)SOG that organized resistance movements
Op-35	Component of MAC(V)SOG responsible for cross-border operations into Cambodia and Laos
OPEC	Organization of Petroleum Exporting Countries
OSS .	US Office of Strategic Services, the forerunner of the CIA
PBR	Patrol Boat, Riverine
PCF	Patrol Craft, Fast or Swift Boat
PDF	Panama Defense Forces
PRAF	People's Revolutionary Armed Forces
PRU	Provincial Reconnaissance Unit: an indigenous South Vietnamese para-military unit
Psyops	Psychological Operations
PTF	Patrol Torpedo Boat, Fast
RCMP	Royal Canadian Mounted Police
ROE	Rules of Engagement
RPG	Rocket Propelled Grenade
SACSA	Special Assistant for Counter-insurgency Activities for the Joint Chiefs of Staff
SAM	Surface-to-Air Missile

SAS	British 22 Special Air Service Regiment
SASR	Special Application Sniper Rifle
SAW	Squad Automatic Weapon
SBI	SEAL Basic Indoctrination
SBU	Special Boat Unit
SCUBA	Self-Contained Underwater Breathing Apparatus
SDV	Swimmer Delivery Vehicle
SEAL	US Navy special warfare officer or enlisted person: acronym stands for Sea, Air, Land
SF	US Army Special Forces
SITREP	Situation Report
SOAR	Special Operations Aviation Regiment
SOCCENT	Special Operations Command – USCENTCOM
SOCEUR	Special Operations Command – USEUCOM
SOC-K	Special Operations Command – Korea
SOCLANT	Special Operations Command – USACOM
SOCPAC	Special Operations Command – USPACOM
SOCSOUTH	Special Operations Command – USSOUTHCOM
SOF	Special Operations Forces
SOG	Special Operations Group
SOS	Special Operations Squadron
SOW	Special Operations Wing
SOWT	Special Operations Weather Team
Sqdn	Squadron
STAB	SEAL Tactical Assault Boat
STAR	Surface-To-Air Recovery
SWCL	Special Warfare Craft, Light
TOC	Tactical Operations Center
TOW	Tracked-Optically Wire guided command missile

UBA	Underwater Breathing Apparatus
UDT	Underwater Demolition Team
UNODIR	Acronym for UNless Otherwise DIRected
USACAPOC	US Army Civil Affairs and Psychological Operations Command
USACOM	US Atlantic Command
USAFSOC	US Air Force Special Operations Command
USASOC	US Army Special Operations Command
USCENTCOM	US Central Command
USEUCOM	US European Command
USPACOM	US Pacific Command
USSOCOM	United States Special Operations Command
USSOUTHCOM	US Southern Command
VC	Viet Cong
VNAF	South Vietnamese Air Force
WATC	West African Training Cruise
WHITE STAR	Code name for the deployment of US Army Special Forces personnel to southeast Asia in the latter part of the 1950s

SELECT BIBLIOGRAPHY

To Free the Oppressed; a Pocket History of the U.S. Special Forces (The John F. Kennedy Special Warfare Center and School Public Affairs Office, October 1990)

United States Special Operations Command, pamphlet published by the U.S. Special Operations Command Public Affairs Office, MacDill Air Force Base, Florida

Adams, James, *Secret Armies* (New York, The Atlantic Monthly Press, 1987; London, Hutchinson, 1987)

Adkin, Mark, *Urgent Fury; The Battle for Grenada* (London, Leo Cooper, 1989)

Ballard, Jack S., *Development and Employment of Fixed-Wing Gunships 1962–1972* (Washington, Office of Air Force History)

Beckwith, Colonel Charlie A., USA (Ret) and Donald Knox, Delta Force (New York, Harcourt Brace Jovanovich, 1983; London, Arms and Armour, 1984)

Bidwell, Shelford, *The Chindit War; Stilwell, Wingate, and the Campaign in Burma* (New York, Macmillan, 1979)

de la Billiere, General Sir Peter, *Storm Command; A Personal Account of the Gulf War* (London, HarperCollins, 1992)

Bolger, Daniel P., *Americans at War 1975–1986; An Era of Violent Peace* (Novato, California, Presidio, 1988)

Burrus, Lt. Col L.H., US Army (Retired), *Mike Force* (New York, Pocket Books, 1989)

Cleaver, Frederick W., et. al., *U.N. Partisan Warfare in Korea, 1951–1954* (Chevy Chase, Maryland, The Johns Hopkins Research Office, June 1956)

Collins, John M., *Green Berets, SEALs, and Spetsnaz; U.S. & Soviet Special Military Operations* (McLean, Pergamon-Brasscy's, 1987)

Donnelly, Thomas, Margaret Roth, and Caleb Baker, *Operation Just Cause; the Storming of Panama* (New York, Lexington Books, 1991)

Frank, B., *U.S. Marines in Lebanon* (Washington, DC, History and Museums Division, HQ, USMC, 1987)

Gaddis, John Lewis, *Strategies of Containment* (Oxford, Oxford University Press, 1982)

Grant, Zalin, *Facing the Phoenix* (New York, W.W. Norton and Company, 1991)

Jackson, Robert, *The Secret Squadrons; Special Duty Units of the RAF and USAAF in the Second World War* (London, Robson, 1983)

Kelly, Orr, *Brave Men Dark Waters*, (Novato, California, Presidio, 1992)

Kissling, Herbert H., *An Air Commando and Special Operations Chronology 1961–1991* (Hurlburt Field, Florida, First Special Operations Wing, Air Force Special Operations Command, United States Air Force)

Kyle, Colonel James H., USAF (Ret.), with John Robert Eidson, *The Guts to Try* (New York, Orion, 1990)

Mauldin, Bill, *The Brass Ring* (New York, W.W. Norton & Company, 1971)

McConnell, Malcolm, *Just Cause* (New York, St. Martins, 1991)

McNamara, Robert S., *Blundering into Disaster* (New York, Random House, 1986; London, Bloomsbury, 1987)

Morris, Dave, 'Salvador's Unsung Heroes; SF Advisers Fight for Recognition,' *Soldier of Fortune*, July 1992

Paddock, Jr, Alfred H., *US Army Special Warfare; Its Origins* (Washington, DC, National Defense University Press, 1982)

Parnell, Ben, *Carpetbaggers; America's Secret War in Europe* (Austin, Eakin Press, 1987)

Rhodes, Jeffrey P., 'Any Time Any Place,' *Air Force Magazine*, June 1988

Rowan, R., *The Four Days of Mayaquez* (New York, W.W. Norton & Co, 1975)

Santoli, Al, *To Bear Any Burden: The Vietnam War and Its Aftermath in the Words of Americans and Southeast Asians* (New York, E.P. Dutton, 1985)

Schemmer, Benjamin F., '8th Special Ops Squadron Nicknamed 8th Bomb Squadron After BLU-82 Missions,' *Armed Forces Journal International*, July 1991

Singlaub, Major General John K., US Army (Retired) with Malcolm McConnell, *Hazardous Duty; an American Soldier in the Twentieth Century* (New York, Summit, 1991)

Simpson III, Charles M., *Inside the Green Berets; The First Thirty Years* (Novato, California, Presidio, 1983)

Stanton, Shelby L., *Green Berets at War; U.S. Army Special Forces in Southeast Asia 1956–1975* (Novato, California, Presidio, 1985 and London, Greenhill, 1986)

Stanton, Shelby L., *Rangers at War; Combat Recon in Vietnam* (New York, Orion, 1992)

Sweetman, Bill, 'Forces of Darkness,' *International Defense Review*, June 1988

Thompson, Leroy, *Dirty Wars* (Devon, David and Charles)

Tilford Jr, E., *Search and Rescue in Southeast Asia* (Washington, DC, Office of USAF History, 1980)

Tuchman, Barbara W., *The First Salute* (London, Sphere, 1990)

VanWagner, R.D., *1st Air Commando Group; Any Place, Any Time, Any Where, Military History Series 86-1* (Maxwell Air Force Base, USAF Air Command and Staff College, 1986)

Watson, Bruce W., et. al., *Military Lessons of the Gulf War* (London, Greenhill Books, 1991, 1993)

Walker, Greg, 'From Refugees to Liberators' *Soldier of Fortune* magazine, June 1992

Waller, Douglas, 'Secret Warriors,' *Newsweek*, 17 June 1991

Woodward, Bob, *The Commanders* (New York, Simon & Schuster, 1991)

Worsham, James J., and Major R.B. Anderson, 'Mosby: The Model Partisan,' *Special Warfare Magazine*, Winter 1989

Index

1st Air Commando Group: 25
1st Air Commando Wing: 86
5th Air Commando Squadron: 85
23rd Air Force: 158
82d Airborne Division:
  in Grenada: 124–5
  in the Gulf War, 1990: 175
1st Battalion, 8th Marines (Battalion
    Landing Tea 1/8): 142
24th Marine Amphibious Unit (MAU):
    142
96th Civil Affairs (CA) Battalion: 191–2
450th Civil Affairs (CA) Company: 197
4400th Combat Crew Training Squadron
    (CCTS): 77–8
1st Ranger Battalion: 121–22
2d Ranger Battalion: 142
3d Ranger Battalion: 122
5th Special Forces Group (Airborne):
  in the battle for Camp A Shau: 52–4
  Project Delta in Vietnam: 50–1
  role in interdiction of the Ho Chi Minh
    Trail: 56
  role in the Gulf War, 1990–1: 193–6
7th Special Forces Group (Airborne):
  role in hostage rescue: 115
  role in the Panama intervention: 188–91
10th Special Forces Group:
  formative years, 1952–60: 33–4
  role in Kurdish relief operations, 1991:
    198–9
  use of atomic demolitions: 33
4th Special Operations Squadron: 80
8th Special Operations Squadron:
  bombing missions in DESERT STORM:
    225–6
  composition: 158
16th Special Operations Squadron:
  destruction of Spirit 03: 226–7
  in the Panama intervention: 218–22
  organization: 158
39th Special Operations Wing: 178

160th Special Operations Aviation
    Regiment:
  in Grenada, 1983: 125–6
  in Panama, 1989: 186–8
  in the Gulf War, 1991: 196
  origins: 125
302d Special Operations Group (EC-130E
    command and control aircraft): 158
919th Special Operations Group (SOG) (AC-
    130A gunships): 158
A Shau battle: 1966:
  role of fixed-wing gunships: 80
  role of Special Forces: 52–4
A Team:
  designation as A Detachments: 48
  first assignment of General James J.
    Lindsay: 171
  initial establishment of 'FA' teams: 33
  role in Operation MA BELL: 190–1
AC-47 Spooky: 79–81
AC-119G/K Shadow/Stinger: 84–5
AC-130 Spectre:
  deployment in Vietnam: 81–4
  in Grenada: 159–60
  in the Gulf War, 1991: 226–7
  modernization: 217
  role in the Iran hostage rescue attempt:
    151, 156
  role in the Mayaguez rescue operation:
    149–51
  role in the Panama intervention: 218–22
AH-6 Little Bird helicopter:
  equipment: 186
  role in Panama intervention: 187
Air Force Special Operations Command
    (AFSOC): 222–4
Alison, Colonel John R., USAAF: 25–6
Assistant Secretary of Defense for Special
    Operations and Low-Intensity Conflict:
    113

Baker, James A., US Secretary of State: 169

Bank, Colonel Aaron:
    Special Forces training initiatives of: 33–4
    with the 10th SF Group (Abn): 33–4
Beckwith, Charlie:
    as an exchange officer in England in 1962:
    115
    assignment with 22 SAS: 115
    role in forming a hostage rescue unit:
    115–6
    role in the Iran hostage rescue mission:
    116–20
    with Project Delta in Vietnam: 50–1
Beres, Lieutenant Colonel Thomas, USAF:
    225
Bishop, Maurice, Prime Minister of Grenada:
    96
Blackjack operations in Vietnam: 51–2
Blair, Captain John D.: 52–4
Boland Amendment, 1984: 94
Bush, George Herbert Walker, US
    President:
    first team as President: 165
    role in Kurdish relief effort in Iraq: 177
    role in the Gulf War, 1990–1: 175–6
    role in the Panama intervention: 167–9

Calero, Adolpho, Nicaraguan Contra: 94
Caristo, First Lieutenant Fred: 48–9
Carter, Captain Tennis 'Sam': 53–4
Carter, Jimmy, US President: 92, 117, 156
Central Intelligence Agency (CIA):
    role in Bay of Pigs, 1961: 40
    role in Korean war: 31–2
    role in Operation WHITE STAR, 1959:
    34
    role in Vietnamese 'pacification'
    campaign: 43
Chrisafulli, James (Monk), Chief Warrant
    Officer, US Army: 196
Civil affairs:
    Air Force civil affairs operations outside
    Vietnam: 66
    functions and missions of civil affairs units:
    191
    role in Panama intervention: 191–2
    role in the Gulf war, 1990–1: 196–9
    USACAPOC: 197
Civil War, American: 22
Civilian Irregular Defense Group:
    at Camp A Shau: 52–4
    at Nam Dong: 49

composition: 49
Cochran, Colonel Philip G., USAAF: 25
Collins, Captain Willard, USAF: 80
Couvillon, Major Michael, USAF: 159–60

Dakota, C-47: 26, 77–8
de la Billiere, Lieutenant General Peter,
    British Army: 177
Diem, President Ngo Dinh:
    indigenous resistance to: 42
    overthrow of: 43
    President Kennedy's support of: 42
    role in 'pacification' campaign: 41
    role in the partition of Vietnam: 41
Donlon, Captain Roger H.C.: 49–50

Eisenhower, Dwight D., US President: 41
Erie, Captain Carl, US Navy: 139

Fisher, Major Bernard: 54
Flexman, Ralph E., Bell Aerosystems: 79
Ford, Gerald R., US President: 91

Gairy, Sir Eric, Prime Minister of Grenada:
    95
Gemayel, Amin, President of Lebanon: 95
Geraghty, Colonel Timothy J., USMC: 95
Gray, Colonel George III, USAF: 225
Grenada intervention, 1983:
    events leading to US intervention: 95–6
    role of Air Force special operations forces:
    159–60
    role of Army special operations forces:
    121–6
    role of Naval special warfare forces:
    136–42
Guertz, Major Robert P., USAF: 78
Gulf of Tonkin incident: 44
Gulf War, 1990–1:
    events leading coalition action against
    Iraq: 172–6
    role of Air Force special operations forces:
    224–31
    role of Army special operations forces:
    192–9
    role of Naval special warfare forces: 211–5

Hall, Staff Sergeant Billie, Special Forces
    Medic: 53
HC-130 Hercules Tankers (Shadow Tanker):
    158

Higgins, Major Kevin, US Army: 189
Horner, Lieutenant General Charles, USAF: 226
Horsley, Chief Warrant Officer Fred: 187
Hussein, Saddam, President of Iraq:
    role in the Gulf War, 1990–1: 165, 174–5
    role in the Iran/Iraq war: 174

Iran hostage rescue attempt, 1980:
    role of Air Force special operations: 151–8
    role of Army Special Forces: 116–20
    takeover of the US Embassy in Tehran: 92

Jackson, Dr. Robert E., USAID: 86
Jacobelly, Colonel Jake, US Army:
    as commander, 7th Special Forces Group (Airborne): 188
Johnson, Colonel Jesse L., US Army: 225
Johnson, Lyndon B., US President: 44
Joint Chiefs of Staff:
    role in the formation of Special Forces: 33
    role in the Iran hostage rescue mission: 92–3
    role in the Panama intervention: 169
    role in the Son Tay raid: 57
Jones, General David, USAF, Chairman, JCS: 92–3
JUNGLE JIM, 1961: 77–8

Kennedy, President, John F.:
    decision to reinvigorate special operations forces: 39
    direction of initial deployments to Vietnam: 42
    role in Bay of Pigs, 1961: 40
    role in Vietnam strategy: 41–2
Khrushchev, Nikita, Leader of the USSR: 39
Kingston, Major General Robert C., US Army:
    command of the JFK Center for Military Assistance: 115
    concepts for hostage rescue: 115
    role in creating a Special Forces hostage rescue force: 115–6
Kit Carson Scouts: 65–6
Korean War:
    8240th Army Unit: 29–30
    Air Force special operations support: 32–3
    Combined Command for Reconnaissance Activities in Korea (CCRAK): 31

Joint Advisory Commission Korea (JACK): 31–2
    Rangers: 32
Kunkel, Captain George, US Army: 187
Kurdish Relief, from 1991:
    background: 177–8
    role of Army special operations forces: 198–9

Lasyone, Captain Bryan A., USAF: 160
LeMay, General Curtis, USAF: 79
Leonik, Major Bob, USAF: 228–9
Lien Doc Nguoi Nhia (LDNN): 64
Low-intensity-conflict (LIC) doctrine:
    in Vietnam: 41–2
    role of ASD-SOLIC: 113
    role of the fixed-wing gunship: 78
Lucas, Captain Keith, US Army: 126

MAC(V)SOG:
    air force support: 80–1
    origins: 44–5
    South Vietnamese Sea Commando support: 66
MacArthur, General of the Army Douglas:
    recognition of Filipino guerilla commander: 27
    role in Korean War: 29
Mao Tse-tung, effect on Viet Cong strategy: 42
Marine Helicopter Squadron 162 (HMM-162): 142
Marine Service Support Group 24 (MSSG 24): 142
Marion, Major Francis, the 'Swamp Fox': 21
MC-130 Combat Talon:
    equipment: 152–3
    in Grenada: 159
    in Kurdish relief operations: 198
    in the 8th SOS: 158
    in the Iran rescue attempt: 151, 152–3, 155–8
    role in the Gulf War: 224–6
McDonald, Gilmore Craig, Bell Aerospace: 79
McKean, Colonel Bill, Commander 5th SF Group (Abn): 50
Meadows, Richard
    as a Master Sergeant in MAC(V)SOG: 56–7
    as a Captain in the Son Tay Raid: 57–8

as a civilian in the Iran rescue mission: 118
Metcalf, Vice Admiral Joseph, US Navy: 139, 141
Mexico, US Army punitive expedition, 1916: 22
MH-3 'Pave Pig': 230–1
MH-53 Pave Low:
  equipment: 227–8
  role in Kurdish relief operations in Iraq: 198
  role in the Gulf War, 1990–1: 238–40
Mike Force: 52–4
Montagnards: 49
Mosby, Colonel John, the 'Gray Ghost': 22

Nixon, Richard M., US President: 91
Noriega, Manuel, President of Panama: 166–9
Norton, Charlie: 33

O'Dwyer, Lieutenant Colonel Phillip, USAF: 78
Operation BAHAMAS AND TURKS (BAT), counter drug operation: 158–9
Operation BOOKS: 86
Operation FARMGATE, USAF special operations in Vietnam: 78–9
Operation PROVIDE COMFORT, Iraqi Kurdish relief effort: 178, 198–9
Operation SANDY BEACH I: 77–8
Operation THUNDERHEAD, SEAL POW rescue in Vietnam: 74–5

Panama intervention, 1989:
  events leading to US intervention: 166–8
  roles of Air Force special operations units: 219–22
  roles of Army special operations forces: 181–92
  roles of Naval Special Warfare units: 209–10
Pastora, Eden, Nicaraguan Contra: 94
Paz, Robert, 1st Lieutenant, USMC: 168
Pershing, General John J.: 22
Peterson, Lieutenant Delbert, USAF: 80
Phoenix Program:
  impact on Communist expansion: 43
  media coverage: 114
  origins: 36
Piehl, Major Gerald H., USAF: 84

Powell, General Colin, US Army, Chairman, JCS: 168
Pratt, Captain William, USAF: 81
Project Delta, 5th SF Group (Airborne) in Vietnam: 50–1
Project Tailchaser, gunship development program: 79
Provincial Reconnaissance Units (PRUs): 64–5

Rangers:
  75th Ranger Regiment: 21, 121
  accession and training: 42
  ARVN or Vietnamese: 48–9
  civil affairs support to: 191–2
  Darby's: 23
  formation of Ranger companies: 55
  in Somalia: 239
  Korean War: 32
  long-range patrol detachments: 54–5
  Merrill's Marauders: 24–5
  operations with 1st SOW: 122–3, 159
  post-Vietnam roles: 121–2
  reduction of recruitment standards: 114
  rescue of British Governor-General in Grenada: 140
  Richmond Hill Prison rescue mission: 125–6
  Rogers': 21
  role in the Iran hostage rescue: 118
  role in the Panama intervention: 183–6
  role in Urgent Fury, 1983: 122–5
  US Army Ranger School: 122
  Vietnamese training of: 48
  with Project Delta: 51
Reagan, Ronald, US President: 125–6
Revolution, American: 21
Richmond Hill Prison rescue operation: 125–6
Rolle, Lieutenant Colonel Lawrence, USAF: 231
Roosevelt, Theodore, US President: 22

Saint Georges University, Grenada: 96, 122–3, 138
Sasaki, Lieutenant Edwin, USAF: 79
Schwarzkopf, General Norman H., US Army:
  command of USCENTCOM: 176
  decision to use special operations forces in Gulf War: 177

Schwehm, Lieutenant Colonel William,
USAF: 83–4
Sea Commandos (South Vietnamese): 71
SEAL Team One:
at Solid Anchor, Vietnam: 69
in battle of Khafji, Saudi Arabia, 1991:
213
losses in Vietnam: 75
operations with PRU units in Vietnam:
64–5
organization: 67
origins: 60
Oscar Platoon: 69–70
POW Rescue, 1972: 74–5
role in *Mayaguez* rescue operation: 128
SEAL Team Two:
In FLINTLOCK exercises: 131–2
in the Panama intervention: 205–7
losses in Vietnam: 75
MTT to Beirut, Lebanon: 142–4
origins: 60
SEAL Team Four:
in Grenada, 1983: 139
in Latin America: 145
in Lebanon, 1983: 143
SEALS:
in Grenada, 1983: 136–42
in Latin America: 144–6
in Operation JUST CAUSE, 1989: 205–7
in the Gulf War, 1990–1: 211–5
in the *Mayaguez* rescue operation: 128
operations against Iran: 201–4
operations in Lebanon, circa 1983: 142–4
post-Vietnam sea craft: 132–4
post-Vietnam training: 129–31
POW rescue attempt, 1972: 74–5
riverine operations in Vietnam: 67–74
roles in Vietnam: 63, 66–7
training: 61
training the South Vietnamese: 63–4
types of operations, circa 1965: 61–3
types of support craft in Vietnam: 68
unilateral operations in Vietnam: 66–75
US Embassy rescue in Somalia, 1991: 238
Simons, Arthur 'Bull':
command of Operation WHITE STAR:
34
in command of Task Force Ivory Coast
(Son Tay Raid): 57–8
with Department Op-35, MAC(V)SOG:
56

Simons, Captain John C., USAF: 79
Sincere, Major Clyde, US Army:
command of Blackjack 23, Vietnam,
March 1967: 52
role in formation of 10th SF Group: 33
Singlaub, Major General John K.:
support to Nicaraguan Contras after his
retirement: 94
with JACK: 31
Solid Anchor, South Vietnam: 69
Special Air Service (SAS), Great Britain:
effect on the formation of US hostage
rescue team: 115
role in training American Special Forces:
33–4
Special Boat Units:
in the Philippine insurrection, 1990:
210–1
in Vietnam: 67–8
post-Vietnam development: 134–6
training in Latin America: 145
Special Forces:
accession and training: 47–8
as advisors to ARVN: 48
at Pacora River Bridge, Panama:
188–90
at Richmond Hill Prison in Grenada:
125–6
border camps in Vietnam: 49–50
early hostage rescue capabilities of: 114
in Africa, 1992: 240–1
in Blackjack operations: 51–2
in DESERT SHIELD: 193–4
in DESERT STORM: 195–6
in Operation PROVIDE COMFORT:
198
in Operation PROVIDE HOPE: 240
in Southeast Asia, 1956–9: 34
in support of MAC(V)SOG: 56–7
in the Greek Letter projects: 50–1
in the Mike Forces: 52–3
in the Son Tay raid: 57–8
initial role in Vietnam: 43
Operation MA BELL, Panama: 190–1
Operation WHITE STAR, 1959: 34
reduction in recruitment standards: 114
role in Operation NIMROD DANCER,
1989: 170
role in the Iran hostage rescue mission:
116–20
Salvador MTTs: 120–1

Special Operations Command, Europe
(SOCEUR):
role in Kurdish relief operations in Iraq:
198
Spirit 03, AC-130 attack on Khafji in
DESERT STORM: 226–7
SS *Mayaguez:*
Air Force special operation support:
149–51
Naval Special Warfare support to: 128–9
seizure by Cambodian forces: 91
Stephens, Chief Warrant Officer Randy, US
Army: 196
Stiner, Carl W.:
as a General in command of USSOCOM:
176–7
as a Lieutenant General in command of
XVIII Airborne Corps: 169–70
Sullivan, William H., US Ambassador to
Laos: 81

Taylor, Lieutenant Colonel Wesley, US
Army: 123
Terry, Captain Ronald W., USAF: 79
Thatcher, Margaret, Prime Minister of Great
Britain: 177
Thieu, Nguyen Van, President of the
Republic of Vietnam: 43
Thurman, General Maxwell, US Army:
168–9
Trask, Captain Tom, USAF: 230
Troglen, SSgt Jack W., USAF: 83–4
Truman, Harry, US President: 29
Truman Annex, Florida, SEAL infiltration of:
132–3

Ubon Air Base, Thailand: 82
Udorn Royal Thai Air Force Base, Thailand:
81
United States Atlantic Command: 170
United States Central Command
(USCENTCOM):
area of responsibility: 170
role in the Gulf War, 1990–1: 176–7

United States European Command
(USEUCOM): 171
United States Pacific Command
(USPACOM): 171
United States Southern Command
(USSOUTHCOM): 171
United States Special Operations Command
(USSOCOM):
in Operation JUST CAUSE: 170–3
organization: 172
origins: 96–7
US Army Ranger School, Fort Benning: 122
US Marine Barracks, Beirut bombing, 1983:
95
USS *Grayback*: 74
USS *Tunney*: 62
USSOUTHCOM: 169–73

Vaught, Major General James B., US Army:
92–3, 154–5
Viet Cong:
Army SOF and: 48–54
origins, strategy and tactics of: 42
use of Ho Chi Minh Trail: 42
Vietnamese 1st Observation Group: 48
Villa, Pancho: 21

Westmoreland, General William:
appointment as MAC(V) Commander: 44
role in fielding the first AC-130: 82
role in forming long-range patrol
detachments: 54
Woerner, General Frederick F., US Army:
role in the Panama intervention: 166, 168
World Anti-Communist League (WACL):
94
World War Two:
European theater: 22–4
naval special warfare origins: 27–8
rebuilding a special operations capability:
22
role of the British in special operations: 22

Zumwalt, Admiral Elmo: 69